HERITAGE
of LIGHT

HERITAGE of LIGHT

THE SPIRITUAL DESTINY OF AMERICA

by

Janet A. Khan

Bahá'í
PUBLISHING

Wilmette, Illinois

Bahá'í Publishing
415 Linden Avenue, Wilmette, Illinois 60091-2844

Copyright © 2009 by the National Spiritual Assembly of the
Bahá'ís of the United States

12   11   10   09   4   3   2   1

Library of Congress Cataloging-in-Publication Data

Khan, Janet A. (Janet Adrienne), 1940–
  Heritage of light : the spiritual destiny of America / by Janet A.
Khan.
     p. cm.
  Includes bibliographical references and index.
  ISBN 978-1-931847-73-5 (alk. paper)
  1. Bahai Faith—History. 2. Bahai Faith—United States. I. Title.
BP330.K43 2009
297.9'30973—dc22

                                    2009023091

Cover design by Bob Reddy
Book design by Patrick Falso

CONTENTS

INTRODUCTION

This book examines in detail one of the most distinctive features of the Bahá'í Faith: the role assigned to the American Bahá'í community and to the American nation in the development of a unified global society and the eventual inauguration of a world civilization.

Integral to the exploration of this theme is the mysterious linkage between the followers of this religion in America and those in Iran, epitomized by the designation of the American Bahá'ís as "the spiritual descendants of the dawn-breakers,"[1] those Iranian Bahá'ís of an earlier time who displayed an unparalleled staunchness of faith and heroism in the face of unspeakable brutality and oppression.

To address this issue adequately, it is necessary to analyze in depth some of its aspects, such as the attributes of the dawn-breakers of Iran, the subsequent expression of those characteristics in the constructive endeavors of the American Bahá'ís to execute their assigned tasks, and the far-reaching significance of their actions. This analysis is illuminated by the definitive statements in the Bahá'í writings on these themes, as well as the historical record.

As an introduction to this subject, it is necessary to provide a brief overview of some of the main features of the Bahá'í Faith, its system of organization and vision of the future, and to introduce "the dawn-breakers"[2] of the early days of the religion in Iran.

THE BAHÁ'Í FAITH—AN OVERVIEW

The Bahá'í Faith was inaugurated in 1844 by the declaration of Mírzá 'Alí Muḥammad (1819–50), known as the Báb (meaning in

Arabic, "the Gate"), that He was the bearer of a message from God, and that He was the Herald and Forerunner of a second Prophet, Whose advent was imminent and Whose mission would usher in an era of righteousness and peace. The dawn of the religion coincided with a period of millennial expectation and its progressive teachings generated a high degree of interest and ferment among the population, initially in the Middle East and subsequently throughout the Western world. The Bahá'í Faith is a religion of change and regards all human beings as having the true purpose of participating in an ever-advancing civilization. It aims to create unity between the diverse elements of humankind. Its teachings include principles that are directed to all aspects of human thought and conduct and which promote individual and social development. Central to Bahá'í belief is the view that

> religious truth is not absolute but relative, that Divine Revelation is a continuous and progressive process, that all the great religions of the world are divine in origin, that their basic principles are in complete harmony, that their aims and purposes are one and the same, that their teachings are but facets of one truth, that their functions are complementary, that they differ only in the non-essential aspects of their doctrines, and that their missions represent successive stages in the spiritual evolution of human society.[3]

The aim of the new revelation is, thus, not to belittle the station of the Prophet-Founders of past religions, nor to diminish their teachings. Rather, it is "to restate the basic truths which these teachings enshrine in a manner that would conform to the needs, and be in consonance with the capacity, and be applicable to the problems, the ills and perplexities, of the age in which we live."[4]

The teachings of the religion were, nevertheless, perceived by the authorities in the Middle East as both a challenge to their power and to the established social and ecclesiastical order. The reaction of the fanatical Muslim clergy was swift and merciless. The organized forces of church and state immediately launched a severe persecution against the Báb, precipitating His exile, imprisonment, and finally His execution by firing squad. Their concerted efforts were, likewise, directed toward the extermination of the nascent community. The earliest followers of the Báb, who are characterized as the dawn-breakers—those who participated in the activities that coincided with the dawn of the new religion—were caught up in this maelstrom of violent opposition. Indeed, the early history of the religion is drenched with the blood of thousands of its adherents, with the thirst for vengeance unquenched by the martyrdom of the Báb in 1850.

Mírzá Ḥusayn 'Alí (1817–92), a Persian nobleman titled Bahá'u'lláh (meaning in Arabic, "the Glory of God"), Whose advent was foretold by the Báb, and to Whom the Báb's followers turned naturally for leadership after His martyrdom, was also assailed by the repressive forces of fanaticism. He was imprisoned for a period in an underground dungeon in Ṭihrán in 1852 and upon His release was exiled to Baghdad along with the members of His immediate family and a number of His followers. Bahá'u'lláh's declaration of His prophetic mission in 1863 brought the full force of the civil ecclesiastical opposition upon Him and His followers. He remained a prisoner and an exile for the rest of His life, and was transferred successively to the Ottoman cities of Constantinople (present-day Istanbul) and Adrianople (present-day Edirne). Finally, He was incarcerated for a period of twenty-four years in the notorious prison-city of Acre on the Mediterranean coast, where He passed away in 1892. His remains were interred at Bahjí, on the outskirts of Acre.

Unique to the Bahá'í Faith are its provisions to avoid the enduring schisms that have grievously diminished the strength and cohesion of many religions as a consequence of disagreements over authority and organization after the passing of the Founder. These provisions are contained in the covenant of Bahá'u'lláh, which sets out explicitly in writing the arrangements for authority and organization after His passing. The covenant designates the appointed successor and provides for the establishment of Bahá'í administrative institutions to guide the affairs of the religion. Bahá'u'lláh appointed His eldest son, 'Abdu'l-Bahá, as His successor and head of the religion, and subsequently, 'Abdu'l-Bahá appointed his eldest grandson, Shoghi Effendi, as Guardian of the Faith in his Will and Testament.

To bring into being the Bahá'í administrative structure, specified in the covenant of Bahá'u'lláh, Shoghi Effendi gave special attention to establishing and consolidating the administrative institutions throughout the world and to elucidating both the principles and methods of operation of this evolving administrative system. By discharging his functions, which included acting as the authorized interpreter of the Faith, Shoghi Effendi successfully completed his mission to expand and protect the fledgling Faith by the time of his own passing in 1957.

The Bahá'í Faith has no priesthood and is free from the privileges, prerogatives, and rituals that are generally associated with ecclesiastical structures. The Bahá'í Administrative Order has two arms. It consists on the one hand of democratically elected assemblies operating at the local and national levels of society. These bodies are endowed with the authority to administer the affairs of their Bahá'í community through the exercise of legislative, judicial, and executive powers in matters relating to religious practice. An internationally elected body, the Universal House of Justice, was formed in 1963 and acts as head of the Bahá'í Faith. The Universal House of Justice was alluded to in the writings of Bahá'u'lláh, and its functions and the means for its establishment were elucidated by 'Abdu'l-Bahá and Shoghi Effendi.

The second arm of the Administrative Order is composed of individuals of high standing in the community who are appointed to act in an advisory capacity to Assemblies and individuals. They offer counsel, foster adherence to the spiritual values of the religion, and call attention to those measures required to protect the Bahá'í Faith from inadvertent or malicious corruption of its teachings with the passage of time. These individuals are designated as Counselors and Auxiliary Board members, and, along with their assistants, are organized into five boards of Counselors, one for each continental area of the world. Their work is coordinated and supervised by the International Teaching Center, which is located at the Bahá'í World Center and functions under the guidance of the Universal House of Justice.

The Bahá'í Dispensation is anticipated to endure no less than one thousand years. It is divided into three ages: the Heroic Age, the Formative Age, and the Golden Age. The Heroic Age began in 1844, inaugurated by the declaration of the Báb, and closed with 'Abdu'l-Bahá's passing in 1921. It is the Age associated with the turbulent years of the birth of the religion, with the exploits of its saints and martyrs in the land of its birth, and with the initial spread of its teachings throughout the world.

The second of the three ages in the Dispensation of Bahá'u'lláh is the Formative Age, with its distinguishing feature being the establishment throughout the world by Bahá'ís of an Administrative Order for their Faith. This system of organization and administration of the Bahá'í community is based on principles laid down by Bahá'u'lláh and further elaborated by 'Abdu'l-Bahá in his Will and Testament within his capacity as authorized interpreter of his father's writings. The Formative Age is also destined to witness the establishment by the nations of the world of the Lesser Peace, characterized as a binding treaty for the political unification of the world. Furthermore, it will lead to the emancipation of the Bahá'í Faith from the fetters of religious orthodoxy and to the universal recognition of its independent status as a world religion.[5]

The third and final age of the Bahá'í Dispensation is its Golden Age, which lies hundreds of years in the future, when the transformation of human society through the influence of the Bahá'í teachings and as a practical consequence of the spiritualization of the world will give rise to the Most Great Peace and to the birth and efflorescence of a world civilization having a dazzling splendor far beyond our capacity to visualize.[6]

INTRODUCTION TO THE DAWN-BREAKERS

The men and women in Iran who recognized the Báb as the bearer of a new divine message, and who witnessed the dawning influence of His Revelation and participated in the turbulent events that marked its advent in the land of its birth, are referred to in the Bahá'í writings as the "dawn-breakers," those who were present at the beginning of the new day. The dramatic impact of the Báb's prophetic mission on His early followers and the tenor of this stirring period are captured in the following description:

> We behold, as we survey the episodes of this first act of a sublime drama, the figure of its Master Hero, the Báb, arise meteor-like above the horizon of Shíráz, traverse the somber sky of Persia from south to north, decline with tragic swiftness, and perish in a blaze of glory. We see His satellites, a galaxy of

God-intoxicated heroes, mount above that same horizon, irradiate that same incandescent light, burn themselves out with that self-same swiftness, and impart in their turn an added impetus to the steadily gathering momentum of God's nascent Faith.[7]

While the names of some of these heroic figures are known, and their exploits will be described in later chapters, what is of particular interest is the significance and linkages between the exploits and qualities of the dawn-breakers and their "spiritual descendants,"[8] the followers of the Bahá'í Faith in North America, in contemporary times. While the exploits of the dawn-breakers, the first followers of the Báb who witnessed the birth of a new revelation and participated in the turbulent events that marked its advent, took place during the Heroic Age of the religion, the significance of their contribution bridges both the Heroic and Formative Ages.

The following chapters portray the drama of and some of the major events associated with the Faith's Heroic Age; examine the Bahá'í conception of martyrdom, comparing it with other contemporary forms of this phenomenon; describe the transition to the Formative Age, the Age associated with the rise of the Bahá'í Administrative Order; and survey a number of historical parallels between major events that transpired in Iran during the Dispensation of the Báb and contemporary religious and other crises which impacted the Bahá'í community. These seminal and often tragic events set in motion processes that, though at a later time are manifested in a different form, are also critical to the evolutionary needs of the developing Bahá'í community in the Formative Age.

Throughout the book consideration is given to the enduring inspiration and motivation to be derived from an appreciation of the outstanding characteristics and qualities of the dawn-breakers of the

Heroic Age, and the relationship between their contribution to the evolution of the religion and the present-day requirements of the Formative Age of the Bahá'í Faith are explored.

Detailed attention is given to analyzing the significance and implications of the unique role played by the members of the American Bahá'í community in their capacity as the "spiritual descendants of the dawn-breakers of the Heroic Age of the Bahá'í Dispensation."⁹ In particular, attention is given to the outstanding contributions they made to the worldwide expansion of the Bahá'í Faith, to raising the framework of the Faith's administrative machinery, to laying the foundations of a future world civilization, and to protecting the Faith from persecution and oppression. All these areas of responsibility were willingly embraced by the American Bahá'ís.

The final chapter addresses the Bahá'í perspective of the destiny of the American Bahá'í community and examines its complex relationship to the American nation of which it forms a creative and potentially vital component.

1

DRAMA OF
THE HEROIC AGE

A comprehensive treatment of the history of the inception of the Faith of the Báb and Bahá'u'lláh has been recounted in the inspirational chronicle by Nabíl entitled *The Dawn-Breakers: Nabíl's Narrative of the Early Days of the Bahá'í Revelation*, which details in graphic language the saga of the birth of the Bahá'í religion, and in *God Passes By*, Shoghi Effendi's sweeping history of the first one hundred years of the Bahá'í Era, which describes the circumstances surrounding the subsequent expansion of the nascent religion, the development of its Administrative Order, and the emergence of the Bahá'í Faith as a world-embracing religious movement.

In this chapter we will examine some of the events surrounding the advent of the Bahá'í Faith, a new universal religion that had its origins in Iran in the middle of the nineteenth century. We will describe the tumultuous impact of these events and the persecutions that ensued. We will review the heroic exploits of the spiritually perceptive men and women who witnessed the rise of the sun of the new revelation, acknowledged the truth of its message, and sacrificed their substance, and often their lives, to aid its spread throughout the land of its birth and beyond, and, reflecting briefly on the nature of history, we will consider the significance of these exploits for the present day.

BIRTH AND RISE OF THE NEW REVELATION

From a Bahá'í perspective, the course of history is, in large part, shaped by the intermittent intervention of the divine will in the historical process itself. At the heart of Bahá'í belief is the concept of progressive revelation, which involves the coming of divine Educators, or Manifestations of God, at periodic intervals in various parts of the world over the span of thousands of years. Each of these Manifestations of God, who are the Founders of the world's great religious systems, brings teachings appropriate to the needs of the age in which they appear, providing the inspiration and values for the advance of civilization and moving humanity forward toward a promised time of world unity, human rights, and peace. Their seminal teachings and creative impulse, when translated into constructive action, unlock individual potential and stimulate social development. The Báb, the Forerunner, and Bahá'u'lláh, Whose advent He foretold, are the Founders of the Bahá'í Faith. They are the most recent of these Educators, and as such, fit into this historical process. Their teachings are designed to promote global unity and world order.

The Bahá'í revelation emerged from the matrix of Shi'íh Islam and was for a time mistakenly regarded as an obscure sect, an offshoot of Islam. While some of its teachings make reference to certain aspects of Islam, it is now more generally recognized that the Bahá'í Faith represents a restatement of the essential spiritual verities underlying all the great world religious systems. It also contains social teachings and administrative principles tailored to the needs of contemporary society and designed to promote its constructive evolution.

The birth and rise of the new religion were chronicled by the Iranian historian Nabíl, who was himself a participant in some of the scenes he described. With meticulous care he assembled the facts, verified the accuracy of the historical accounts, and painted a vivid picture of the deeds of the Faith's early champions. The tale he recounts is one of struggle and martyrdom and of the combined efforts of the forces of corruption, fanaticism, and cruelty to destroy the cause of reformation and modernity. The events described by Nabíl are of such far-reaching significance that Shoghi Effendi attests that they "greatly enriched, through their tragedy and heroism, the religious annals of mankind."[1]

To understand the nature of the intense struggle between the call to a new age raised by the Báb and the forces opposed to change, it is necessary to examine the conditions prevailing in Iran at the time. George Townshend provides the following description of the state of society:

> All observers agree in representing Persia as a feeble and backward nation divided against itself by corrupt practices and ferocious bigotries. Inefficiency and wretchedness, the fruit of moral decay, filled the land. From the highest to the lowest there appeared neither the capacity to carry out methods of reform nor even the will seriously to institute them. National conceit preached a grandiose self-content. A pall of immobility lay over all things, and a general paralysis of mind made any development impossible.[2]

The sháh, who wielded untrammeled power, and the largely incompetent government were "utterly subservient" to the powerful and fanatic Muslim ecclesiastical order.[3] Is it any wonder that when these civil and religious authorities became aware of the challenge posed to the structure of their society and to their own influence by the new religious doctrines and laws, ethical standards, and social principles proclaimed by the Báb, they made a concerted effort to destroy His nascent religion?

Commenting on the role of "the divines of Persia" in instigating the attacks on the new revelation, Shoghi Effendi indicates that these religious leaders were "the first who hoisted the standard of revolt, who inflamed the ignorant and subservient masses against it, and who instigated the civil authorities, through their outcry, their threats, their lies, their calumnies, and denunciations, to decree the banishments, to enact the laws, to launch the punitive campaigns, and to carry out the executions and massacres that fill the pages of its history . . ." He further attests: "So abominable and savage was the butchery committed in a single day, instigated by these divines, and so typical of the 'callousness of the brute and the ingenuity of the field' that Renan, in his *Les Apôtres*, characterized that day as 'perhaps unparalleled in the history of the world.'"[4]

The fierce spiritual contest that subsequently engulfed the country pitted "at once people, clergy, monarch and government" against the "trail-breakers of the New Day," the resolute and heroic disciples and companions of the Báb.[5]

THE COMMENCEMENT OF THE HEROIC AGE

May 23, 1844 marks the commencement of the Heroic Age of the Bahá'í Era. It was ushered in by the declaration of the Báb that He was the bearer of a divine message, "the mouthpiece of God Himself, promised by the Prophets of bygone ages, . . . the Herald of One immeasurably greater than Himself." In addition, He summoned the kings of the earth to investigate His claim, warned the corrupt government officials concerning their behavior, and challenged the rulers of the world to acknowledge the value of His Cause, and to deliver His message "to lands in both the East and the West."[6] This momentous declaration took place in the city of Shíráz during a meeting with the young Mullá Husayn, who was the first person to believe in the Báb.

During the following forty days, seventeen other individuals accepted the Báb's claim and, together with Mullá Husayn, they constitute the group known as the "Letters of the Living," the Báb's chosen disciples. Shoghi Effendi provides the following insight into this fascinating and mystical process and underlines the particular significance of two of these early disciples, both of whom were destined to play an important role in the early history of the religion:

Gradually, spontaneously, some in sleep, others while awake, some through fasting and prayer, others through dreams and visions, they discovered the Object of their quest, and were enlisted under the banner of the new-born Faith. The last, but in rank the first, . . . was the erudite, the twenty-two year old Quddús. . . . Immediately preceding him, a woman [Ṭáhirih], the only one of her sex, who, unlike her fellow-disciples, never attained the presence of the Báb, was invested with the rank of apostleship in the new Dispensation.[7]

The Báb summoned to His presence these disciples, assigned to each a specific task and prior to their departure, He prepared them for their mission with the following words of counsel and encouragement: "O My beloved friends! You are the bearers of the name of God in this Day. You have been chosen as the repositories of His mystery. It behooves each one of you to manifest the attributes of God, and to exemplify by your deeds and words the signs of His righteousness, His power and glory." He called to mind the words Jesus addressed to His disciples as they set out to teach His Cause:

Ye are even as the fire which in the darkness of the night has been kindled upon the mountain-top. Let your light shine before the eyes of men. Such must be the purity of your character and the degree of your renunciation, that the people of the earth may through you recognize and be drawn closer to the heavenly Father who is in heaven. You who are His spiritual children must

by your deeds exemplify His virtues, and witness to His glory.
You are the salt of the earth, but if the salt have lost its savor,
wherewith shall it be salted?

In this same address, the Báb stressed the magnitude of their responsibility, and emphasized the greatness of the New Day. He counsels
His followers in these terms:

O My Letters! Verily I say, immensely exalted is this Day above
the days of the apostles of old. Nay, immeasurable is the differ-
ence! You are the witnesses of the Dawn of the promised Day of
God. You are the partakers of the mystic chalice of His Revelation. . . . The days when idle worship was deemed sufficient are
ended. The time is come when naught but the purest motive,
supported by deeds of stainless purity, can ascend to the throne
of the Most High and be acceptable unto Him. . . . You have
been called to this station; you will attain to it, only if you arise
to trample beneath your feet every earthly desire, and endeavor
to become those "honored servants of His who speak not till He
hath spoken, and who do His bidding."

Finally the Báb informs His disciples that He is preparing them for
the advent of an even mightier Day to come. He calls upon them
to put their trust in God and to "Scatter throughout the length and
breadth of this land, and, with steadfast feet and sanctified hearts,
prepare the way for His coming."[8]

The Báb's disciples were galvanized into action by the mandate
conferred upon them. They scattered throughout the provinces of
Iran, attracting receptive individuals, especially from the clerical and
merchant classes, to the religion of the Báb. Indeed, as the fame of
the Báb spread, the "wave of passionate inquiry" that swept the whole

country resulted not only in widespread interest in the new revelation but also provoked a countervailing negative reaction.[9] The clergy, fearful of losing their power and authority, and under the pretext of preserving peace and public security, prevailed upon the representative of the government in Shíráz to arrest the Báb. The tumult that ensued convulsed the nation and prompted the sháh to dispatch Siyyíd Yaḥyáy-i-Dárábí, surnamed Vaḥíd, one of the most influential and learned of his subjects, to interview the Báb and to report on his findings.

It is recounted that Vaḥíd, who was renowned for his knowledge of Islam, planned to interrogate the Báb and demonstrate the falsity of His claim, thereby increasing his own prestige. Three interviews took place. By the third interview, however, Vaḥíd found the Báb's responses to be so compelling and convincing that he embraced the new religion and immediately arose to dedicate his life to its service.[10] He died in Nayríz, during one of the violent upheavals in which the followers of the Báb were embroiled as a result of their refusal to recant their belief.

The sháh's chief minister, Ḥájí Mírzá Áqásí, who conspired with the clergy to denounce the Báb as a heretic, induced the sháh in 1847 to banish the Báb to the fortress of Máh-Kú, situated in the remotest corner of Ádhirbáyján, on the frontiers of the Ottoman and Russian empires, where He was held for a period of nine months.[11] The Báb Himself describes the pitiful conditions of His confinement in a letter addressed to the sháh:

> I swear by the Most Great Lord! Wert thou to be told in what place I dwell, the first person to have mercy on Me would be thyself. In the heart of a mountain is a fortress [Makú] . . . the inmates of which are confined to two guards and four dogs. Picture, then, My plight . . . I swear by the truth of God! Were

he who hath been willing to treat Me in such a manner to know Who it is Whom he hath so treated, he, verily, would never in his life be happy. Nay—I, verily, acquaint thee with the truth of the matter—it is as if he hath imprisoned all the Prophets, and all the men of truth and all the chosen ones . . .[12]

With the passage of time, the local population was charmed by the personality of the Báb, sought His guidance, and flocked in increasing numbers to attain His presence. Alarmed when some of the followers of the Báb travelled to Máh-Kú and were able to meet their leader, Ḥájí Mírzá Áqásí resolved to transfer the Báb to a new and even more inhospitable place of confinement. Thus, in 1848 the Báb was banished to the fortress of Chihríq in an effort to diminish the influence of the new revelation. Shoghi Effendi describes the paradoxical impact of this new banishment, noting, "the turmoil raised in Chihríq eclipsed the scenes which Máh-Kú had witnessed. Siyyíds of distinguished merit, eminent 'ulamás, and even government officials were boldly and rapidly espousing the Cause of the Prisoner."[13]

Seeking to allay the excitement caused by growing interest in the Cause of the Báb, Ḥájí Mírzá Áqásí instructed that the Báb be conducted to Tabríz to be interrogated by the ecclesiastical dignitaries of that city. While the primary purpose of this meeting was to humiliate Him and to devise steps to exterminate the new religious movement, Shoghi Effendi attests that "It instead afforded Him the supreme opportunity of His mission to assert in public, formally and without any reservation the claims inherent in His Revelation."[14]

Nabíl provides a dramatic account of this gathering. He describes the impact of the person of the Báb on the assemblage, the deep silence that suddenly fell upon the group before the interrogation began, and how, when questioned about His identity and message the Báb loudly exclaimed:

I am, I am, I am the Promised One! I am the One Whose name
you have for a thousand years invoked, at Whose mention you
have risen, Whose advent you have longed to witness, and the
hour of Whose Revelation you have prayed God to hasten. Verily, I say, it is incumbent upon the peoples of both the East
and the West to obey My word, and to pledge allegiance to My
person." 15

Such a bold assertion concerning His station electrified the assembled
clerics and led to His denunciation as a heretic. When the ensuing
discussion degenerated into a futile dispute about the Báb's usage
of the Arabic language, He arose and walked out of the gathering,
and the assembly broke up in confusion. The Báb was subsequently
returned to Chihríq where He remained incarcerated until just before
His martyrdom.

Though the intention of the authorities in banishing the Báb was to
stifle the new religion at its birth, in reality the prolonged confinement
providentially afforded Him with a degree of security and enabled Him
to reveal His book of laws, the *Báyan*, which, among other things,
"abrogated the laws and ceremonials enjoined by the Qur'án regarding
prayer, fasting, marriage, divorce and inheritance," and to compose
some of His major works, including prayers, "scientific treatises, doc-
trinal dissertations, exhortations, commentaries on the Qur'án and on
various traditions, epistles to the highest religious and ecclesiastical dignitaries of the realm, and laws and ordinances for the consolidation of
His Faith and the direction of its activities." Furthermore, conscious of
the approach of His death, the Báb, in His writings, increasingly made
reference to the author of a revelation that was soon to supersede His
own. From the beginning of His ministry He was cognizant that His
was a twofold mission—as the bearer of a wholly new and independent
revelation and as the Herald of One still greater than His own. In fact,

the *Bayán*, the repository of the laws and precepts of the new Dispensation, explicitly names the Promised One and anticipated the Order that was to be identified with Bahá'u'lláh's revelation.[16]

The isolation of the Báb prompted His disciples to begin to apply the teachings of the new religion, an action that not only required great personal courage but also provoked violent opposition. In 1848, while the Báb was still incarcerated in Chihríq, a number of His followers assembled in three adjacent gardens in the hamlet of Badasht at the invitation of Bahá'u'lláh. The main purpose of the gathering was "to implement the revelation of the Bayán by a sudden, a complete and dramatic break with the past," and to find the means by which the Báb might be released from confinement. Eighty-one disciples gathered for this historic conference. It reached its climax when Ṭáhirih, the only female Letter of the Living, renowned for the purity of her character and her extensive knowledge, and who was the sole woman present, stunned her assembled companions by appearing unveiled before them. Not only did she violate the time-honored code of conduct, but she also "sounded the clarion-call, and proclaimed the inauguration of a new Dispensation." This symbolic act challenged the assembled followers of the Báb and gave rise to "a veritable revolution in the outlook, habits, ceremonials and manner of worship" among her coreligionists, who hitherto had been "zealous and devout upholders" of Islamic law. Each day the group confirmed a provision of the Bayán, abrogating one of the laws of the Qur'án. The way was now clear for the proclamation of the laws and precepts destined to usher in the new Dispensation.[17]

The public and formal declaration of the Báb as the Promised One, which took place in 1848 during His examination in Tabríz, unloosed "a veritable avalanche of calamities" on His Faith. It provoked a "heated and prolonged controversy" throughout the nation and polarized the population. At the same time, the failure of the weak and vacillating government to address the issue emboldened the clerics to incite their superstitious congregations to take up arms against the followers of the new religion. This fierce nationwide controversy consisting on the one hand of the clergy's denunciations of the Báb and the cogent arguments and treatises prepared by His followers on the other, resulted in "a systematic campaign in which the civil and ecclesiastical powers were banded together" in active and violent opposition to the helpless followers of the Báb. The situation was further exacerbated by the death in that year of Muḥammad Sháh, the ascension to the throne of the young Náṣiri'd-Dín Sháh, and the appointment of Mírzá Ṭaqí Khán as the chief minister. The latter immediately decreed that merciless punishment be inflicted on the followers of the Báb. Shoghi Effendi captures the extent of this campaign in the following terms:

> Government, clergy and people arose, as one man, to assault and exterminate their common enemy. In remote and isolated centers the scattered disciples of a persecuted community were pitilessly struck down by the sword of their foes, while in centers where large numbers had congregated measures were taken in self-defense, which, misconstrued by a cunning and deceitful adversary, served in their turn to inflame still further the hostility of the authorities, and multiply the outrages perpetrated by the oppressor. In the East at Shaykh Ṭabarsí, in the south in Nayríz, in the west in Zanján, and in the capital itself, massacres, upheavals, demonstrations, engagements, sieges, acts of treachery proclaimed, in rapid succession, the violence of the storm which had broken out, and exposed the bankruptcy, and blackened the annals, of a proud yet degenerate people.

Thus began a period of ceaseless commotion, which might well be regarded as "the bloodiest and most dramatic of the Heroic Age of the Bahá'í Era."[18]

UPHEAVALS IN MÁZINDARÁN, ṬIHRÁN, NAYRÍZ, AND ZANJÁN

The ministry of the Báb was marked by several great upheavals in different parts of Iran. Bahá'í historian and writer, Moojan Momen, characterizes the general pattern of these cataclysmic events, as follows: "A band of Bábís, who were armed but for the most part unskilled in warfare, being peasants, traders and mullás, would come into conflict with the local populace incited by the 'ulamá. Troops would be called in and the Bábís besieged by the army equipped with firearms and cannons. After a prolonged and heroic defense, the defenders would be overcome through treachery and massacred."[19]

MÁZINDARÁN — SHAYKH ṬABARSÍ

The first and perhaps the most significant of these upheavals took place in October 1848 in Mázindarán in the precincts of a building that served as a shrine and place of pilgrimage in honor of one Shaykh Ṭabarsí. It involved two of the Báb's most outstanding disciples, the audacious Mullá Ḥusayn and the erudite Quddús, along with over 300 of His other followers. Shoghi Effendi states that this contest, which lasted eleven months (beginning in 1848 and ending in 1849), was caused "by the unconcealed determination of the dawn-breakers of a new Age to proclaim, fearlessly and befittingly, its advent, and by a no less unyielding resolve, should persuasion prove a failure, to resist and defend themselves against the onslaughts of malicious and unreasoning assailants."[20] He also underlines the immediate significance of this event and alludes to the future implications of its outcome:

It demonstrated beyond the shadow of a doubt what the indomitable spirit of a band of three hundred and thirteen untrained, unequipped yet God-intoxicated students, mostly sedentary recluses of the college and cloister, could achieve when pitted in self-defense against a trained army, well equipped, supported by the masses of the people, blessed by the clergy, headed by a prince of the royal blood, backed by the resources of the state, acting with the enthusiastic approval of its sovereign, and animated by the unfailing counsels of a resolute and all-powerful minister. Its outcome was a heinous betrayal ending in an orgy of slaughter, staining with everlasting infamy its perpetrators, investing its victims with a halo of imperishable glory, and generating the very seeds which, in a later age, were to blossom into world-wide administrative institutions, and which must, in the fullness of time, yield their golden fruit in the shape of a world-redeeming, earth-encircling Order.[21]

In a later chapter of this book, details of the seminal events that transpired at Shaykh Ṭabarsí and the developmental processes to which these events gave rise will be elaborated. We will also explore the parallels that exist between this great upheaval in Iran and the heroic actions taken by the American Bahá'ís in the Formative Age of the Bahá'í Era to further the establishment and consolidation of the Bahá'í Administrative Order.

Confined as He was in the remote fortress of Chihríq, news of the events at Shaykh Ṭabarsí brought immeasurable sorrow to the Báb. It is reported, that for a period of five months, "He was crushed with grief, a grief that stilled His voice and silenced His pen."[22] When, at last, He began to write again, He composed eulogies in honor of Quddús and Mullá Ḥusayn and the other heroic souls who met their death at Ṭabarsí, and dispatched one of His followers to Mázindarán to visit their graves and to recite prayers on His behalf.

SEVEN MARTYRS OF ṬIHRÁN

The next great tragedy to befall the beleaguered community occurred in the first part of 1850 with the arrest in Ṭihrán of a number of prominent followers of the Báb. Immortalized as the Seven Martyrs of Ṭihrán, the victims included the maternal uncle of the Báb and a well-known dervish. Far from being religious fanatics or drawn from the marginalized elements of society, they represented "all the more important classes in Persia—divines, dervishes, merchants, shopkeepers, and government officials; they were men who enjoyed the respect and consideration of all." The prisoners were offered their freedom in exchange for recanting their newfound Faith. Despite entreaties by the officials, material inducements, and even the offer of ransom by influential friends, the prisoners confounded the civil and ecclesiastical authorities by refusing to yield. As a result, they were subjected to the most appalling torture and eventual death, which took place in the full glare of public attention. Commenting on their behavior, an observer noted "they died fearlessly, willingly, almost eagerly, declining to purchase life by mere lip-denial . . . ; they were not driven to despair of mercy as were those who died at Shaykh Ṭabarsí . . . ; and they sealed their faith with their blood in the public square of the Persian capital . . ." For three days and nights their dismembered bodies remained unburied and exposed in the square while untold unspeakable indignities were heaped upon them by the masses.[23]

NAYRÍZ

The violent conflagration in Nayríz in the province of Fárs in mid-1850 was of a much briefer duration than the upheaval at Shaykh Ṭabarsí, though of equally devastating consequences. The central figure of the Nayríz upheaval was Siyyid Yaḥyáy-i-Dárábí, better known as Vaḥíd. He was supported by "a handful of men, innocent, law-abiding, peace-loving, yet high-spirited and indomitable, consisting partly, . . . of untrained lads and men of advanced age." Included among the latter was a shoemaker of more than ninety years of age. Ranged against the hapless Bábís were the combined forces of the civil and ecclesiastical authorities. The governor of Nayríz and other officials feeling threatened by the increasingly positive response to the Faith of the Báb, initially sought to arouse the populace against the Bábís and later, with the assistance of the governor of Shíráz, raised an army to eradicate the Cause. Once again, this episode illustrates "the restraint and forbearance of the victims, in the face of the ruthless and unprovoked aggression of the oppressor."[24]

Though the army had at its disposable vast resources and the active support of the government officials and the inhabitants of the province, it was unable to defeat the small, untrained band of the companions of Vaḥíd fairly in the field. They consequently resorted to treachery, hypocritically raising the call of peace. Feigning inadequate prior knowledge about the nonpolitical aims of the message of the Báb and the relationship of the new Faith to Islam, they invited Vaḥíd and several other representatives to a meeting in which he could explain to them the true character of the Báb's religion. They proposed a truce while the matter was discussed.

Aware of their designs, Vaḥíd, nevertheless, felt duty bound to take the opportunity to set forth the teachings of the new religion. The meeting lasted for three days and produced no tangible results. Impatient to bring the gathering to a close, the authorities called for Vaḥíd's immediate execution. The manner of his death was brutal. His turban was wound around his neck; he was bound to a horse and dragged through the streets. His corpse was attacked by the fanatic mobs "to the accompaniment of drums and cymbals."[25]

The companions of Vaḥíd were induced to surrender by means of subterfuge. Though promised security, they were hounded and refused refuge. They were ultimately seized, chained, tortured, and many were slaughtered. Their women and children were also captured and subjected to unspeakable brutalities; their property was confiscated and their houses were destroyed. After being paraded through the streets of Nayríz, the companions of Vaḥíd were subjected to atrocious treatment in the hope of extorting some financial advantage for their persecutors. Indeed, "Every instrument of torture their executioners could devise were utilized to quench their thirst for revenge. They were branded, their nails were pulled out, their bodies were lashed, an incision was made in the nose through which a string was driven, nails were hammered into their hands and feet, and in that piteous state each of them was dragged through the streets, an object of contempt and derision to all the people."[26]

News of the horrific tragedy in Nayríz generated a great deal of interest in the new religion throughout the land, increasing, thereby, the consternation of the civil and ecclesiastical officials. Though the forces of the army had triumphed, it became clear that the spirit responsible for the heroism of the followers of the Báb was by no means vanquished. Before long, another and yet more devastating upheaval began in the west of the country in the area around the city of Zanján

ZANJÁN

The Zanján upheaval was unprecedented both in its duration and in the number of lives that it claimed. It is centered around the exploits of Mullá Muḥammad-'Alí, known as Ḥujjat. Described as "one of the ablest ecclesiastical dignitaries of his age," who after embracing the Cause of the Báb, became one of its most "formidable champions," Ḥujjat was renowned for his "scholarship and keen intelligence," while "his outspokenness and the strength of his character made him the terror of his adversaries." Jealous of his knowledge and the large following he was attracting, and challenged by the modern, liberal principles he advocated, which they perceived as a threat to their power and their institutions, the religious authorities denounced him as an advocate of a heresy and as a repudiator of the teachings of Islam.[27]

Determined to wipe out all who followed the new religion, the clergy compelled the governor to send forth a town-crier to proclaim throughout Zanján that whoever was willing to endanger his life, to forfeit his property, and expose his wife and children to misery and shame, should throw in his lot with Ḥujjat and his companions, and that those desirous of ensuring the well-being and honor of themselves and their families, should withdraw from the neighborhood in which those companions resided and seek the shelter of the sovereign's protection. This action immediately divided the population into distinct camps. Nabíl describes its heartrending results:

> It gave rise to the most pathetic scenes, caused the separation of fathers from their sons and the estrangement of brothers and of kindred. Every tie of worldly affection seemed to be dissolving on that day, and the solemn pledges were forsaken in favor of a loyalty mightier and more sacred than any earthly allegiance. Zanján fell prey to the wildest excitement. The cries of distress which members of divided families, in a frenzy of despair, raised to heaven, mingled with the blasphemous shouts which a threatening enemy hurled upon them.[28]

In pursuit of their avowed aim to destroy the Bábís, the authorities summoned reinforcements from the surrounding villages. Meanwhile Ḥujjat, along with some 3,000 of his followers—including men, women and children—was forced to take refuge within a fort. The defenders of the fort were cautioned by Ḥujjat "against shedding unnecessarily the blood of their assailants. He constantly reminded them that their action was of a purely defensive character, and that their sole purpose was to preserve inviolate the security of their women and children. 'We are commanded,' he was frequently heard to observe, 'not to wage holy war under any circumstances against the unbelievers, whatever be their attitude towards us.'"[29]

Seeking to gain relief from the constant onslaughts of the enemy, Ḥujjat wrote a letter to the sh́áh appealing for justice. However, the letter was intercepted and replaced with one that heaped abuse upon the sh́áh. The hostilities dragged on, and though suffering from hunger and lack of resources, the Bábís refused to surrender. In desperation, the authorities brought in seventeen regiments of cavalry and infantry and directed fourteen big guns against the fort. Yet they were still unable to obtain victory.

As the casualties among the Bábís mounted, women played an increasingly important role in the defense of the fort. Shoghi Effendi attests that some "disguised in the garb of men, rushed to reinforce its defenses and to supplant their fallen brethren, while others ministered to the sick, and carried on their shoulders skins of water for the wounded, and still others, like the Carthaginian women of old, cut off their long hair and bound the thick coils around the guns to reinforce them."[30] The spirit of solidarity that characterized the exertions of the Bábís and the heroism of their acts led the authorities to believe that they numbered no less than ten thousand. Unable to overcome the defenders of the fort, despite having the resources of the state and the advantage of the massive military might at their disposal, the exasperated authorities once more resorted to deceit and treachery. They called for the suspension of hostilities on the pretext that the sh́áh had decided to abandon the enterprise. A message indicating that the sh́áh had forgiven Ḥujjat and his companions was conveyed to the fort. As a testimony to this pledge, the message was placed in a sealed Qur'án. To test the sincerity of the enemy, Ḥujjat dispatched a delegation consisting of nine boys all under ten and a number of men all aged over eighty. When the delegation was attacked the true intention of the authorities became clear. What followed was a renewal of hostilities, reinforced by sixteen regiments, each equipped with ten guns. The siege continued for a whole month, with attacks during the day and night. The onslaught was fierce and inflicted heavy casualties. While reinforcements for the enemy continued to pour in, the ranks of the defenders of the fort were diminished.

In all, no less than eighteen hundred companions of Ḥujjat perished during the upheaval at Zanján. When Ḥujjat died in January 1851 from wounds he had earlier received, the army, clergy, and populace threw themselves upon the survivors and exacted barbarous revenge. Shoghi Effendi commented on the fate of the hapless victims, calling attention to

the exposure of the captives, of either sex, hungry and ill-clad, during no less than fifteen days and nights, to the biting cold of an exceptionally severe winter, while crowds of women danced merrily around them, spat in their faces and insulted them with the foulest invectives; the savage cruelty that condemned others to be blown from guns, to be plunged into ice-cold water and lashed severely, to have their skulls soaked in boiling oil, to be smeared with treacle and left to perish in the snow; and finally, the insatiable hatred that impelled the crafty governor to induce through his insinuations the seven year old son of Ḥujjat to disclose the burial-place of his father, that drove him to violate the grave, disinter the corpse, order it to be dragged to the sound of drums and trumpets through the streets of Zanján, and be exposed, for three days and three nights, to unspeakable injuries.[31]

THE MARTYRDOM OF THE BÁB

It was becoming increasingly clear to the authorities that the repressive measures taken against the followers of the Báb were proving counterproductive. The isolation of the Báb and the persecutions imposed on His struggling community simply served to inflame the zeal of His followers and confirm their loyalty to their new Faith. While the siege of Zanján was still in progress, the chief minister of the sháh instructed the governor of Ádhirbáyján, the province in which the fortress of Chihríq was located, to arrange for the execution of the Báb.

The Báb was conducted under guard to the city of Tabríz, where amid great turmoil He was taken to the barracks, and, together with one of His companions by the name of Anís, who was to die with His beloved Leader, He was placed in a cell until His execution. The Báb was executed by firing squad in the barracks square in Tabríz on 9 July 1850. Nabíl describes the dramatic and indeed miraculous circumstances surrounding this tragic event—the fact that the Báb walked away, unhurt, surviving the bullets fired by the first regiment, the replacement of this regiment by another which succeeded in snuffing out His life, the gale-force winds that swept the city, causing the dust to obscure the light of the sun from noon until evening, and the consternation that gripped the inhabitants of the city.[32]

The mangled remains of the Báb and Anís were transferred from the barracks square to the edge of the moat outside the gate of the city, where some forty guards were stationed. On the following morning the Russian consul in Tabríz visited the spot and arranged for an artist to make a drawing of the remains. On that same night, an intrepid follower of the Báb succeeded in removing the remains to a place of safety. Their remains were, at the instruction of Bahá'u'lláh, moved from place to place, and later in the time of 'Abdu'l-Bahá, they were transferred to the Holy Land where they were ceremoniously interred in a specially designed edifice on the slopes of Mt. Carmel.

The persecutions of the new religious community did not come to an end with the martyrdom of the Báb. Rather, the community was confronted by a fresh calamity when two of the Bábís, "driven by a frenzy of despair to avenge" the death of the Báb, made an attempt on the life of the sháh, who they mistakenly believed to be responsible for His execution. Their disgraceful act had immediate consequences for the whole community. "An army of foes—ecclesiastics, state officials and people, united in relentless hate" launched a "reign of terror" that was, in the words of Shoghi Effendi, "revolting beyond description." He states:

> The spirit of revenge that animated those who had unleashed its horrors seemed insatiable. Its repercussions echoed as far as the press of Europe, branding with infamy its bloodthirsty participants. The Grand Vizir [chief minister], wishing to reduce the chances of blood revenge, divided the work of executing those condemned to death among the princes and nobles, his principal fellow-ministers, the generals and officers of the Court, the representatives of sacerdotal and merchant classes, the artillery and the infantry. Even the Sháh himself had his allotted victim . . .

The atrocities committed against the Bábís were so horrendous that an Austrian officer, in the employ of the sháh, who was obliged to witness such cruel and inhuman behavior, felt compelled to tender his resignation.[33]

Swept up in this vortex were not only the rank and file of the community but also several of its prominent members who had performed outstanding services to the infant Cause. Included among them was the immortal heroine, Ṭáhirih, an outstanding and fearless teacher of the religion, whose discourses on the tenets of the Faith captivated the "flower of feminine society in the capital," and whose vital role at the Conference of Badasht has already been mentioned. This "great Bábí heroine, the first woman suffrage martyr" met her death in a garden in the city of Ṭihrán. There she was strangled and her body thrown into a pit.[34]

Another of those caught up in the reign of terror was Bahá'u'lláh, Who from the early days of the new religion had dedicated Himself to its service and played an important role in stimulating and protecting the nascent community. It was to Bahá'u'lláh that the Báb, prior to His martyrdom, had, in a profoundly symbolic act, entrusted His papers and seals, and to Whom the Bábís turned for leadership after the Báb's death. Because of His prominence in the community Bahá'u'lláh was falsely accused of involvement in the attempt on the life of the sháh. He was arrested in 1852 and incarcerated in a foul and pestilential underground dungeon in Ṭihrán. Upon His release in 1853 He was exiled to Baghdad along with the members of His immediate family and a number of His companions.

The purge of the community of the Báb was not confined to Ṭihrán but spread throughout the whole country. The carnage that ensued replicated the atrocities already perpetrated in Nayríz and Zanján. Nabíl captures the horrific nature of these sufferings in his account of the incident in which forty women and children were incinerated by being forced into a cave in which a vast quantity of firewood had been heaped up, soaked with naphtha, and set alight.[35] Shoghi Effendi characterizes the Ministry of the Báb (1844–1853) as "a chapter which records for all time the bloodiest, the most tragic, the most heroic period of the first Bahá'í century." He writes:

The torrents of blood that poured out during those crowded and calamitous years may be regarded as constituting the fertile seeds of the World Order which a swiftly succeeding and still greater Revelation was to proclaim and to establish. The tributes paid the noble army of heroes, saints and martyrs of that Primitive Age, by friend and foe alike, from Bahá'u'lláh Himself down to the most disinterested observers in distant lands, and from the moment of its birth until the present day, bear imperishable witness to the glory of the deeds that immortalize that Age.[36]

In a later chapter we describe the remaining periods of the Heroic Age, outline the events leading up to the inception of the Formative Age, characterize its distinguishing features and introduce the concept of the dawn-breakers of the Formative Age, those members of the Bahá'í Faith in the West who are designated as the spiritual descendants of the dawn-breakers of the Heroic Age of the religion.

2

THE ROLE OF
THE MARTYR

The birth of every great world religion has been distinguished both by the mobilization of the forces of fierce opposition to the person of the Founder of the religion and to His spiritually transforming and innovative teachings, and by the concerted oppression of its followers by those who seek to halt the spread of the new revelation. In Christianity, for example, the first three hundred years were marked by recurrent persecutions and unnumbered martyrs—individuals who faced their oppressors with courage and heroism. The pattern of persecution and martyrdom is a soul-stirring and familiar theme that repeats itself with the advent of each new religious dispensation.

The martyr's willingness to face ignominy, unpopularity, imprisonment, and death to vindicate the message of the Prophet serves not only as a dramatic example of an unyielding personal commitment to a set of noble beliefs but also as a thought-provoking inspiration to those who witness the martyr's sacrifice. In recent years, however, the concept of martyrdom has been applied more broadly and as a consequence has been perverted by being associated with notions of holy war, fanaticism, and terrorism or by acts such as suicide bombing—phenomena that, in the modern world, have strong political implications, are in many instances divorced from true religious belief, and often arise from the cynical manipulation of ignorant and gullible members of an aggrieved society.

As a context within which to understand the uniqueness of the Bahá'í conception of martyrdom and the behavior of the dawn-breakers, the early followers of the Báb and Bahá'u'lláh, we explore, in this chapter, the characteristics of martyrs, examine the relationship between martyrdom and suicide, and consider some of the modern manifestations of martyrdom.

CHARACTERISTICS OF THE MARTYR

The word "martyr" derives from the Greek word *martus* meaning "witness," one whose knowledge derives from personal observation. In all monotheistic religions a martyr is defined as "one who knows that to profess their faith may result in death, but chooses to profess faith through their life." Martyrdom has been described as "a radical protest on behalf of transcendent values against social conventions that always threaten those values." Martyrs, then, are those who refuse to compromise their faith in the face of persecution and abuse. Death becomes the ultimate witness to the truth of the individual's belief when all other alternatives are refused. Martyrs are condemned to death due to their refusal to recant their belief. Death is not sought but imposed by external forces beyond the individual's control. Martyrs die by the hands of others.[1]

Describing the underlying dynamics of martyrdom, Fields, a psychologist interested in terrorism and contemporary manifestations of trauma and abuse, including martyrdom, calls attention to the life-enhancing orientation of the individual who is martyred, to his or her willingness to make a courageous choice, and the basis on which this choice is made. She explains that the action of the martyr "is predicated on a *choice to live* to profess the faith. The act of living is itself a profession of faith, and the struggle to overcome obstacles to life is fueled by belief mixed with hope."[2]

According to Fields, "Dying for a cause would negate the importance of living to fulfill that cause and its attendant obligations." Further, it is her view that "The martyr takes actions that transcend but do not negate the self." Commenting on the "religious martyr," who "might say or believe 'it's in God's hands,'" Fields states that "that belief does not alter his or her recognition of their ultimate responsibility." Hence her observation, "The essence of martyrdom is the choice to live and the courage to take responsibility for life or death." Finally, Fields identifies "a fervent hope and belief in the future" as the critical underlying motivation for the martyr's willingness to sacrifice self.[3]

DISTINCTION BETWEEN MARTYRDOM AND SUICIDE TERRORISM

Theologians Berenbaum and Firestone argue that people choose to end their lives for three essential reasons, namely, "they do not value life or at least *this* life; they value something more than life or something more than *this* life and they are prepared to offer their life for that which they value more than life; and they despair of this life or of the cost of remaining alive in suffering indignity, shame, or pain." In relating these categories to the martyr, Berenbaum highlights the importance of both the martyr's altruistic motivation for acting in a sacrificial manner, and the way in which "credible" belief supports the martyr's behavior. He writes: "Martyrdom requires either a renunciation of this life as unimportant or unworthy or the sense that something is much more important than this life and that sense must be credible to the individual and perhaps to the community."[4]

While the martyr accepts suffering and sacrifice with altruism and in anticipation of a more positive future, suicide involves the willful ending of one's own life. It is a deliberate and determined act. In most societies it is not only considered to be irrational, but is condemned and subject to taboo. In the Abrahamic religions suicide is generally prohibited. There is no glorification of deliberately inviting death. Rather, these religions make a distinction between actively willing to end one's life in suicide and accepting one's death as the divine will by means of martyrdom at the hands of another as a consequence of adherence to a belief.

While there is not one single cause of suicide, it may well be precipitated by psychological factors such as despair, depression, extreme sorrow, or unbearable pain and physical suffering. Suicide may also take the form of defiance and protest, or, in some instances, be directed toward the achievement of political or ideological goals.

In modern usage, the terms "martyr" is often misapplied to members of organizations and groups who die while perpetrating violent acts of terrorism, which are inconsistent with the ideas and values of the religions they purport to uphold or represent. They act in the name of organizations and conduct campaigns designed to achieve specific political ends. The ideal of martyrdom is exploited for military and political purposes. While martyrs sacrifice their life in the name of faith and their death can be directly attributed to the cause or faith they have refused to recant, the suicide bomber is neither condemned to death nor suffers death at the hands of another. The suicide bomber willfully acts to take his or her own life, often in a way that is intended to cause death and destruction to others and to promote a cause. Death is avoidable, but is chosen to serve ideological or political ends. Hence on the political stage the use of the word "martyr" ceases to have a literal meaning and becomes metaphorical. The figure of the "martyr" is used to maintain national or group identity, to rally support in crisis situations.[5]

Ami Pedahzur, an Israeli scholar, calls attention to the propaganda value of sensational and shocking terror events. Not only do they demoralize the adversary but they also serve to arouse the emotional support of the oppressed group for a political or ideological ambition to which it aspires. Commenting on the tradition of public rituals for the commemoration and celebration of suicide attacks, Pedahzur observes that "social support for suicide terrorism, of the 'culture of death,' . . . is very rarely a grassroots phenomenon. The organization's leadership is engaged in trying to mobilize support and one of the prominent ways of doing this—among societies which are oppressed and feel weak and hopeless—is by supplying heroes and hope."[6]

Given the socially destructive nature of suicide terrorism, many explanations have been sought in an attempt to understand what motivates individuals such as suicide bombers to commit violence against others. Various theories have been tried, modified, and discarded. For example it has been argued that the willingness to commit indiscriminate acts of violence against others is the result of subjection to oppression and the deprivation of human rights. Others assert that such actions spring from deep frustration, from a profound disappointment and disenchantment, and a sense of alienation, both spiritual and cultural, from the society in which the individual resides. Still others depict the behavior as representing the power of the weak, as the only available response in face of a powerful, technologically advanced adversary. Furthermore it has been reported that those who commit such deadly acts often claim as their rationalization the fact that the cause to which they are committed is so great and so important that it justifies the death of innocent people.[7]

While the motivation for acts of suicide, perpetrated by terrorists and others, is obviously very complex, the political connection between terrorism and self-imposed "martyrdom" is a recurrent theme. Commenting on this linkage, Fields calls attention to the underlying motive of revenge. She observes that "the act of killing others while killing oneself becomes the political objective that incorporates the intention of vendetta." Ghadirian, a psychiatrist interested in trauma, also suggests that "self-imposed 'martyrs'" are likely to be inspired by hate and that their actions are instigated to punish or kill those perceived as enemies. Such a perspective stands in sharp contrast to the altruistic attitudes of the true martyr.[8]

BAHÁ'Í CONCEPTIONS OF MARTYRDOM

From a Bahá'í perspective, martyrs are those who bear witness to the truth of their Faith by their willingness to sacrifice their life in its path. They refuse to compromise their belief in the face of persecution, and when given the opportunity to save their life by recanting their faith, they courageously decline. In this regard, Shoghi Effendi attests, "the martyrs were called upon to deny their faith or die; as men of principle they preferred to die."[9]

In the Bahá'í teachings, suicide is strongly discouraged, being regarded as an act contrary to the Will of God. Bahá'í martyrs, therefore, do not commit suicide; they meet their death at the hands of others. Further, Bahá'í martyrs are neither fanatics nor religious zealots motivated by an apocalyptic or political vision. Their motivation is altruistic, life-affirming, and future-oriented. Commenting on the reasons for the sacrificial behavior of the martyrs in the time of the Báb, Shoghi Effendi affirms:

It was not through a blind religious zeal but because they desired to bring about for the future generations that promised era that the Faith of the Báb promised to start—an era of peace, good-will and full realization of the spiritual significance of the life of man upon the earth. They suffered that we may be happy. They died that we may live in perfect bliss. What a sacred debt, therefore, we owe to them! How much we ought to labour to repay them for their sacrifices, and how willing and earnest we should be in consecrating our life in the path they trod![10]

While the Bahá'í writings extol the station of the martyr and pay tribute to the heroism of the martyrs of the Heroic Age of the Faith of the Báb, it is important to note that the followers of the religion are cautioned to act with prudence and care and not volunteer to give their lives. Indeed, following the turbulent years of the Heroic Age, when the sacrifices of the martyrs had resulted in the establishment of embryonic Bahá'í communities in Iran, the concept of martyrdom was enlarged to embrace the idea of a life of service. In essence, this conception emphasizes the sacrificial spirit and intention of the action, rather than the action itself—the balance is shifted from the willingness to suffer death for the Cause to the willingness to work actively for the religion throughout one's life. For example, when one of the early believers supplicated Bahá'u'lláh to grant him the station of martyrdom, he received the following response: "Today the greatest of all deeds is service to the Cause. Souls that are well assured should with utmost discretion teach the Faith, so that the sweet fragrances of the Divine Garment will waft from all directions. This martyrdom is not confined to the destruction of life and the shedding of blood. A person enjoying the bounty of life may yet be recorded a martyr in the Book of the Sovereign Lord." Elaborating on this theme, Bahá'u'lláh discourages physical violence and stresses the importance of teaching His Faith with wisdom. Addressing His followers, He counsels: "Beware lest ye shed the blood of any one. Unsheathe the sword of your tongue from the scabbard of utterance for therewith ye can conquer the citadel of men's hearts."[11]

The uniqueness of the Bahá'í view on martyrdom is characterized by Ghadirian as follows: as standing "in contrast to some of the fundamentalists' indoctrinations to engage in violent suicide attacks and 'martyrdom' to promote their cause." It also differs from the "mental attitude of fanatics," which he describes as being "charged with emotions such as hate and rage, culminating in a self-imposed 'martyrdom.'" "In contrast," he asserts "the pages of history of the persecution and martyrdom of Bahá'ís show that these individuals, even in the moments before their death, were submissive and prayed that their tormentors and executioners be guided and forgiven."[12]

DAWN-BREAKERS OF THE HEROIC AGE

Against the background of the foregoing discussion of the role of martyrs and differing perspectives on the subject of martyrdom, we will now explore the unique quality of the deeds performed by the dawn-breakers of the Heroic Age, describe their outstanding characteristics, and examine both their contribution to the early history of the Bahá'í Faith and to its continuing evolution.

As already mentioned, the dawn-breakers of the Heroic Age were the early believers of Persia who recognized the prophetic station of the Báb and arose to dedicate their lives to the promotion of His teachings and the establishment of the new universal religion. The message of the Báb and the challenging teachings set forth in His revelation were promulgated at a time of great Messianic expectation and thus struck a responsive chord in the hearts of the people. The dawn-breakers traveled throughout the country, announcing to their fellow-citizens the advent of the new day in religious history. Their activities generated an air of feverish excitement and attracted a positive response among the general population. Though the Bábís disavowed any interest in interfering in the political realm, the civil and ecclesiastical authorities felt challenged by the rising tide of interest in the new revelation. Anxious that their absolute powers were being undermined, they instituted savage persecutions and attacks against the helpless followers of the Báb, culminating in the martyrdom of the Báb in 1850, and the deaths of thousands of His innocent followers.

QUALITY AND SIGNIFICANCE OF THE DEEDS

In assessing the unique quality and significance of the actions of the dawn-breakers, which contributed to the birth and establishment of the Bahá'í Faith, a number of themes emerge, which will be explored below. These include the dynamic role of sacrifice, the link between steadfastness and conscious awareness of the teachings of the religion the martyrs chose to accept, and the scrupulous adherence to spiritual and ethical principles.

In relation to the dynamic principles underlying the operation of sacrificial behavior, the Báb in one of His tablets, explicates the transcendent significance and purpose of the sacrifices of the early dawn-breakers. He indicates that their actions served to proclaim and glorify the new revelation. Their lives testify to the willingness of enlightened souls to engage in heroic and sacrificial actions in service to the spiritual values they espouse, and their example serves as an inspiration to the spiritually perceptive. Meditating on these mysterious processes and the operation of the divine will, the Báb in His tablet addresses the divinity in the following terms:

> How numerous the souls raised to life who were exposed to dire humiliation in Thy Path for exalting Thy Word and for glorifying Thy divine Unity! How profuse the blood that hath been shed for the sake of Thy Faith to vindicate the authenticity of Thy divine Mission and to celebrate Thy praise! How vast

the possessions that were wrongfully seized in the Path of Thy love in order to affirm the loftiness of Thy sanctity and to extol Thy glorious Name! How many the feet that have trodden upon the dust in order to magnify Thy holy Word and to extol Thy glory! How innumerable the voices that were raised in lamentation, the hearts that were struck with terror, the grievous woes that none other than Thee can reckon, and the adversities and afflictions that remain inscrutable to anyone except Thyself; all this to establish, O my God, the loftiness of Thy sanctity and to demonstrate the transcendent character of Thy glory.

These decrees were ordained by Thee so that all created things might bear witness that they have been brought into being for the sake of naught else but Thee. Thou hast withheld from them the things that bring tranquility to their hearts, that they might know of a certainty that whatever is associated with Thy holy Being is far superior to and exalted above aught else that would satisfy them; inasmuch as Thine indomitable power pervadeth all things, and nothing can ever frustrate it.

Indeed Thou hast caused these momentous happenings to come to pass that those who are endued with perception may readily recognize that they were ordained by Thee to demonstrate the loftiness of Thy divine Unity and to affirm the exaltation of Thy sanctity.[13]

In His writings, Bahá'u'lláh identifies two specific aspects of the sacrificial services of the early followers of the Báb, which He characterizes as being amongst the proofs that demonstrate the truth of the new revelation. The first pertains to the fact that spiritually minded individuals are invariably attracted to the Messenger of God, investigate and accept His claim to be a Revealer of divine truth, and commit themselves to service to His Cause. The second relates to the quality of steadfastness. Commenting on the nature of the outstanding services of the early disciples of the Báb, Bahá'u'lláh states:

> All these were guided by the light of that Sun of divine Revelation, confessed and acknowledged His truth. Such was their faith, that most of them renounced their substance and kindred, and cleaved to the good-pleasure of the All-Glorious. They laid down their lives for their Well-Beloved, and surrendered their all in His path. Their breasts were made targets for the darts of the enemy, and their heads adorned the spears of the infidel. No land remained which did not drink the blood of these embodiments of detachment, and no sword that did not bruise their necks. Their deeds, alone, testify to the truth of their words.[14]

Bahá'u'lláh affirms that the willingness of the martyrs to sacrifice "their life, their substance, their wives, their children, their all" constitutes conclusive evidence of the truth of the revelation. Likewise, He states, their "[s]teadfastness in the Faith is a sure testimony, and a glorious evidence of the truth." To illuminate the extent of their steadfastness, He describes the challenges that confronted the followers of the Báb at the hands of the authorities and the nature of their response:

> In every city, all the divines and dignitaries rose to hinder and repress them, and girded up the loins of malice, of envy, and tyranny for their suppression. How great the number of those holy souls, those essences of justice, who, accused of tyranny, were put to death! And how many embodiments of purity, who showed forth naught but true knowledge and stainless deeds, suffered an agonizing death! Notwithstanding all this, each of these holy beings, up to his last moment, breathed the Name

of God, and soared in the realm of submission and resignation. Such was the potency and transmuting influence which He exercised over them, that they ceased to cherish any desire but His will, and wedded their soul to His remembrance.[15]

Bahá'u'lláh identifies the fundamental reason for their resignation and He relates it to the transforming power that comes from aligning oneself to the Will of God. He asks:

Who in this world is able to manifest such transcendent power, such pervading influence? All these stainless hearts and sanctified souls have, with absolute resignation, responded to the summons of His decree. Instead of complaining, they rendered thanks unto God, and amidst the darkness of their anguish they revealed naught but radiant acquiescence to His will. It is evident how relentless was the hate, and how bitter the malice and enmity entertained by all the peoples of the earth towards these companions. The persecution and pain they inflicted on these holy and spiritual beings were regarded by them as means unto salvation, prosperity, and everlasting success.

Indeed, to underscore the severity of the sufferings of the martyrs, Bahá'u'lláh poses the following question:

Hath the world, since the days of Adam, witnessed such tumult, such violent commotion? Notwithstanding all the torture they suffered, and manifold the afflictions they endured, they became the object of universal opprobrium and execration. Methinks, patience was revealed only by virtue of their fortitude, and faithfulness itself was begotten only by their deeds.[16]

OUTSTANDING CHARACTERISTICS

The personal qualities the dawn-breakers exemplified in their lives highlight the level of individual responsibility to which the followers of all new religions are called. Their duty is not only to broadcast the socially transforming principles of the new revelation, but also to demonstrate the efficacy of its message in daily life. The behavior of the followers of the Báb constituted a challenge and an admonition to the surrounding population. In contrast to the decadent Persian society in which they lived, the dawn-breakers were renowned for their personal integrity, high moral standards, and sense of discipline and order. They were motivated by a spirit of optimism, they were open to new ideas, and they aligned themselves with the spirit of the emergent era of peace and justice.

It is noteworthy that the very existence of the early followers of the Báb, the "trail-breakers of the New Day," and their presence in society constituted a challenge to the traditional way of life of their fellow-citizens and set them apart from their countrymen. The sharpness of this contrast is highlighted by Shoghi Effendi's characterization of the various elements of Persian society at the time of the appearance of the Báb. For example, the populace is described as being "the most decadent race in the civilized world, grossly ignorant, savage, cruel, steeped in prejudice, [and] servile in their submission to an almost deified hierarchy," while the reactionary Shi'íh priesthood was viewed as "Fiercely fanatic, unspeakably corrupt, enjoying unlimited ascendancy over the masses, jealous of their position, and irreconcilably opposed to all liberal ideas." Further, Shoghi Effendi attests that the government was not only corrupt, idle, bloated, and parasitical but also "incompetent, tenaciously holding to their ill-gotten privileges, and utterly subservient to a notoriously degraded clerical order."[17]

Shoghi Effendi employs a series of sharply antithetical images to illustrate the extent of the contrast between the behavior of the dawn-breakers and the population at large. For example, he testifies that in opposition to the "intrigue, ignorance, depravity, cruelty, superstition and cowardice" demonstrated by the members of Persian society, the Báb's followers manifested in their behavior "a spirit exalted, unquenchable and awe-inspiring, a knowledge surprisingly profound, an eloquence sweeping in its force, a piety unexcelled in fervor, a courage leonine in its fierceness, a self-abnegation saintly in its purity, a resolve granite-like in its firmness, a vision stupendous in its range, . . . a power of persuasion alarming to its antagonists. . . ." Indeed, Shoghi Effendi asserts that the transforming influence of the standard of their faith and their code of conduct was so powerful that it "challenged and revolutionized the lives of their countrymen."[18]

Perhaps nowhere is this contrast more noticeable than when comparing the behavior of the Báb's followers and those who attacked them during the bloody upheavals at Shaykh Ṭábársí, Nayríz, and Zanján. Here the disorder, confusion, lack of discipline, drunkenness and gambling, and the treacherous acts of the attackers differs sharply from the faith and prayerful devotion, the high moral standard and detachment from material possessions, and the discipline and order that characterized the beleaguered Bábís in times of stress and crisis. Indeed, even implacable enemies of the new religion were impressed by the quality of their lives and astounded at the degree of their solidarity and forbearance.[19]

The dawn-breakers of the Heroic Age were individuals from all walks of life who were open to new ideas and understood the spirit of the times and the need for spiritual and social change. Many of them embraced the message of the Báb after a period of spiritual search. Others, like Ḥujjat, accepted His message immediately after reading a single page from one of the Báb's tablets.[20] They were spiritually transformed by their acceptance of His revelation, by their willingness to endeavor to put the laws for the new day into practice in their personal lives, and by their eagerness to share His message with their countrymen, a step that inevitably brought them into conflict with the powerful ecclesiastical and civil structures. Examples of such transformation abound in the early history of the Faith, included among them being that of the sedentary student, Mullá Ḥusayn, who was the first to recognize the Báb. Mullá Ḥusayn was not only spiritually transformed by his encounter with the Báb, but, at a later time, he experienced a transformation that enabled him to overcome his physical weakness to perform extraordinary feats of swordsmanship during the upheaval at Shaykh Ṭábársí. Nabíl provides the following account:

> Unsheathing his sword and spurring on his charger into the midst of the enemy, Mullá Ḥusayn pursued, with marvelous intrepidity, the assailant of his fallen companion. His opponent, who was afraid to face him, took refuge behind a tree and, holding aloft his musket, sought to shield himself. Mullá Ḥusayn immediately recognized him, rushed forward, and with a single stroke of his sword cut across the trunk of the tree, the barrel of the musket, and the body of his adversary. The astounding force of that stroke confounded the enemy and paralyzed their efforts. All fled panic-stricken in the face of so extraordinary a manifestation of skill, of strength, and of courage.[21]

Those who embraced the Faith of the Báb immediately and unhesitatingly arose to serve it. The early history of the Faith provides many examples. One such example concerns the humble sifter of wheat, Mullá Muḥammad Ja'far, who was the first to accept the Báb's message in Iṣfáhán, a city whose distinguished and learned divines failed to grasp the significance of the new revelation. The Báb, in His writings, immortalizes the spiritual insight and the zealous advocacy of the sifter of wheat, and Nabíl describes how, when Mullá Muḥammad Ja'far became aware of the siege of Shaykh Ṭábársí,

> he felt an irresistible impulse to throw in his lot with those heroic companions of the Báb who had risen for the defense of their Faith. Carrying his sieve in his hand, he immediately arose and set out to reach the scene of that memorable encounter. "Why leave so hurriedly?" his friends asked him, as they saw him running in a state of intense excitement through the bazaars of Iṣfahán. "I have risen," he replied, "to join the glorious company of the defenders of the fort of Shaykh Ṭábársí! With this sieve which I carry with me, I intend to sift the people in every city through which I pass. Whomsoever I find ready to espouse the Cause I have embraced, I will ask to join me and hasten forthwith to the field of martyrdom."[22]

The lives of the dawn-breakers were characterized by a willingness to make sacrifices for the Cause they had embraced. They demonstrated a high degree of detachment from the material world. Some, like the Seven Martyrs of Ṭihrán, resisting the pressures of the authorities and their families encouraging them to recant as a means of saving their lives, were prepared to sacrifice their lives. Others, like the erudite Váḥid, sacrificed their status and position in the community. Still others, like the great Ṭahírih, were cast out by their family for daring to take such an unpopular stand. And many sacrificed all their possessions when that was necessitated by circumstances.

Their strength, sense of orientation, and motivation derived from their knowledge of the teachings of the Báb and their conviction that these teachings described the path to true happiness. Their vision of the advent of the Promised One, of the dawning of a New Day, and the transformation of the condition of the world, allowed them to see beyond the challenges of the present crisis. They understood the spiritual significance of their suffering, the possibility of sacrificing their all to their Beloved, and they were sustained by a strong belief in the power of God to assist and reinforce their actions. 'Abdu'l-Bahá characterizes the paradoxical meekness and strength in the following passage in one of His tablets: "Their grave offence was to display a glimpse of the beauty of the heavenly Peacock. To do this they spread out the plumage of sanctity and intoned sweet melodies even as the warbling of a nightingale. This was the only guilt they had committed; their faithfulness was regarded as a crime, and their sincerity as deceit."[23]

The courage of the early believers was remarkable. They fearlessly proclaimed the new and controversial teachings of the Báb, aware that their actions were likely to provoke persecution. It is important to note that they did not adopt a passive stance in the face of persecution, nor did they attempt to overthrow the government. While their motives were clearly not political, they interceded actively with the government and took steps to protect themselves; and, they would not recant, even to save their lives. In addition, they refuted with cogent arguments the misrepresentations of the teachings of their faith by the clergy.

The dawn-breakers of the Heroic Age did not shrink from attacks. They were undeterred by the number and military might of their opponents, yet they did not overstep the bounds of moderation. Their actions were motivated solely by self-defense. Their behavior was always principled; as soon as they were told that no further attacks would be attempted against them they were willing to leave their fortifications and depart for their homes. Nevertheless, Nabíl tells how, in every instance, they were treacherously deceived by an unprincipled enemy. However, it can be argued that the very fact that these disciples were ready and willing to emerge from the fort and return to their homes after receiving the assurance that they would be no more molested is itself evidence that they were not contemplating any action against the authorities.

Shoghi Effendi provides the following testimony concerning the uniqueness of the contribution of the dawn-breakers of the Heroic Age of the Bahá'í Faith:

> Has Christianity or Islám, has any Dispensation that preceded them, offered instances of such combinations of courage and restraint, of magnanimity and power, of broadmindedness and loyalty, as those which characterized the conduct of the heroes of the Faith of Bahá'u'lláh? Where else do we find evidences of a transformation as swift, as complete, and as sudden, as those effected in the lives of the apostles of the Báb? Few, indeed, are the instances recorded in any of the authenticated annals of the religions of the past of a self-abnegation as complete, a constancy as firm, a magnanimity as sublime, a loyalty as uncompromising, as those which bore witness to the character of that immortal band which stands identified with this Divine Revelation—this latest and most compelling manifestation of the love and the omnipotence of the Almighty![24]

3

TRANSITION TO THE FORMATIVE AGE

The Heroic Age of the Bahá'í Faith consists of three distinct but related periods which spanned a total of some eighty years. The first period (1844–53) coincided with the ministry of the Báb. It begins with His declaration, culminates in His martyrdom, and "ends in a veritable orgy of religious massacre revolting in its hideousness." Underlining the main features of this dramatic period, Shoghi Effendi indicates that "It is characterized by nine years of fierce and relentless contest, whose theatre was the whole of Persia, in which above ten thousand heroes laid down their lives, in which two sovereigns of the Qájár dynasty and their wicked ministers participated, and which was supported by the entire Shí'ih ecclesiastical hierarchy, by the military resources of the state, and by the implacable hostility of the masses."[1]

LATER PERIODS OF THE HEROIC AGE

In the first chapter we examined some of the major events that transpired during these turbulent years and described the qualities of the early followers of the Báb who arose to promulgate the teachings of the new religion. In the present chapter we will briefly describe the remaining two periods of the Heroic Age, outline the events leading to the inception of the Formative Age, describe some of its characteristics, and introduce the concept of the dawn-breakers of the Formative Age, the members of the Bahá'í Faith in the West who are designated as the spiritual descendants of the dawn-breakers of the Heroic Age of the religion.

THE MINISTRY OF BAHÁ'U'LLÁH, 1853–92

The second period of the Heroic Age extends over thirty-nine years (1853–92). It encompasses the mission of Bahá'u'lláh, Whose advent was foretold and anticipated by the Báb. It opens in 1853 with the coming of revelation to Bahá'u'lláh during His incarceration in the Síyáh-Chál, the notorious underground prison in Ṭihrán, and terminates with His death in 1892. Included among its distinguishing features are Bahá'u'lláh's proclamation of His revelation to the kings and ecclesiastical leaders of the world; the spread of the religion beyond the confines of the land of its birth to the neighboring territories of present-day Turkey, Russia, Iraq, Syria, Egypt, and India; and the intensity of the hostility directed toward it by "the united attacks launched by the sháh of Persian and the sulṭán of Turkey, the two admittedly most powerful potentates of the East, as well as by the opposition of the twin sacerdotal orders of Shí'ih and Sunní Islám."[2] This hostility was the cause of the successive exiles of Bahá'u'lláh and His family to Baghdad, Constantinople, Adrianople, and ultimately to the prison-city of Acre.

The aim of these banishments was to eradicate the Faith of Bahá'u'lláh from the face of the earth. At the same time, the officials in the land of its birth unleashed renewed persecutions against the steadily expanding community. Though these persecutions were on "a far smaller scale than the blood baths which had baptized the birth of the Faith," they were wide-ranging and "marked by an even greater degree of ferocity." The members of the defenseless community were hunted down, plundered, and exterminated. In accordance with the instructions of Bahá'u'lláh they offered no armed resistance, even in self-defense. Harassed by "arrests, interrogations, imprisonment, vituperation, spoliation, tortures and executions," the struggling Faith was, for a time, driven underground.[3]

Included among those who met their deaths during this convulsive period was Áqá Buzurg, known as Badí', who was designated the "Pride of Martyrs" by Bahá'u'lláh. Badí' was a seventeen-year-old youth, who during his visit to Bahá'u'lláh in Acre, accepted the responsibility of delivering, in person, the tablet Bahá'u'lláh addressed to the Persian king, Náṣiri'd-Dín Shah. Upon handing the Tablet to the sháh, Badí' was "arrested, branded for three consecutive days, his head beaten to a pulp with the butt of a rifle, after which his body was thrown into a pit and earth and stones heaped upon it."[4] It is reported that Bahá'u'lláh was so moved by the sacrifice of Badí' that for a period of three years He continued to extol Badí''s great heroism and courage in His writings.

Likewise, Bahá'u'lláh extolled the qualities of the two eminent brothers from Iṣfáhán, Mírzá Muḥammad-Ḥasan and Mírzá Muḥammad-Ḥusayn, known respectively as the King of Martyrs and the Beloved of Martyrs, and He expressed grief at the circumstances of their tragic passing. The brothers were renowned for their "generosity, trustworthiness, kindliness and piety." A dishonest religious leader who owed the brothers a great deal of money set in train the events that led to their martyrdom. Seeking to free himself from the responsibility of repaying this debt, he denounced the brothers as Bábís to the civil authorities, an action, which in the climate of general hostility against the followers of the new religion precipitated their death. In the words of Shoghi Effendi, the brothers "were put in chains, decapitated, dragged to the Maydán-i-Sháh, and there exposed to the indignities heaped upon them by a degraded and rapacious populace." Reflecting on the gravity of the injustice of these heinous actions, 'Abdu'l-Bahá attests that "In such wise was the blood of these two brothers shed that the Christian priest of Julfá cried out, lamented and wept on that day."[5] These are but a few typical examples of the treatment meted out to the followers of the Bahá'í Faith by its adversaries during this stage of its development in the country of its birth.

Despite the relentless persecution and Bahá'u'lláh's continued incarceration in the prison-city of Acre, the Faith was not crushed. Indeed, the range and scope of His writings increased. Bahá'u'lláh continued to proclaim His message to the kings and religious leaders of the world. Included among these was His "significant summons issued to the Presidents of the Republics of the American continent to seize their opportunity in the Day of God, and to champion the cause of justice." In 1873 Bahá'u'lláh revealed His book of laws, the Kitáb-i-Aqdas (Most Holy Book), in which He defined the functions of the institution of the House of Justice and alluded to the other institutions that are progressively to be brought into being as part of His visionary system of world governance. His later tablets explained in greater detail the fundamental tenets and principles underlying His Dispensation. They stressed, for example, the importance of the principle of the oneness and wholeness of the human family and of justice. They emphasized the role of consultation, the importance of education, and the encouragement of the arts and sciences, and they outlined the principle of collective security, with its emphasis on the reduction of national armaments and the convening of "a world gathering in which the kings and rulers of the world will deliberate for the establishment of peace among the nations."[6]

Prior to His death Bahá'u'lláh established a covenant with the members of the religion. This was contained in the Book of Bahá'u'lláh's covenant, which was written entirely in His own handwriting. The purpose of the covenant was to safeguard the unity and integrity of the world-embracing community by clearly specifying the transfer of authority and the means by which the religion was to be organized and administered after the passing of its Founder. According to the explicit provisions of Bahá'u'lláh's covenant, 'Abdu'l-Bahá, Bahá'u'lláh's eldest son, was named as His successor and head of the Bahá'í Faith, and Bahá'u'lláh conferred upon him the authority to interpret the meaning of the Bahá'í writings.

The second period of the Heroic Age is brought to a close with the passing of Bahá'u'lláh in Acre in 1892.

THE MINISTRY OF 'ABDU'L-BAHÁ, 1892–1921

The third and final stage of the Heroic Age spans the period from 1892 until 1921. It revolves around the person of 'Abdu'l-Bahá, Bahá'u'lláh's eldest son. This stage begins with the announcement of Bahá'u'lláh's covenant and 'Abdu'l-Bahá's appointment, according to the clear and written provisions of the Book of His Covenant, as the head of the Bahá'í Faith and the authorized interpreter of Bahá'u'lláh's writings. He likewise served as "the Delineator" of the Faith's "future institutions." Shoghi Effendi explains the unique and significant implications of 'Abdu'l-Bahá's appointment:

He had been elevated to the high office of Center of Bahá'u'lláh's Covenant, and been made the successor of the Manifestation of God Himself—a position that was to empower Him to impart an extraordinary impetus to the international expansion of His Father's Faith, to amplify its doctrine, to beat down every barrier that would obstruct its march, and to call into being, and delineate the features of, its Administrative Order, the Child of the Covenant, and the Harbinger of that World Order whose establishment must needs signalize the advent of the Golden Age of the Bahá'í Dispensation.[7]

'Abdu'l-Bahá's ministry is marked by persistent attempts to undermine his authority and to subvert the covenant of Bahá'u'lláh by those
few who were jealous of his position and allied with those who wanted
to destroy the foundations of the religion. In addition, the Bahá'í
communities in the East continued to be oppressed by antagonistic
regimes. While these attempts to impair the unity of the community
and to curtail its influence were the cause of great distress, and in the
short-term retarded the growth of the Faith, in the longer term, they
failed utterly to split the community and served instead to fortify its
foundations and to demonstrate its resilience.[8]

One of the first objectives of 'Abdu'l-Bahá when he assumed the
headship of the religion was to arrange for the entombment of the
remains of the Báb on Mount Carmel, in accordance with the explicit
instruction of Bahá'u'lláh. This task, which was made much more
difficult by the machinations of the enemies of the Faith in the Holy
Land, was finally accomplished in 1909. It ranks as one of the outstanding achievements of 'Abdu'l-Bahá's ministry.[9]

During the lifetime of 'Abdu'l-Bahá the Bahá'í Faith spread to
the continent of Europe, Australasia, the Far East, and the North
American continent. Indeed, in the estimation of Shoghi Effendi, the
establishment of the Faith of Bahá'u'lláh in the Western Hemisphere
constitutes "the most outstanding achievement that will forever be
associated with 'Abdu'l-Bahá's ministry." When the Ottoman Empire
collapsed, 'Abdu'l-Bahá was freed from forty years of exile and captiv-
ity. Soon after, he embarked on an extended period of travel, which
lasted from September 1910 until December 1913. His journeys took
him to a number of cities in Egypt, England, France, the United
States and Canada, and on the return trip, in addition to spending
more time in England and France, he visited Germany and the Central
European cities of Budapest and Vienna. 'Abdu'l-Bahá's eight-month-
long tour of North America marks the climax of these journeys. This

historic tour lasted from April until December 1912 and entailed a journey of over five thousand miles on that continent, a journey that took him from the Atlantic to the Pacific coast and back. Shoghi Effendi attests that 'Abdu'l-Bahá's mission to the Western world is "so momentous that it deserves to rank as the greatest exploit ever to be associated with His ministry."[10]

'Abdu'l-Bahá's purpose in making these arduous tours was to make known the teachings of the Bahá'í Faith to the general public and to encourage and educate the small communities of individuals who had recently identified themselves with the religion. Shoghi Effendi states:

> It was in the course of these epoch-making journeys and before large and representative audiences, at times exceeding a thousand people, that 'Abdu'l-Bahá expounded, with brilliant simplicity, with persuasiveness and force, and for the first time in His ministry, those basic and distinguishing principles of His Father's Faith, which together with the laws and ordinances revealed in the Kitáb-i-Aqdas constitute the bed-rock of God's latest Revelation to mankind. The independent search after truth, unfettered by superstition or tradition; the oneness of the entire human race, the pivotal principle and fundamental doctrine of the Faith; the basic unity of all religions; the condemnation of all forms of prejudice, whether religious, racial, class or national; the harmony which must exist between religion and science; the equality of men and women, the two wings on which the bird of human kind is able to soar; the introduction of compulsory education; the adoption of a universal auxiliary language; the abolition of the extremes of wealth and poverty; the institution of a world tribunal for the adjudication of disputes between nations; the exaltation of work, performed in the spirit of service, to the rank of worship; the glorification of justice as the ruling

principle in human society, and of religion as a bulwark for the protection of all peoples and nations; and the establishment of a permanent and universal peace as the supreme goal of all mankind—these stand out as the essential elements of that Divine polity which He proclaimed to leaders of public thought as well as to the masses at large in the course of these missionary journeys.[11]

As the architect of the World Order foreshadowed in the writings of the Báb and Bahá'u'lláh, 'Abdu'l-Bahá during his ministry delineated in his writings some of the features of the Administrative Order that would come into being after his passing, and would herald the advent of that Order. He actively fostered the development of the rudimentary Bahá'í administrative, spiritual, and educational institutions being reared in the Bahá'í communities throughout the world and he encouraged the translation, publication, and dissemination of Bahá'í literature. He composed his last Will and Testament, whose provisions were to usher in the Formative Age of the Bahá'í Faith, and revealed the Tablets of the Divine Plan which conferred upon the Bahá'ís in the North American continent the unique and primary responsibility for spreading the religion throughout the world and for erecting its administrative structure.

The death of 'Abdu'l-Bahá in 1921 and the interment of his remains on Mount Carmel brought to an end the Heroic Age of the Bahá'í Era. Shoghi Effendi attests to the uniqueness of this "Primitive Age." It was, he states, "unapproached in spiritual fecundity by any period associated with the mission of the Founder of any previous Dispensation, was impregnated, from its inception to its termination, with the creative energies generated through the advent of two independent Manifestations and the establishment of a Covenant unique in the spiritual annals of mankind."[12]

INCEPTION OF THE FORMATIVE AGE (1921–)

The inception of the Formative Age of the Bahá'í Era synchronizes with the founding of the Bahá'í Administrative Order, based primarily on the execution of principles laid down by Bahá'u'lláh and the provisions of 'Abdu'l-Bahá's Will and Testament. This administrative system is destined to be "at once the harbinger, the nucleus and pattern" of the future World Order of Bahá'u'lláh, and which in the fullness of time will inaugurate no less than "the Kingdom of the Father upon earth as promised by Jesus Christ Himself." Envisaged as an age of transition, the Formative Age is, in the words of Shoghi Effendi, "to be identified with the rise and establishment of the Administrative Order, upon which the institutions of the future Bahá'í World Commonwealth must needs be ultimately erected in the Golden Age that must witness the consummation of the Bahá'í Dispensation."[13]

It is interesting to note that the features of this World Order and the means by which it is to be implemented have been, and will continue to be progressively disclosed. While held in a remote prison, the Báb, in His writings, announced the advent of this Order and associated it with the name of Bahá'u'lláh, Whose mission He foretold. In the Báb's Persian Bayán we find the following prophetic allusion: "Well is it with him who fixeth his gaze upon the Order of Bahá'u'lláh, and rendereth thanks unto his Lord! For He will assuredly be made manifest . . ." At a later time Bahá'u'lláh revealed the laws and principles that are to govern the operation of His World Order, and referred to its universal significance in the Kitáb-i-Aqdas, His book of laws. We read: "The world's equilibrium hath been upset through the vibrating influence of this most great, this new World Order. Mankind's ordered life hath been revolutionized through the agency of this unique, this wondrous System—the like of which mortal eyes have never witnessed."[14]

The next stage in the progressive unfoldment of the World Order was marked by the revelation by 'Abdu'l-Bahá of his Will and Testament, a seminal document, characterized as the "Charter" of the Administrative Order, which is destined to precede the emergence of World Order. Indeed, the Will and Testament "called into being, outlined the features and set in motion the processes of, this Administrative Order."[15] The early years of the Formative Age are marked by the efforts of the Bahá'ís in the East and the West to lay the foundations of the embryonic institutions of the Administrative Order.

As the membership of the Bahá'í community grows, the influence of its Administrative Order extends to a greater proportion of society. Bahá'ís believe that its methods of operation, with an emphasis on maintenance of a careful balance between centralized and decentralized functioning, the use of democratic procedures in the election of its administrative bodies, measures to preserve individual freedom and initiative, and safeguards for fostering cultural diversity, provide both a pattern and a nucleus for a future world society. Bahá'ís anticipate that the Formative Age will reach its culmination, perhaps centuries into the future, with the evolution of its Administrative Order into an inclusive entity known as the World Order of Bahá'u'lláh animated by the Bahá'í spiritual and administrative principles.

THE WILL AND TESTAMENT
OF 'ABDU'L-BAHÁ — THE CHARTER

In order to understand the significance of this seminal document, it is necessary to examine the contents of 'Abdu'l-Bahá's Will and Testament, in particular, the provisions it contains for the designation of the successor to 'Abdu'l-Bahá and the establishment of the institutions of the Bahá'í Administrative Order, and to describe in brief some of the features of the Bahá'í system of administration, which is destined to serve as the vehicle for the systematic spread of Bahá'í values and social order throughout the world.

The Will and Testament is described by Shoghi Effendi as "the Charter of a future world civilization" and as 'Abdu'l-Bahá's "greatest legacy to posterity, the brightest emanation of His mind and the mightiest instrument forged to insure the continuity of the three ages which constitute the component parts of His Father's Dispensation." Written entirely in 'Abdu'l-Bahá's own handwriting, this historic document might be regarded, in some of its features, as supplementary to Bahá'u'lláh's book of laws, the Kitáb-i-Aqdas. It reiterates the fundamental beliefs of the religion and underlines the stations of the Báb and Bahá'u'lláh. It establishes the institution of the Guardianship and appoints his great grandson, Shoghi Effendi as the first Guardian of the Bahá'í Faith. It sets out the measures for the election of the Universal House of Justice by the members of Secondary Houses of Justice (currently called National Spiritual Assemblies). It also defines the functions and responsibilities of the institution of the Hands of the Cause, and stresses the importance of obedience to the covenant by the adherents of the Faith.[16]

Just as there were attacks on the covenant of Bahá'u'lláh by those who sought to undermine the religion during 'Abdu'l-Bahá's ministry, following the death of 'Abdu'l-Bahá, a small number of disaffected individuals arose to question the provisions of his Will and Testament concerning succession and the organization of the religion. In addition, some who were more comfortable with the purely individualistic leadership of 'Abdu'l-Bahá took a little time to accommodate to the existence and authority of elected Spiritual Assemblies, whose establishment was to be a feature of the new Formative Age. However, the vast majority of the believers readily accepted the newly appointed Guardian, and endeavored to understand the needs of the new stage in the evolution of the administration of the Faith. They embraced change and set about erecting its administrative structure and enlarging its worldwide community.

THE BAHÁ'Í ADMINISTRATIVE ORDER—
THE ROLE OF SHOGHI EFFENDI

The Bahá'í administrative system is unique. The Bahá'í Faith has no priesthood, and is free from the privileges, prerogatives, and rituals associated with an ecclesiastical structure. In its basic and current form, the Administrative Order has two arms, one consisting of elected individuals who act as members of Spiritual Assemblies, local and national, which are endowed with the authority to administer the affairs of their Bahá'í community through the exercise of legislative, judicial, and executive powers in matters pertaining to religious practice. An internationally elected body, the Universal House of Justice, formed in 1963, acts as the head of the Faith to which all believers turn for guidance.

The other arm of the Administrative Order is composed of individuals of high standing in the community who act in an advisory capacity to Assemblies and individuals, offering counsel, fostering adherence to the spiritual values of the religion, and calling attention to those measures required to protect the Bahá'í Faith from the inadvertent corruption of its teachings with the passage of time. These individuals are designated as Hands of the Cause, Counselors, Auxiliary Board members, and assistants. The Counselors and their auxiliaries are organized into five Boards of Counselors, one for each continental area of the world. Their work is coordinated and supervised by the International Teaching Center, which is located at the Bahá'í World Center and functions under the guidance of the Universal House of Justice.

To bring this structure into being 'Abdu'l-Bahá appointed his eldest grandson, Shoghi Effendi, as Guardian of the Faith. Through the discharge of his functions, which included that of being the authorized interpreter of the Faith, Shoghi Effendi successfully completed his mission by the time of his passing in 1957. Upon taking up his appointment, Shoghi Effendi addressed letters to the worldwide Bahá'í community in which he formulated the basic principles for the operation and systematic establishment of Local and National Spiritual Assemblies throughout the East and the West and set in motion processes that were to lead to the election of the Universal House of Justice. He thus translated the provisions in the Will and Testament into practical guidance, which served to motivate, mobilize, and empower the Bahá'í world to successfully negotiate its transition from the Heroic Age to the Formative Age of the Faith. In the following passage, Shoghi Effendi captures the eager and immediate response of the Bahá'í community to meeting the needs of a new stage in the development of the Bahá'í Faith for systematic action and the adoption of a long-term perspective:

No sooner had the provisions of that Divine Charter, delineating the features of the Administrative Order of the Faith of Bahá'u'lláh been disclosed to His followers than they set about erecting, upon the foundations which the lives of the heroes, the saints and martyrs of that Faith had laid, the first stage of the framework of its administrative institutions. Conscious of the necessity of constructing, as a first step, a broad and solid base upon which the pillars of that mighty structure could subsequently be raised; fully aware that upon these pillars, when firmly established, the dome, the final unit crowning the entire edifice, must eventually rest . . . the pioneer builders of a divinely-conceived Order undertook, in complete unison, and despite the great diversity in their outlook, customs and languages, the double task of establishing and of consolidating their local councils, elected by the rank and file of the believers, and designed to direct, coordinate and extend the activities of the followers of a far-flung Faith.[17]

The requirements of the Formative Age not only called for a change in the nature of the activities to be undertaken by the Bahá'í community and for reevaluation of its priorities, but also for a change in personal orientation on the part of its individual members. In this regard, a letter written on behalf of Shoghi Effendi characterizes the distinctive qualities required of the believers and the needs of the transitional age in the following terms:

> Every day has certain needs. In those early days the Cause needed Martyrs, and people who would stand all sorts of torture and persecution in expressing their faith and spreading the message sent by God. Those days are, however, gone. The Cause at present does not need martyrs who would die for the faith, but servants who desire to teach and establish the Cause throughout the world. To live to teach in the present day is like being martyred in those early days. It is the spirit that moves us that counts, not the act through which that spirit expresses itself; and that spirit is to serve the Cause of God with our heart and soul.[18]

4

SEEDS OF WORLD ORDER

There is both a mystical and existential relationship between the Heroic Age of the Bahá'í Faith and its Formative Age. The Heroic Age, associated with the dawn and rise of the religion in the land of its birth, is characterized by the leadership of charismatic individuals, the heroic exploits of its martyrs and saints, and the stirring deeds of the rank and file members of the community. It is distinguished by clashes with the forces of society and religion that were instigated by political and ecclesiastical leaders who felt threatened by the vision and values of the new revelation. The Formative Age, which is an age of transition to a more distant Golden Age, which is destined to witness the emergence of enduring peace and the establishment of the Bahá'í World Commonwealth, is associated with the building of the Bahá'í Administrative Order, the global system for the administration of the affairs of the Bahá'í community. In the following terms, Shoghi Effendi describes the generative influence of "the most tragic, the most heroic period of the first Bahá'í century," and he foreshadows its potential impact on the future development of the Faith: "The torrents of blood that poured out during those crowded and calamitous years may be regarded as constituting the fertile seeds of that World Order which a swiftly succeeding and still greater Revelation was to proclaim and establish."[1]

More specifically, Shoghi Effendi links the heroic and seminal clash that took place at the fort of <u>Sh</u>ay<u>kh</u> Ṭabarsí during the lifetime of the Báb with the very inception of the embryonic World Order envisioned in the Bahá'í teachings, whose establishment is a hallmark of the Formative Age. He writes:

> Its outcome was a heinous betrayal ending in an orgy of slaughter, staining with everlasting infamy its perpetrators, investing its victims with a halo of imperishable glory, and generating the very seeds which, in a later age, were to blossom into world-wide administrative institutions, and which must, in the fullness of time, yield their golden fruit in the shape of a world-redeeming, earth-encircling Order.[2]

And, he draws attention to Bahá'u'lláh's eulogy to the heroism of the martyrs:

> "The whole world," is Bahá'u'lláh's matchless testimony in the Kitáb-i-Íqán, "marveled at the manner of their sacrifice. . . . The mind is bewildered at their deeds, and the soul marveleth at their fortitude and bodily endurance. . . . Hath any age witnessed such momentous happenings?" And again: "Hath the world, since the days of Adam, witnessed such tumult, such violent commotion? . . . Methinks, patience was revealed only by virtue of their fortitude, and faithfulness itself was begotten only by their deeds." "Through the blood which they shed," He, in a prayer, referring more specifically to the martyrs of the Faith, has significantly affirmed, "the earth hath been impregnated with the wondrous revelations of Thy might and the gem-like signs of Thy glorious sovereignty. Ere-long shall she tell out her tidings, when the set time is come."[3]

In this chapter we examine the salient features of the heroic episode that took place at the fort of Shaykh Ṭabarsí and explore the basis for considering how this event serves as "the very seeds" of the Bahá'í Administrative Order. In addition, we describe the motivation and behavior of the Bábís who sought refuge within the fort, and the system of disciplined organization with which they conducted the defense of the fort, and we use features of this historic event to draw parallels with the purpose and functioning of the Bahá'í Administrative system.

THE EPISODE AT THE FORT OF SHAYKH ṬABARSÍ

The formal announcement by the Báb of His station as the Promised One during His public interrogation was, in the words of Shoghi Effendi, "the explosive force that loosed a veritable avalanche of calamities which swept down upon the Faith and the people among whom it was born." A systematic campaign against the new religion was launched by the combined forces of the civil and ecclesiastical authorities. In isolated and remote centers the Bábís were mercilessly attacked wherever they were found. They had no recourse but to band together for self-protection, a move that was typically misconstrued and interpreted as an act of hostility against the authority of the government and clergy, and which further increased the determination to wipe out this new faith community. The tragic events that transpired at the fort of Shaykh Ṭabarsí took place against this backdrop.[4]

In the events that immediately preceded the seven-month siege, Mullá Ḥusayn, the first Letter of the Living, was instructed by the Báb to go to the aid of Quddús who was being held in detention in the town of Sárí in the province of Mázindarán. As they proceeded on this journey, Mullá Ḥusayn and his companions attracted so many others to embrace the call of the new day that the swelling band of supporters aroused such anxiety and hostility that the entire group could not stay within the walls of any town or within the limits of any village. As they approached the town of Bárfurúsh, its leading cleric denounced Mullá Ḥusayn so vehemently that the whole town rose up in opposition to the Bábís. Though 'Abbás-Qulí Khán-i-Lárijání, the head of the military in the province, promised safe passage to Mullá Ḥusayn and his companions, so great was the leading cleric's hostility toward the Bábís that he persuaded Khusraw, the officer assigned to escort the Bábís to safety, to violate his commander's order and instead to attack those he was charged to protect. 'Abdu'l-Bahá describes how Mullá Ḥusayn and his companions were treacherously attacked in the heart of the forest, and he captures the moment when the hapless Bábís first became aware of their betrayal: "Khusraw dispersed his horsemen and footmen and set them in ambush in the forest of Mazíndáran, scattered and separated the Bábís in that forest on the road and off the road, and began to hunt them down singly. When the reports of muskets arose on every side the hidden secret became manifest . . ."[5] In the ensuing fray there were a number of casualties, including the treacherous officer who led the charge. Though the army dispersed in disarray, the Bábís continued to be harried by the attacks on their camp by hostile villagers. Mullá Ḥusayn was forced to seek a place where the Bábís could be safely lodged.

On 12 October 1848, Mullá Ḥusayn quartered his followers near the burial place of Shaykh Ṭabarsí,* about fourteen miles southeast of Bárfurúsh, and gave orders for the construction of a fort around the shrine. He assigned to each group a section of the work, and

---

* Shaykh Ṭabarsí was one of the transmitters of the traditions ascribed to the Imams of the Muslim Faith. His burial place was visited by people of the neighborhood. See *The Dawn-Breakers: Nabíl's Narrative of the Early Days of the Bahá'í Revelation*, p. 343.

encouraged its early completion. From the very first day, the Bábís were, at the instigation of the leading cleric, harassed by the villagers in the surrounding areas, and they were forced to defend themselves. Nabíl attests:

> Every attack of the enemy ended in failure and shame. Undeterred by the fierceness of their repeated onsets, the companions valiantly withstood their assaults until they had succeeded in subjugating temporarily the forces which had hemmed them in on every side. When the work of construction was completed Mullá Ḥusayn undertook the necessary preparations for the siege which the fort was destined to sustain, and provided, despite the obstacles that stood in his way, whatever seemed essential for the safety of its occupants.[6]

When the work was completed the companions in the fort received a visit from Bahá'u'lláh. In the course of His visit He inspected the fort, judged it to be satisfactory, and consulted with Mullá Ḥusayn about outstanding matters that pertained to the welfare and safety of his companions. Bahá'u'lláh advised Mullá Ḥusayn to arrange for Quddús, the last Letter of the Living, to join the companions in the fort. His advice was immediately put into action. Prior to His departure, Bahá'u'lláh expressed His desire to return, in the near future, to lend His assistance to the defenders of the fort, a desire which was to be thwarted by circumstances beyond His control. Bahá'u'lláh addressed the occupants of the fort in the following portentous words—words that capture both the purpose and the vision of the significance of the events in which they were soon to engage: "You have been chosen of God to be the vanguard of His host and the establishers of His Faith. His host verily will conquer. Whatever may befall, victory is yours, a victory which is complete and certain."[7]

Toward the end of 1848 Quddús arrived at the newly built fort and, at the insistence of Mullá Ḥusayn, assumed the overall leadership. He immediately called for the number of the inhabitants of the fort to be counted. They numbered 313 individuals, the majority of whom were students and theologians, known for their character, their learning and literary accomplishments, rather than those trained in the arts of war. Indeed, throughout the whole episode, Quddús himself set an example of devotion by continuing to compose commentaries on various religious and theological subjects. A daily routine of activities was also instigated, which included the recitation of prayers and chanting of the writings of the Báb and Quddús. These periods of devotion were to prove a source of spiritual upliftment and sustenance in the difficult days ahead.

The completion of the fort excited the curiosity of the villagers in the surrounding areas and further inflamed the animosity of the clerics. While the Bábís sought simply to live peacefully within the walls of their fortification, the clergy misrepresented their purpose and appealed to the government to intervene on the grounds that the followers of the Báb were aiming to direct a campaign against the sháh. Fearful, the sháh called for a military response. An army of 12,000 men was raised and marched to the vicinity of the fort, where it encamped and erected barricades to prevent the delivery of bread and water to those within. As the army's preparations for an attack were nearing completion, early one morning, Quddús, escorted by Mullá Ḥusayn and a number of companions on horseback, followed by the entire company on foot, sallied out of the fort and uttered the call, "Yá Ṣáḥíbu'z-Zamán,"* with such intensity that it spread

---

* "Yá Ṣáḥíbu'z-Zamán," literally, "O Thou Lord of the Age." "Yá Ṣáḥíbu'z-Zamán" is one of the titles of the Promised One. See, *The Dawn-Breakers: Nabíl's Narrative of the Early Days of the Bahá'í Revelation*, p. 675.

consternation among the enemy lying in ambush in the forest, caus-ing them to flee and abandon their possessions. Having repulsed their assailants, Quddús instructed the Bábís to return to their fort. He did not press for a final and decisive victory, explaining his motivation as follows:

> We need not carry further the punishment. Our purpose is to protect ourselves that we may be able to continue our labors for the regeneration of men. We have no intention whatever of causing unnecessary harm to anyone. What we have already achieved is sufficient testimony to God's invincible power. We, a little band of His followers, have been able, through His sustain-ing grace, to overcome the organized and trained army of our enemies.[8]

Before long, it became apparent that the opposing military, now led by a prince of the realm, had been reinforced with several regiments of infantry and cavalry, and was beginning to regroup in prepara-tion for a renewed attack. As a defensive measure and to increase the security of their position, Quddús instructed his companions to dig a moat around the fort. They labored intensively day and night for nineteen days to complete the task.

No sooner was the moat completed than the prince dispatched a messenger to the fort to inquire, on behalf of the sháh, about the activities in which the occupants of the fort were engaged. Mullá Husayn, their spokesman, assured the messenger that the Bábís had absolutely no intention either of subverting the foundation of the monarchy or of usurping the authority of the sháh. He stressed that their concern was to vindicate the Cause of the Promised One. He, therefore, called upon the prince to assemble the religious leaders so the Bábís could demonstrate the validity of the revelation proclaimed by the Báb. Addressing the messenger, Mullá Ḥusayn issued the following challenge: "Let the Qur'án decide as to who speaks the truth. Let the prince himself judge our case and pronounce the verdict. Let him also decide as to how he should treat us if we fail to establish, by the aid of verses and traditions, the truth of this Cause."[9]

The prince failed to take up Mullá Ḥusayn's offer. Three days later, while it was yet dark, as the army prepared to launch an attack on the occupants of the fort, Quddús ordered the gates of the fort to be opened and the Bábís sallied forth in the direction of the stronghold that served as the operational headquarters of the army. Observing the indifference of the Bábís to the hail of bullets, and fearing for his life, the prince fled, escaping barefooted through an open window. "His host," writes Nabíl, "deprived of their leader and struck with panic, fled in disgraceful rout before that little band which, despite their own overwhelming numbers and the resources which the imperial treasury had placed at their disposal, they were unable to subdue."[10]

Later that same day, 23 December 1848, there was another attack and Quddús received a bullet wound in his mouth. With renewed determination Mullá Ḥusayn and his companions fought a desperate battle in which they displayed marvelous heroism and succeeded not only in rescuing the wounded Quddús but also in putting the entire army to flight.

In time the demoralized army regrouped and was further reinforced with additional manpower and heavy equipment. In preparation for a renewed attack on the Bábís, the army constructed seven barricades around the fort. At dawn on 2 February 1849, Mullá Ḥusayn led his last sortie. He succeeded in overcoming the resistance of the third barricade before being struck by a bullet after his horse became entangled in the rope of a tent. Carried back to the fort by his companions, he subsequently died and was interred in the grounds of the fort. Testifying to the exploits and the character of Mullá Ḥusayn, Nabíl writes:

> From each of these hot and fierce engagements Mullá Ḥusayn emerged, in spite of the overwhelming forces arrayed against him, unscathed and triumphant. In each encounter he distinguished himself by such acts of valour, of chivalry, of skill, and of strength that each one would alone suffice to establish for all time the transcendent character of a Faith for the protection of which he had so valiantly fought, and in the path of which he had so nobly died. The traits of mind and of character which, from his very youth, he displayed, the profundity of his learning, the tenacity of his faith, his intrepid courage, his singleness of purpose, his high sense of justice and unswerving devotion, marked him as an outstanding figure among those who, by their lives, have borne witness to the glory and power of the new Revelation. He was six and thirty years old when he quaffed the cup of martyrdom.[11]

Despite the untimely death of Mullá Ḥusayn the occupants of the fort again confounded the army. However, some ninety companions were wounded in the day's engagements, most of whom later succumbed. In the camp of the adversary, news of Mullá Ḥusayn's death served to strengthen the resolve of the army and new attacks were planned. Quddús appointed Mírzá Muḥammad-Báqir to replace Mullá Ḥusayn in leading the companions. Sallying forth with eighteen companions, they once more routed the military forces leagued against them. This stunning victory served to cement the unity of the defenders of the fort and to remind them of the efficacy of the power with which their Faith had endowed them.

The spirit that motivated the companions in the fort who engaged in these recurrent defensive exploits was clearly articulated by Quddús, who uttered the following words during this most difficult period:

> Never . . . have we under any circumstances attempted to direct any offensive against our opponents. Not until they unchained their attack upon us did we arise to defend our lives. Had we cherished the ambition of waging holy war against them, had we harboured the least intention of achieving ascendancy through the power of our arms over the unbelievers, we should not, until this day, have remained besieged within these walls. The force of our arms would have by now, as was the case with the companions of Muḥammád in days past, convulsed the nations of the earth and prepared them for the acceptance of our Message. Such is not the way, however, which we have chosen to tread. Ever since we repaired to this fort, our sole, our unalterable purpose has been the vindication, by our deeds and by our readiness to shed our blood in the path of our Faith, of the exalted character of our mission. The hour is fast approaching when we shall be able to consummate this task.[12]

The pressure of the forces arrayed against the Bábís inexorably increased. Cannon fire was directed at them. Their food and other supplies were completely exhausted. 'Abdu'l-Bahá depicts the extent of the sufferings of the occupants of the fort in the following terms:

> The believers . . . went eighteen days without food. They lived on the leather of their shoes. This too was soon consumed, and they had nothing left but water. They drank a mouthful every morning, and lay famished and exhausted in their Fort. When attacked, however, they would instantly spring to their feet, and

manifest in the face of the enemy a magnificent courage and astonishing resistance . . . Under such circumstances to maintain an unwavering faith and patience is extremely difficult, and to endure such dire afflictions a rare phenomenon.[13]

The siege ultimately ended not through surrender, but when the prince who commanded the attacking forces swore an oath on the Qur'án, to which he affixed his seal, and solemnly promised that the lives and property of the companions in the fort would be preserved should they come out of the fort and disperse in peace. Though wary of the intention of the prince, out of respect for the Qur'án and the prince's solemn oath, Quddús and his companions determined to test the sincerity of the promise by agreeing to leave the fort. In their willingness to replace conflict with cooperation they displayed a critical form of courage.

As soon as Quddús together with two hundred and two of his companions left the fortress, the true intention of the prince became tragically evident. The promise of safety was immediately broken. The Bábís were massacred, their corpses were violated, and the fort was pillaged and razed to the ground. Of the original three hundred and thirteen occupants only a few survived. Quddús was taken to Bárfúrush, where at the hands of the leading cleric of that town, he suffered fiendish torture and was killed in the public square. His martyrdom took place in May 1849, seven months after his fellow-Bábís took refuge in the fort of Shaykh Ṭabarsí.

When news of the fate of the defenders of the fort reached the Báb, He was heartbroken, and, for some months, He was overcome with grief. The Báb penned eulogies of Quddús and of Mullá Ḥusayn and of all those who immortalized their names in the defense of the fort. He then instructed one of His followers to undertake a pilgrimage on His behalf to the place of their martyrdom. While there, this believer was further instructed to recite special tablets revealed by the Báb in memory of the martyrs of Ṭabarsí, and as a souvenir of his visit, the Báb requested that he bring for Him "a handful of that holy earth" which covers the remains of His loved ones.[14]

The historian Nabíl, as a befitting tribute to those who sacrificed their lives in this momentous and historic episode, provides a partial list of the names of those involved. He prefaces his list with the following words:

> It would be appropriate at this juncture to place on record the names of those martyrs who participated in the defense of the fort of Shaykh Ṭabarsí, in the hope that generations yet to come may recall with pride and gratitude the names, no less than the deeds, of those pioneers who, by their life and death, have so greatly enriched the annals of God's immortal Faith.[15]

SALIENT FEATURES OF THE EPISODE

In *God Passes By*, Shoghi Effendi identifies the "salient features" of the "tragic episode" that transpired at Shaykh Ṭabarsí. They include elements that highlight the nature of the motivation of the defenders of the fort, the quality of their leadership, the dynamic impact of their discipline and order, and their resilience in the face of overwhelming obstacles.[16]

MOTIVATION

It is evident from a description of the events that took place at the fort of Shaykh Ṭabarsí that the followers of the Báb were forced to band together for self-protection and survival. They were compelled to take up residence in the fort, to reinforce its perimeter, and later to dig a moat and build towers, primarily as a means of protecting themselves from the increasing hostility and the fierce and concerted attacks orchestrated by the combined forces of the civil and ecclesiastical authorities and executed by the forces of the imperial army. Even when the Bábís took to the field of battle, their desire was to preserve the fledgling community of the Báb, and to ensure the continuity of His religion and the ultimate spread of its society-transforming tenets. At no time did they set out to oppose or attempt to undermine the government, though they were frequently accused of disloyalty to the sháh, and dark political motives were attributed to them. Indeed, to any impartial witness it was clear that such allegations were false. Shoghi Effendi attests in a letter written on his behalf that, "the very fact that these disciples were ready and willing to emerge from the fort and return to their homes after receiving the assurance that they would be no more molested is itself an evidence that they were not contemplating any action against the authorities."[17] And, for their compliance, the followers of the Báb were treacherously deceived.

Likewise, the Bábís did not engage in any form of holy war, in the sense of a war for God and for the true faith waged against an infidel enemy. The notion of a holy war, sanctioned or even commanded by God, is a common and recurring theme in the history of religions. In the Muslim tradition, for example, jihad [holy war] was most commonly interpreted to mean armed struggle for the defense or advancement of Muslim power. "Those who fight in the jihad qualify for rewards in both worlds—booty in this one, paradise in the next." While the religion of the Báb emerged from an Islamic context, and, to some extent, the conceptions and ideas of the Bábís were influenced by former custom, in His writings, the Báb had not given any instructions or endorsement concerning aggressive warfare, even for religious purposes, and since He was being held in an isolated prison, it was not possible for His followers to seek His guidance. 'Abdu'l-Bahá captures the position of the Bábís in the following terms: "In towns where there were but a limited number, all of them with bound hands became food for the sword, while in cities where they were numerous, they arose in self-defense in accordance with their former beliefs, since it was impossible for them to make enquiry as to their duty, and all doors were closed."[18]

In later years, Bahá'u'lláh clarified any ambiguity that might have existed concerning what to do when under attack. He categorically "abolished the law to wage holy law," affirming, "It is better to be killed than to kill."[19]

When forced to fight for their lives, the Bábís did so with determination, skill, and strength, however, their response was moral and principled. Shoghi Effendi pays tribute to "the sublime patience, the noble restraint" exercised by Mullá Ḥusayn and the other defenders of the fort who refused to unsheathe their swords until attacked. Indeed, Nabíl emphasizes that "Even in the midst of a fierce conflict they would not drive home an advantage nor strike an unnecessary blow." They did not seek revenge nor did they attempt to exact retribution.[20]

On a personal level, the defenders of the fort were not motivated by any desire for personal gain or worldly riches. The Bábís were aware of the challenges that confronted them, and calm in the face of danger. In this regard, Shoghi Effendi underlines,

the spirit of renunciation that prompted those sore pressed sufferers to contemptuously ignore the possessions left behind by their fleeing enemy; that led them to discard their own belongings, and content themselves with their steeds and swords; ... and impelled those same companions to disdain, and refuse even to touch, the costly furnishings and the coffers of gold and silver which the demoralized and shame laden ... commander of the army of Mázindárán . . . had left behind in his headlong flight from his camp.[21]

Throughout the extended campaign, from time to time, Quddús, being acutely conscious of the danger involved, offered the inhabitants of the fort the opportunity to remove themselves from immediate harm by leaving the fortress. Few chose to avail themselves of this opportunity. On one such occasion, at the time of the New Year in 1849, Quddús alluded to the approach of an intensification of the trials of his companions that would bring in its wake the martyrdom of a considerable number of them. He addressed them with these words:

Beware lest you allow the encroachments of self and desire to impair so glorious a station. Fear not the threats of the wicked, neither be dismayed by the clamour of the ungodly. Each one of you has his appointed hour, and when that time is come, neither the assaults of your enemy nor the endeavours of your friends will be able either to retard or to advance that hour. If the powers of the earth league themselves against you, they will be powerless, ere that hour strikes, to lessen by one jot or tittle the span of your life. Should you allow your hearts to be agitated for but one moment by the booming of the guns which, with increasing violence, will continue to shower their shot upon this fort, you will have cast yourselves out of the stronghold of Divine protection.[22]

Motivated by spiritual values, the Bábís did not actively court death, though they willingly accepted it in order to demonstrate the transforming power of their religion and to ensure that the Cause might live and prosper. In making this ultimate personal sacrifice, it was not their aim to harm others or to embroil them in danger. Rather, they went out of their way to protect the innocent.

QUALITY OF LEADERSHIP

The leadership of Quddús and the tactical brilliance of Mullá Ḥusayn are characterized by a rare combination of discipline and resourcefulness, by a consciousness of the importance of both the interdependence and practical necessity of drawing on the inspiration of the spiritual and on logical thought and planning.

It is interesting to note that recent studies in the fields of psychology and business management stress the importance of resourcefulness and creativity in effective leadership behavior. Bennis, for example, writing about the challenges of leadership in the modern world, states that "creativity is an essential characteristic of leaders," and Reardon, exploring the operation of courage in business, identifies resourcefulness in decision-making as a key element. She observes, "Contingency planning is really about resourcefulness. People who take bold risks and succeed are versatile thinkers; they ready themselves with alternative routes." Reardon concludes that, with "well-developed contingency plans managers are better empowered to make bold moves that serve their organization, their careers, and their own sense of personal worth."[23]

The current state of the world and the apparent dearth of leadership skills of those in power have given rise to a renewed interest in the study of leadership. Stressing the vital importance of "exemplary leadership" for the solution of "the major threats to world stability," Bennis identifies six competencies which he believes all exemplary leaders possess. He writes: "They create a sense of mission, they motivate others to join them on that mission, they create an adaptive social architecture for their followers, they generate trust and optimism, they develop other leaders, and they get results."[24]

The uniqueness of the leadership styles of Quddús and Mullá Ḥusayn become evident when examined in light of contemporary understandings of leadership. Each assumed leadership at different times. At first, Mullá Ḥusayn was in command of the fort. He was responsible for coordinating the reinforcement of the fortress, and fending off attacks while preparing the structure for the major onslaught that was to come. When Bahá'u'lláh came to inspect the completed fortifications, He directed Mullá Ḥusayn to arrange for Quddús to join the companions in the fort. Cognizant of Quddús's superior station, Mullá Ḥusayn, with true humility, instructed his companions to observe toward Quddús "a reverence such as they would feel prompted to show to the Báb, Himself." He commanded that they should consider him as Quddús's "lowly servant," and, in stressing the strength and determination of his intent, he addressed his companions, thus: "You should bear him such loyalty that if he were to command you to take my life, you would unhesitatingly obey."[25]

Nabíl recounts how some of the inhabitants of the fort initially supposed that the profound reverence which Mullá Ḥusayn showed toward Quddús was "dictated by the exigencies of the situation rather than prompted by a spontaneous feeling of devotion to his person." Such views were soon dispelled as they observed the "knowledge and sagacity which Quddús displayed . . . , the confidence with which he spoke, and the resource and enterprise which he demonstrated in the instructions he gave to his companions." By such means, his authority was reinforced and his prestige enhanced.[26]

The transfer of command proceeded without challenge. The historical record shows that there was no conflict of leadership between Quddús and Mullá Ḥusayn. They worked together in concert. Their relationship was one of loving support and collaboration. Each recognized the unique rank and special functions of the other. But, beyond that, they derived their sense of mission from the same source.

Both Quddús and Mullá Ḥusayn had a clear grasp of the significance of the Báb's revelation and its relationship to the forces of historical change. They understood that the teachings of the Báb were an expression of the divine will, and these teachings outlined the path to true spiritual fulfillment, and defined the path to a new future social order. Their desire to promulgate and implement the life-transforming teachings of the Báb, and to make their contribution to the creation of a new world was the source of their motivation and at the heart of the sense of mission that they embraced—a mission to which all the followers of the Báb also subscribed to the extent to which they were able to grasp its significance.

The underlying motivation of their mission was fundamentally spiritual, but also had practical implications. It engendered deep faith in the power of God, which not only enabled the defenders of the fort to believe in their ability to accomplish the tasks at hand, but also to cope with hardship and to surmount the obstacles with which they were confronted. This sense of mission brought comfort and strength to the individual and led to wise actions that were measured against the guiding principles of the religion.

Quddús fostered the sense of mission among his companions by increasing their knowledge of the teachings of the Báb, and their appreciation of the vision contained within His writings. Each day, Quddús gathered the defenders of the fort to listen to the chanting of the utterances of the Báb and to the commentaries he, himself, had composed. The regularity of these study and devotional sessions was unbroken either by the threats of the enemy or the ferocity of their attacks. Indeed, the understanding and spiritual sustenance gained from such gatherings, and by the recitation in unison of certain prescribed verses, reinforced the strength and the resolve of the heroic and beleaguered Bábís.

While Quddús and Mullá Ḥusayn shared the same sense of mission, which they communicated to their companions, Quddús attracted their support by his knowledge and personal qualities. Shoghi Effendi pays tribute to his "serenity and sagacity," and to "the confidence" he instilled in his followers through the vision he imparted to them and through deepening their conscious awareness of the power and protection of God. Shoghi Effendi also calls attention to Quddús's "resourcefulness," illustrated by his understanding of his opponents, and by the manner in which he adjusted to changing circumstances both in terms of dwindling resources and the increasingly violent assaults of the forces leagued against the defenders of the fort.[27]

Working in close collaboration with Quddús, Mullá Ḥusayn motivated others by heroic deeds. He led by example. Though by training a sedentary scholar, more at home with books and pens than with a sword, Mullá Ḥusayn proved himself an intrepid and brilliant tactician, not only in the careful contingency planning that went into the preparation of the fort, but also in his ability to achieve remarkable results in the field against a formidable army. On the signal from Quddús, Mullá Ḥusayn would mount his horse and lead the companions into the fray. Undeterred by the bullets that rained upon them, Mullá Ḥusayn and his tenacious companions pressed forward until the objectives had been accomplished and the adversary was in retreat. Shoghi Effendi attests to the "super-human prowess" exhibited by Mullá Ḥusayn and to "the magnificent courage" of the defenders of the fort in the face of vastly superior numbers.[28]

As leaders Quddús and Mullá Ḥusayn were undoubtedly creative and resourceful. Yet, each met a martyr's death. How, then, to assess the results of what they achieved? It is suggested that their lives, their exploits, and the sacrifices they willingly made might be viewed as a contribution to an ongoing, evolving historical process. Paradoxically, the tragic events at the fort of Shaykh Ṭabarsí ensured the survival of the teachings of the Báb and prepared the way for the advent of the promised day of unity and peace that was to be ushered in by Bahá'u'lláh, Whose advent was foretold by the Báb. In the following statement, Balyuzi, a Bahá'í historian, captures the significance of this unfolding process:

> It was in the path of that Supreme Manifestation of the Godhead that the Báb had shed His blood. It was to pave the way for His coming that martyrs had fallen at Shaykh Ṭabarsí, at Zanján, at Nayríz. Indeed the whole *raison d'être* of the Bábís was to know and acknowledge "Him Whom God shall make manifest." "I am preparing you for the advent of a mighty day"—these had been the words of the glorious Báb addressed to the Letters of the Living, His first disciples, when He laid upon them the mandate to go out, "scatter throughout the length and breadth" of the land and with "steadfast feet and sanctified hearts, prepare the way for His coming." The Báb had assured His people of "ultimate victory," but that "ultimate victory" had surprisingly and cruelly eluded them. It must, therefore, of a certainty, be theirs under the standard of that Supreme Manifestation of the Godhead, Whose advent had also been promised to them, and Whom they eagerly awaited.[29]

THE DYNAMIC FORCE OF UNITY

The events that took place at the fort at Shaykh Ṭabarsí illustrate the impact of the dynamic interplay between discipline and order on the behavior of the defenders of the fort and what they were able to accomplish. Indeed, their distinctive behavior stands in sharp contrast to the actions of the people who arose to eliminate them. Underlining the exemplary nature of the conduct of the occupants of the fort, Shoghi Effendi calls attention to "the fortitude, the intrepidity, the discipline and the resourcefulness of its heroes" and he compares these qualities with "the turpitude, the cowardice, the disorderliness and the inconstancy of their opponents."[30]

While the fort provided a physical stronghold for its heroic defenders, it might also be said that their faithful adherence to the teachings of the Báb served as a spiritual refuge for the Bábís. Their personal discipline and commitment to implement His laws enabled the defenders of the fort to vindicate the sacredness and timeliness of the Báb's religion. The dynamic interaction between individual and community spiritual practices transformed the atmosphere within the fortress. It produced not only a sense of personal well-being but also enabled the defenders of the fort to endure the terrible physical privations with which they were afflicted, and it firmed their resolve to carry on. Nabíl provides the following insight into their plight:

> Their food, alas, was by this time reduced to the flesh of horses, which they had brought away with them from the deserted camp of the enemy. With steadfast fortitude they endured the afflictions which beset them from every side. Their hearts were set on the wishes of Quddús; all else mattered but little. Neither the severity of their distress nor the continual threats of the enemy could cause them to deviate a hairsbreadth from the path which their departed companions had so heroically trodden.[31]

On a material level, the collective action required to construct the fort and to fend off the attacks of the adversary required both discipline on the part of the individual and a system of organization, supported by all, which served to channel and focus the actions of the individuals toward the achievement of the desired goals.

In the first instance, the fort had to be built. Mullá Ḥusayn entrusted its design to one of the believers experienced in the field of construction, then assigned his companions to a number of teams, each of which had a defined responsibility. While the plan of operation gave overall direction to the project and ensured that the necessary tasks were completed in the appropriate sequence, the dedicated effort of each individual was also critical, since the work had to be completed within a short period of time, and attempts were made by the antagonists to impede the progress of the venture. At a later stage, it was necessary to reinforce the fortifications. Quddús called upon his companions to dig a moat around the fort as a safeguard against renewed attack. Nabíl records, "Nineteen days elapsed during which they exerted themselves to the utmost for the completion of the task they had been charged to perform. They joyously laboured by day and by night in order to expedite the work with which they had been entrusted."[32]

Likewise, at the time of battle, Quddús and Mullá Ḥusayn established the plan of action, formulated the strategy, and specified who was to lead the charge and how many companions were to participate. They chose the time at which the defenders sallied forth from the fort and decided when the objectives had been achieved. The discipline of the individual and his willingness to support the plan with his actions, irrespective of the dangers involved, produced astonishing results.

The system of organization introduced by Mullá Ḥusayn and Quddús served as a vehicle for ensuring united action. The system appears to have been flexible and to adjust to changing circumstances. It served as a force for unity. Concerted action, in conformity with the stated plan, not only ensured the security of the fort, but it focused and greatly magnified the potential impact of limited available resources and enhanced the capacity of the small band of heroic Bábís to achieve outstanding victories in the face of overwhelming opposition. Shoghi Effendi recounts how, in the end, the commander of the army, astounded by the inexhaustible vitality of the Bábís, frustrated by their intrepid courage, and unable to defeat them in an honorable manner, resorted to "abject treachery" to overcome them. After promising safe passage to the occupants of the fort if they were to return to their homes, the commander of the force violated his solemn oath. When they accepted his offer, he exerted no effort to intervene to prevent the slaughter of Quddús and his companions.[33]

SEEDS OF THE BAHÁ'Í ADMINISTRATIVE ORDER

Shoghi Effendi underlines the significance and continuing historical impact of the episode that took place at the fort of Shaykh Ṭabarsí on the development of the Bahá'í Administrative Order, which, in the distant future, is destined to evolve into the World Order of Bahá'u'lláh and to overshadow all humankind. He links the events that transpired at the fort during the Heroic Age of the Bahá'í Faith with the birth and establishment of the system of Bahá'í administration that emerged during the Faith's Formative Age, and he foreshadows events that will happen in the Golden Age of the Faith. Commenting on the outcome of the episode, Shoghi Effendi observes that it generated "the very seeds which, in a later age, were to blossom into worldwide administrative institutions, and which must, in the fullness of time, yield their golden fruit in the shape of a world-redeeming, earth encircling Order."[34]

In exploring the implications of Shoghi Effendi's statement we examine ways in which the episode proved seminal—how it constitutes "the very seeds" of the emerging Bahá'í Administrative Order.[35] We also draw parallels between the events in the fort and the nature and functioning of the administrative institutions of the religion.

ANALOGY OF THE SEEDS

In his letters Shoghi Effendi employs the analogy of the seed to illustrate the invaluable contribution of the early Persian believers to the birth and establishment of the new religion. Consideration of this usage enhances understanding of the seminal nature of their actions. Just as in the physical world, the rupture of the seed is required to allow the shoot to emerge and the plant to grow and bear fruit, on a metaphorical level, a similar phenomenon is observed in the world of religion. For example, in one instance, Shoghi Effendi stresses the relationship between the early believers' willingness to sacrifice and to endure hardships to ensure that, in the long-term, the Cause would flourish. He writes, "upon these heroes of Bahá'u'lláh's native land was bestowed the inestimable privilege of sealing with their life-blood the early triumphs of their cherished Faith, and of paving the way for its approaching victory. In the blood of the unnumbered martyrs of Persia lay the seed of the Divinely-appointed Administration which… is now budding out . . . into a new order, destined to overshadow all mankind."[36]

The image of the bursting of the seed and the sacrifice inherent in the organic process of growth is also applied to the establishment and maturation of the Administrative Order. Shoghi Effendi states: "Its seed is the blood of no less than twenty thousand martyrs who have offered up their lives that it may be born and flourish." The formation of Spiritual Assemblies and the erection of the framework of the Bahá'í administrative structure represents the initial germination of these precious seeds. However this is but a preliminary stage in the evolution toward World Order. Commenting on the future development of the Administrative Order, Shoghi Effendi states: "It will, as its component parts, its organic institutions, begin to function with efficiency and vigor, assert its claim and demonstrate its capacity to be regarded not only as the nucleus but the very pattern of the new

World Order destined to embrace in the fullness of time the whole of mankind." The fecundity of this organic process is far from exhausted! Hence Shoghi Effendi's visionary observation, "the promised Kingdom into which the seed of His institutions must ripen remains as yet uninaugurated."[37]

Implicit in the analogy of the seed is the conscious awareness that growth, and indeed life, is a purposeful evolutionary process. Such an understanding underpins the guiding vision of Bahá'ís. This perspective on life and events, not only gives meaning to life, but also gives direction to setting individual and community goals. It provides a basis for assessing the value of personal and group actions as a contribution to the evolving process, and it offers a context for understanding crises and victories.

PARALLEL THEMES

As noted above, the birth and establishment of a new religion should best be viewed as an organic process that evolves through various stages of development until it reaches the stage of maturity. In this process, the needs and condition of the "plant" will not remain uniform but will differ according to the requirements of the particular stage of development. In its earliest days, the Cause needed martyrs; today it needs people who are willing to dedicate their lives and their resources to the worldwide diffusion of the teachings of the new religion. Hence the needs and conditions that pertained at the time of the turbulent birth of the Bahá'í Faith during the Heroic Age are clearly different from the circumstances that emerged during the Formative Age of the religion where the need for systematic organization became preeminent. It is nevertheless possible to identify a number of parallels between the events that took place in defense of the fort of Shaykh Ṭabarsí and the establishment of the Bahá'í system of administration.

Just as the fortress at Shaykh Ṭabarsí served as a stronghold for the protection of its occupants, the Bahá'í Administrative Order, in the words of Shoghi Effendi, "safeguards and promotes" the Faith of Bahá'u'lláh. Likewise, just as the exploits of the defenders of the fort took place against a background of challenge and attack, and their sacrifices enabled the seeds of the new religion to take root, the Guardian indicates that the purpose of the "administrative machinery" is to "ensure, amid the storms and stress of a struggling civilization, the unity of the Faith, the preservation of its identity, and the protection of its interests."[38]

In the same way that an intensive and sustained effort on the part of the early Bábís was required to construct and reinforce the fortifications, so, too, a supreme effort is required in contemporary times to lay the foundations and establish the institutions of the Administrative Order throughout the world. However, while the fort served as the refuge for its occupants, the Bahá'í administrative system is destined to serve as "the Ark of everlasting salvation," and to embrace the mass of humankind. The scope of the enterprise confronting the Bahá'í community is, therefore, significantly broader and world-embracing. Nevertheless, the qualities of service identified by Shoghi Effendi in relation to the defense of the fort at Ṭabarsí, continue to have relevance in the present. For example, he calls attention to the significance of unity of purpose and action to the achievement of important goals. Indeed, the defense of the fort represents the first significant "collective enterprise" undertaken by the early followers of the Báb, an enterprise characterized by Shoghi Effendi as an outstanding example of "Bahá'í solidarity," in which the actions of the defenders of the fort demonstrated "self-sacrifice," "concerted effort," and the "compelling evidence of the reality of the faith" that was the motivating force of their lives.[39]

In addition to the increased scope of the activities required of the Bahá'ís in the Formative Age, the nature of the endeavors in which they are to engage has to be appropriate to the social milieu and to further the needs of the more advanced stage of evolution of the Bahá'í community. In a letter written on his behalf, Shoghi Effendi captures this shift in emphasis. He writes: "In Persia the Cause was established through the blood of the martyrs shed in its path; in the West it seems it shall prosper as the result of constant sacrifice on the part of its handful of followers. It is only by dedicating our lives to the cause of teaching and our means to establishing its institutions that the Faith of Bahá'u'lláh will conquer the West."[40] In the Formative Age, the priorities are not only to devote one's life to the diffusion of the teachings of the revelation of Bahá'u'lláh throughout the world, but also to invest one's energy and the very substance of one's life in erecting the structure of the Bahá'í administrative system and in developing the Bahá'í community to serve as a model of peace and diversity in a fragmenting and disordered world.

The "birth and primary stages of the erection of the framework of the Administrative Order of the Faith" was characterized by concentration on the formation of Local and National Spiritual Assemblies in all five continents. Shoghi Effendi refers to these embryonic institutions as "strongholds from which the dynamic energies of that Faith can be diffused." It is therefore evident that, while the establishment of these institutions is of great importance, the administration of the religion is not an end in itself. Rather Shoghi Effendi attests that it "is to be conceived as an instrument and not a substitute for the Faith of Bahá'u'lláh, that it should be regarded as a channel through which His promised blessings may flow." The system of elected Spiritual Assemblies provides the machinery for directing the systematic expansion and consolidation of the Bahá'í community, as is discussed in a later chapter.[41]

Just as the authority to direct the events in the fort was the prerogative of Quddús and Mullá Ḥusayn and the companions in the fort willingly abided by their decisions, so too, both the leadership of the present-day Bahá'í community and the authority to direct its affairs are vested in the elected institutions of the Faith, and the power to accomplish the tasks of the community resides primarily in the mass of the believers. Obedience to the decisions of the Assemblies gives rise to orderly and goal-directed activity, and is indispensable to social progress.

One final parallel theme to note is that just as the defenders of the fort were schooled by tribulation, the same might also be said of the Bahá'í Faith and its fast evolving administrative institutions. Despite such difficulties, Shoghi Effendi attests that the religion has "succeeded in maintaining the unity of the diversified and far-flung body of its supporters, and enabled them to launch, unitedly and systematically, enterprises in both Hemispheres, designed to extend its limits and consolidate its administrative institutions." These institutions have also borne the brunt of attacks by adversaries, who in the words of Shoghi Effendi are "jealous" of "its conspicuous victories" and who have "sought to challenge the validity and misrepresent the character of the Administrative Order embedded in its teachings." Far from resulting in defeat, these attacks have "galvanized the swelling army of its defenders to arise and arraign the usurpers of their sacred rights and to defend the long-standing strongholds of the institutions of their Faith."[42]

5

THE DAWN-BREAKERS
OF THE FORMATIVE AGE—
THE ROLE OF THE WEST

While the heroic exploits of the dawn-breakers of the Heroic Age took place mostly in Iran, the land of the birth of the Bahá'í Faith, the exploits of the dawn-breakers of the Formative Age—those members of the religion who are arising with commitment and dedication to serve the Cause they have embraced—are being played out primarily in the West.[1]

The Founders of the Bahá'í Faith singled out the North American Bahá'ís, the "first-born of the communities in the West," for the distinction of raising up the Bahá'í Administrative Order, designed to serve as the vehicle for the worldwide expansion of the religion, and destined to evolve in the distant future into the system of world governance envisaged in the writings of Bahá'u'lláh. As "the cradle of the embryonic World Order of Bahá'u'lláh and the stronghold of its nascent institutions," the American Bahá'í community is called upon to assume primary responsibility for laying the foundations of the administrative system, for establishing its institutions, refining their functioning, and using them as instruments not only for the systematic expansion of the influence of the Bahá'í religion throughout the planet, but also for ministering to the needs of humankind by promoting peace and justice in the world at large.[2]

In this chapter we introduce the subject of the unique role of the West, in particular the role of the American Bahá'í community as the spiritual descendants of the dawn-breakers of the Heroic Age, in the development of the Bahá'í Faith. We explore the magnitude of the tasks involved in building the World Order of Bahá'u'lláh, and in considering the nature of the challenges involved in attempting to bring this Order into being, we reflect on the events that transpired at the conference of Badasht and draw inspiration from the supreme dedication evinced by the early followers of the Báb.

THE ROLE OF THE WEST

There is a mystical linkage between the Heroic and Formative Ages of the Bahá'í Faith and, indeed, between the East and the West. In His book the Qayyúmu'l-Asmá', revealed in the first year of His mission, the Báb directly addressed the "peoples of the West," and called upon them to "issue forth" from their "cities" to aid God, and to "become as brethren" in His "one and indivisible religion." Bahá'u'lláh likewise underlined this organic connection and foreshadowed the fulfillment of the Báb's portentous statement. Bahá'u'lláh attests that the people of Persia failed to appreciate His Cause, and anticipating the rise of the Faith in the West He affirms, "In the East the light of His Revelation hath broken; in the West the signs of His dominion have appeared."[3]

In explaining the unique importance and the significant role played by the West in the history of religion, 'Abdu'l-Bahá calls attention to the operation of a general and dynamic spiritual principle of growth. He testifies that, "From the beginning of time until the present day, the light of Divine Revelation hath risen in the East and shed its radiance upon the West. The illumination thus shed hath, however, acquired in the West an extraordinary brilliancy." To illustrate His point, 'Abdu'l-Bahá refers to the history of the Christian Faith, observing that, "Though it first appeared in the East, yet not until its light had been shed upon the West did the full measure of its potentialities become manifest." He then applies this principle to the development of the Bahá'í Faith, affirming, "The day is approaching when ye shall witness how, through the splendor of the Faith of Bahá'u'lláh, the West will have replaced the East, radiating the light of Divine guidance," and, in the following words, he predicts the spiritual ascendancy of the West, thus: "The East hath, verily, been illumined with the light of the Kingdom. Erelong will this same light shed a still greater illumination upon the West."[4]

A detailed treatment of the rise and consolidation of the Bahá'í Faith in the West is beyond the scope of the present work. Aspects of this subject are addressed in the following chapters. However, mention should be made of the unique role of the West—in particular the North American continent, whose members Shoghi Effendi described as the "champion-builders of the World Order of Bahá'u'lláh"—in forging and establishing the Administrative Order of the Bahá'í Faith. In this regard, Shoghi Effendi refers to the impact of "a remarkable swing of the pendulum," which "caused the administrative center of the Faith to gravitate, away from its cradle [in Persia], to the shores of the American continent." And he underlines the organic connection between the contributions of the dawn-breakers of the Heroic Age and their spiritual descendants in the West: "upon these heroes of Bahá'u'lláh's native land was bestowed the inestimable privilege of sealing with their life-blood the early triumphs of their cherished Faith, and of paving the way for its approaching victory. In the blood of the unnumbered martyrs of Persia lay the seed of the Divinely-appointed Administration which, though transplanted from its native soil, is now budding out, under your loving care, into a new order, destined to overshadow all mankind."[5]

THE ROLE OF THE AMERICAN BAHÁ'Í COMMUNITY

In the writings of the Bahá'í Faith there are many visionary statements that anticipate that the American Bahá'í community and the North American continent are destined, in the future, to make a preeminent contribution to the transformation of spiritual and social values and to the establishment of world order and peace. Shoghi Effendi summarizes some of the most dramatic statements, which illustrate the unique role of America, in the following passage:

The Báb had in His Qayyumu'l-Asmá', almost a hundred years previously, sounded His specific summons to the "peoples of the West" to "issue forth" from their "cities" and aid His Cause. Bahá'u'lláh, in His Kitáb-i-Aqdas, had collectively addressed the Presidents of the Republics of the entire Americas, bidding them arise and "bind with the hands of justice the broken," and "crush the oppressor" with the "rod of the commandments" of their Lord, and had, moreover, anticipated in His writings the appearance "in the West" of the "signs of His Dominion." Abdu'l-Bahá had, on His part, declared that the "illumination" shed by His Father's Revelation upon the West would acquire an "extraordinary brilliancy," and that the "light of the Kingdom" would "shed a still greater illumination upon the West" than upon the East. He had extolled the American continent in particular as "the land wherein the splendors of His Light shall be revealed, where the mysteries of His Faith shall be unveiled," and affirmed that "it will lead all nations spiritually." More specifically still, He had singled out the Great Republic of the West, the leading nation of that continent, declaring that its people were "indeed worthy of being the first to build the Tabernacle of the Most Great Peace and proclaim the oneness of mankind," that it was "equipped and empowered to accomplish that which will adorn the pages of history, to become the envy of the world, and be blest in both the East and the West."[6]

Recognizing, from the outset, the capacity and vitality of the nascent American Bahá'í community, 'Abdu'l-Bahá lavished his attention and guidance upon it. At an advanced age he journeyed to North America, and during his extensive travels he imparted to the membership a more comprehensive understanding of the spiritual, social, and administrative teachings of the Faith. He endorsed and encouraged the initiative of the American Bahá'ís to begin construction of the first House of Worship in the West, personally laying the foundation stone while in the United States. He educated the believers concerning the importance of the covenant and its relationship to the system of administration to which it was to give direction and shape. Finally, in the latter part of his life, during World War I, when contact between the World Center of the Faith and the Bahá'í world was cut off, 'Abdu'l-Bahá revealed a number of tablets to the North American Bahá'ís in which "He unfolded to their eyes His conception of their spiritual destiny." Known as the Tablets of the Divine Plan, these tablets constitute 'Abdu'l-Bahá's "mandate to the community which He Himself had raised up, trained and nurtured, a Plan that must in the years to come enable its members to diffuse the light, and erect the administrative fabric, of the Faith throughout the five continents of the globe."[7]

Shoghi Effendi captures the uniqueness of the relationship between 'Abdu'l-Bahá and the North American continent and the significance of the mandate conferred on this blessed community, when he writes:

The first act of His ministry had been to unfurl the standard of Bahá'u'lláh in the very heart of that Republic. This was followed by His own prolonged visit to its shores, by His dedication of the first House of Worship to be built by the community of His disciples in that land, and finally by the revelation, in the evening of His life, of the Tablets of the Divine Plan, investing His disciples with a mandate to plant the banner of His Father's Faith, as He had planted it in their own land, in all the continents, the countries and islands of the globe. He had, furthermore, acclaimed one of their most celebrated presidents as one who, through the ideals he had expounded and the institutions he had inaugurated, had caused the "dawn" of the Peace anticipated by Bahá'u'lláh to break; had voiced the hope that from their country "heavenly illumination" may "stream to all the peoples of the world"; had designated them in those Tablets as "Apostles of Bahá'u'lláh"; had assured them that, "should success crown" their "enterprise," "the throne of the Kingdom of God will, in the plenitude of its majesty and glory, be firmly established"; and had made the stirring announcement that "the moment this Divine Message is propagated" by them "through the continents of Europe, of Asia, of Africa and of Australasia, and as far as the islands of the Pacific, this community will find itself securely established upon the throne of an everlasting dominion," and that "the whole earth" would "resound with the praises of its majesty and greatness."[8]

SPIRITUAL DESCENDANTS
OF THE DAWN-BREAKERS

The special mandate conferred on the Bahá'ís in North America is not only a great honor and blessing but it also imposes upon them a weighty responsibility to redeem the trust that has been placed in their ability to fulfill the tasks to which they have been called during the Formative Age.

The tasks to be accomplished during the Formative Age build on the accomplishments of the Heroic Age. The goals of the Formative Age, therefore, differ markedly from those of the Age that preceded it. Indeed, each stage in the evolution of the Bahá'í Faith presents its own challenges and requires different kinds of activities that are appropriate to its particular stage of development, activities that enable the community to plan and execute the next steps in its advancement. While the major objective of the Heroic Age was to ensure the spread of the religion in the land of its birth, the evolution of the Bahá'í Faith during the Formative Age calls for involvement in a wide range of activities designed to foster the establishment of the Bahá'í Administrative Order, a system of governance that will serve as a vehicle for the expansion and consolidation of the Bahá'í community and for the spread of the Faith's vision and values in the world at large.

In taking up this challenge the American Bahá'í community is encouraged to draw inspiration, guidance, and motivation from the heroic and sacrificial exploits of the early adherents of the Faith in Persia. Reflection on the courageous and persistent efforts of their spiritual forebears to establish the religion in the land of its birth, in the face of intense hardships and cruel and widespread persecution by the civil and ecclesiastical authorities, serve to remind their present-day spiritual descendants in the West of the sacrifices that are required to lay the foundations of a new religion and to ensure the spread of its transformative worldview. And, on a personal level, contemplation on their attributes serves to underline the nature of the spiritual and moral qualities that must be manifested by the individuals who are engaged in this challenging society-building enterprise.

Shoghi Effendi calls attention to some of the distinctive characteristics of the American Bahá'í community. Implicit in his description of these characteristics is the expectation that this community will make heroic efforts to arise to perform outstanding services for the development of the Bahá'í Faith. He gives expression to his high hopes for this privileged community in the following extract from one of his letters:

> May this Community—the spiritual descendants of the Dawn-breakers of the heroic Age of the Bahá'í Faith, the chief repository of the immortal Tablets of 'Abdu'l-Bahá's Divine Plan, the foremost executors of the Mandate issued by the Center of Bahá'u'lláh's Covenant, the champion-builders of a divinely conceived Administrative Order, the standard-bearers of a future all-conquering army of the Lord of Hosts, the torch-bearers of a future divinely inspired world civilization—arise . . . to secure, as befits its rank, the lion's share in the prosecution of the global crusade designed to diffuse the Light of God's Revelation over the surface of the entire Planet.[9]

To appreciate the significance of the American Bahá'í community's God-given mandate and its designation as "the cradle, as well as the stronghold, of that future New World Order, which is at once the promise and the glory of the Dispensation associated with the name of Bahá'u'lláh,"[10] it is necessary to understand the relationship between the World Order of Bahá'u'lláh and its precursor, the Bahá'í Administrative Order, and the challenges involved in bringing them into existence.

TO BUILD THE WORLD ORDER OF BAHÁ'U'LLÁH

The mission of the Faith of Bahá'u'lláh is to establish world unity. The achievement of this transformative mission involves not only a profound change in human values—the emergence of a deep and abiding appreciation of the oneness and wholeness of humankind—but also the creation of global institutions necessary for the establishment of just and unified relationships between the peoples and nations of the world. War must be eliminated and universal peace firmly established. This far-reaching vision of the future of humanity, set out in the Bahá'í writings is referred to as the World Order of Bahá'u'lláh. Commenting on the uniqueness of this vision and the attitude of the Bahá'ís in relation to it, Hatcher and Martin write: "The conviction of the practicability of world unity, coupled with a dedication and willingness to work toward this goal, is probably the single most distinguishing characteristic of the Bahá'í community."[11]

For Bahá'ís, the institutions that form part of the Bahá'í Administrative Order are an integral part of the Bahá'í Faith that cannot be separated from the purely spiritual and social teachings of the religion. This Administrative Order represents the first shaping of the future World Order. It is the "nucleus" and "pattern" of a new social order destined to bring about the unification of humankind. In this regard, Shoghi Effendi writes: "this Administrative Order is fundamentally different from anything that any Prophet has previously established, inasmuch as Bahá'u'lláh has Himself revealed its principles, established its institutions, appointed the person to interpret His Word and conferred the necessary authority on the body [the Universal House of Justice] designed to supplement and apply His legislative ordinances."[12]

There is a clear distinction between the Administrative Order of the Bahá'í Faith and the future World Order conceived by Bahá'u'lláh. This distinction is characterized by Hatcher and Martin as follows:

In speaking of the World Order, Bahá'ís refer to the full effect which they believe the teachings of the founder of their faith will eventually have on the establishment of a world government, a lasting peace and a united planetary civilization. This World Order obviously does not yet exist; rather, it is the goal towards which the Bahá'í community is striving. But the principal institutions of the Administrative Order already exist and function as an integral part of the international community of Bahá'ís.[13]

While Bahá'ís maintain that their Faith and its Administrative Order have an important role to play in the process of the creation of a united world and they confidently work to establish the future World Order, they do not believe that the new Order will be brought into existence solely through their own efforts or the influence of their Faith. In building for the future, they seek collaboration with peoples and organizations committed to the principle of the oneness of humankind and working to uphold human rights. They also acknowledge the important steps taken by the League of Nations and the United Nations toward the emergence of a system of global governance based on justice.

The Bahá'í teachings indicate that the unfoldment of World Order will occur in three successive stages. The first one, which is well advanced, is that of widespread social breakdown and intense suffering that will afflict both individuals and existing social institutions. It will culminate in a worldwide spiritual, physical, and social crisis, which will mark the end of the first stage and the transition to the second stage of the process.[14]

The second stage of the progress toward World Order will be marked by the establishment of the Lesser Peace, a form of political peace entered into by the nations by international agreement. The Bahá'í teachings envisage that the Lesser Peace will emerge from the suffering and social upheavals of the contemporary world. Indeed, the travail of the age will serve to motivate individuals and nations to strive to put an end to war. According to Hatcher and Martin, "The fundamental feature of the Lesser Peace is the establishment of international safeguards to prevent the recurrence of war among nations. These safeguards would be explicitly outlined in a formal agreement supported by all the nations of the earth, and based on the principle of 'collective security' according to which all the nations should arise collectively to suppress any aggressor nation."[15]

The Lesser Peace is viewed as a necessary prelude to the third stage in the eventual emergence of the World Order, a stage that will, in the distant future, give rise to the Most Great Peace. The potential impact of Bahá'u'lláh's World Order on both individual and social life is captured by Shoghi Effendi's summary of some of its main features:

> The unity of the human race, as envisaged by Bahá'u'lláh, implies the establishment of a world commonwealth in which all nations, races, creeds and classes are closely and permanently united, and in which the autonomy of its state members and the personal freedom and initiative of the individuals that compose them are definitely and completely safeguarded. This commonwealth must, as far as we can visualize it, consist of a world legislature, whose members will, as the trustees of the whole of mankind, ultimately control the entire resources of all the component nations, and will enact such laws as shall be required to regulate the life, satisfy the needs and adjust the relationships of all races and peoples. A world executive, backed by an international Force, will carry out the decisions arrived at, and apply the laws enacted by, this world legislature, and will safeguard the organic unity of the whole commonwealth. A world tribunal will adjudicate and deliver its compulsory and final verdict in all and any disputes that may arise between the various elements

constituting this universal system . . . A world script, a world literature, a uniform and universal system of currency, of weights and measures, will simplify and facilitate intercourse and understanding among the nations and races of mankind. . . .

National rivalries, hatreds, and intrigues will cease, and racial animosity and prejudice will be replaced by racial amity, understanding and cooperation. The causes of religious strife will be permanently removed, economic barriers and restrictions will be completely abolished, and the inordinate distinction between classes will be obliterated.[16]

It is envisioned that the advent of the Most Great Peace will coincide with the emergence of the World Order of Bahá'u'lláh, and that the fruit of this great World Order will be the birth and efflorescence of a world civilization, described by Shoghi Effendi as "the child of the Most Great Peace and hallmark of the Golden Age of the Dispensation of Bahá'u'lláh." All these will come about as a result of the gradual recognition of Bahá'u'lláh's mission by the peoples of the world and by the acceptance and application of the principles contained in His revelation. Anticipating the depth of such changes, Shoghi Effendi writes: "The Most Great Peace . . . as conceived by Bahá'u'lláh—a peace that must inevitably follow as the practical consequence of the spiritualization of the world and the fusion of all its races, creeds, classes and nations—can rest on no other basis, and can be preserved through no other agency, except the divinely appointed ordinances that are implicit in the World Order that stands associated with His Holy Name."[17]

It is evident from the foregoing that building the World Order of Bahá'u'lláh will require centuries of dedicated effort, both on the individual and collective level. Its tasks are challenging and multifaceted. They include understanding the vision of the oneness of the human family, transforming human values and systems of governance, and creating opportunities for peace to emerge. The way forward will not be smooth. Crises will increase the hunger for security and justice, and will strengthen resolve and intensify the search for creative ways to surmount stubborn obstacles to unity.

Undeterred by the challenges involved, the members of the Bahá'í Faith are actively engaged in this visionary process, and, primarily through the establishment of the Bahá'í system of organization within the Bahá'í community, they are taking conscious steps to bring the vision closer to realization. Indeed, the Bahá'í Administrative Order is regarded as the embryonic form of the future World Order. The institutions and laws of the Administrative Order are "destined to be a pattern for future society, a supreme instrument for the establishment of the Most Great Peace and the one agency for the unification of the world, and the proclamation of the reign of righteousness and justice upon the earth."[18]

In the succeeding chapters we examine in detail the ways in which the American Bahá'í community, has, over the years, arisen to carry out its God-given mandate. Since the scope of the tasks involved in raising these administrative structures is so vast and the effort required by the individual so challenging, we begin by reflecting on the events that transpired at the historic Conference of Badasht during the lifetime of the Báb, as a means of drawing parallels between the exploits of the dawn-breakers of the Heroic Age and their contemporary spiritual descendants in the West.

THE CONFERENCE OF BADASHT

In 1848, while the Báb was incarcerated in the fortress of Chihríq, "the independence of the new-born Faith was openly recognized and asserted by His disciples."[19] Eighty-one of the Báb's followers, headed by Bahá'u'lláh, gathered in the hamlet of Badasht in the province of

Khurásán to take counsel together regarding the nature of their Faith and their future course of action. According to Shoghi Effendi,

> The primary purpose of that gathering was to implement the revelation of the Bayán by a sudden, a complete and dramatic break with the past—with its order, its ecclesiasticism, its traditions, and ceremonials. The subsidiary purpose of the conference was to consider the means of emancipating the Báb from His cruel confinement in Chihríq. The first was eminently successful; the second was destined from the outset to fail.[20]

The uniqueness of this conference is that it took place during the actual lifetime of the Manifestation of God.

The conference was orchestrated by Bahá'u'lláh. The participants from different parts of the country were accommodated in three gardens rented by Bahá'u'lláh—one for Himself, and one each for Quddús and Ṭáhirih. They were the guests of Bahá'u'lláh for the twenty-two days the conference lasted.

As if to underline the break with the past, during this time, Bahá'u'lláh disclosed a number of tablets and conferred a new name on each of the assembled believers, names that were subsequently confirmed by the Báb. Furthermore, the independence of the Bábí revelation was progressively asserted. According to Nabíl, "Each day of that memorable gathering witnessed the abrogation of a new law and the repudiation of a long-established tradition. The veils that guarded the sanctity of the ordinances of Islám were sternly rent asunder, and the idols that had so long claimed the adoration of their blind worshippers were rudely demolished."[21]

Working in concert with Quddús and Ṭáhirih, Bahá'u'lláh arranged for the proclamation of the advent of the Báb and the abrogation of

Islamic laws. During the course of the conference various arguments were presented, and there were apparent differences of view and approach between Quddús and Ṭáhirih. The historical record suggests, however, that the seeming differences between the two were part of the overall plan of Bahá'u'lláh.[22] Mindful of the fundamental reform the mission of the Báb was going to make in the faith and lives of the people, the open expression of opposing views eased the shock involved and helped those companions with more conservative views to gradually accustom themselves to the idea of the necessity of change. Harmony was restored by the intervention of Bahá'u'lláh, which made it clear to all that a new Dispensation had, indeed, begun.

The final and dramatic climax of the conference came when Ṭáhirih, who was renowned for her chastity, appeared unveiled before her fellow believers. The impact of this audacious act, which violated prevailing cultural practice, was shocking and immediate. Nabíl vividly captures the drama of what transpired. He records:

Consternation immediately seized the entire gathering. All stood aghast before this sudden and most unexpected apparition. To behold her face unveiled was to them inconceivable. Even to gaze on her shadow was a thing which they deemed improper, inasmuch as they regarded her as the very incarnation of Fáṭimih, the noblest emblem of chastity in their eyes.

Quietly, silently, and with the utmost dignity, Ṭáhirih stepped forward and, advancing towards Quddús, seated herself on his right-hand side. Her unruffled serenity sharply contrasted with the affrighted countenances of those who were gazing upon her face. Fear, anger, and bewilderment stirred the depths of their souls. That sudden revelation seemed to have stunned their faculties. 'Abdu'l-Kháliq-i-Iṣfáhání was so gravely shaken that he cut his throat with his own hands. Covered with blood and shrieking with excitement, he fled away from the face of Ṭáhirih. A few, following his example, abandoned their companions and forsook their Faith. A number were seen standing speechless before her, confounded with wonder. Quddús, meanwhile, had remained seated in his place . . . his face betraying a feeling of inexpressible anger. . . .

His threatening attitude failed, however, to move her. Her countenance displayed that same dignity and confidence which she had evinced at the first moment of her appearance before the assembled believers. A feeling of joy and triumph had now illumined her face. She rose from her seat and, undeterred by the tumult that she had raised in the hearts of her companions, began to address the remnant of that assembly. Without the least premeditation, and in a language which bore a striking resemblance to that of the Qur'án, she delivered her appeal with matchless eloquence and profound fervour.[23]

Ṭáhirih's concluding remarks, which linked her action with the advent of the Promised One and which foreshadowed the impact of His advent, contained this challenging assertion: "I am the Word which the Qá'im is to utter, the Word which shall put to flight the chiefs and nobles of the earth!"[24] She then called upon her companions to rejoice and celebrate this great and joyous occasion.

By her actions Ṭáhirih challenged "the sanctity of the ordinances of Islám, sounded the clarion-call, and proclaimed the inauguration of a new Dispensation." As a symbol of this declaration of independence, she took the courageous step of discarding her veil, an act that constituted a "startling . . . departure from the time-honored traditions of Islám."[25] Underlining the cultural significance of this act at the time, 'Abdu'l-Bahá explains:

All women in Persia are enveloped in veils in public. So completely covered are they that even the hand is not visible. This rigid veiling is unspeakable. Qurratu'l-'Ayn [Ṭáhirih] tore off her veils and went forth fearlessly. She was like a lioness. Her action caused a great turmoil throughout the land of Persia. So excessive and compulsory is the requirement for veiling in the East that the people in the West have no idea of the excitement and indignation produced by the appearance of an unveiled woman. Qurratu'l-'Ayn lost all thought of herself and was unconscious of fear in her attraction to God.[26]

Just as Ṭáhirih resolved to break with the past, so too, did her coreligionists gathered at the conference. Nabíl characterizes the profound effect this historic gathering had on the outlook of its participants, in the following terms: "The object of that memorable gathering had been attained. The clarion-call of the new Order had been sounded. The obsolete conventions which had fettered the consciences of men were boldly challenged and fearlessly swept away. The way was clear for the proclamation of the laws and precepts that were destined to usher in the new Dispensation." And, commenting on the extent of the impact of this gathering on the lives of its participants, Shoghi Effendi attests that it gave rise to a "veritable revolution in the outlook, habits, ceremonials and manner of worship of these hitherto zealous and devout upholders of Muḥammadan law."[27]

Indeed, when the eighty-one Bábís first assembled at Bada<u>sh</u>t, they were not only lovers of the Báb and committed to His message, but they were also still firmly embedded in Islam and its practices. Following the conference they had a much clearer understanding of the claim of the Báb to be the Promised One—that He was the Founder of a new religion, whose teachings represented the expression of the divine will for the new day. With a renewed clarity of vision they arose with determination, from that time forward, to proclaim the advent of the Báb and to follow His teachings. Far beyond the impact on the lives of the individual Bábís, the conference of Bada<u>sh</u>t, which took place in a remote Persian village, marked a great "turning-point in the world's religious history." As with many seminal events, its true significance might not have been fully recognized at the time of its occurrence. Shoghi Effendi leaves no doubt as to the meaning and import of the conference of Bada<u>sh</u>t. He writes:

> No pomp, no pageantry marked so great a turning-point in the world's religious history. Nor was its modest setting commensurate with such a sudden, startling, complete emancipation from the dark and embattled forces of fanaticism, of priestcraft, of religious orthodoxy and superstition. The assembled host consisted of not more that a single woman and a handful of men, mostly recruited from the very ranks they were attacking, and devoid, with a few exceptions, of wealth, prestige and power. The Captain [the Báb] of the host was Himself an absentee, a captive in the grip of His foes. The arena was a tiny hamlet in the plain of Bada<u>sh</u>t on the border of Mázindarán. The trumpeter was a lone woman, the noblest of her sex in that Dispensation, whom even some of her co-religionists pronounced a heretic. The call she sounded was the death-knell of the twelve hundred year old law of Islám.[28]

CONTEMPORARY PARALLELS

In considering the significance of the conference of Bada<u>sh</u>t for contemporary times, it is interesting to note that Shoghi Effendi, addressing the American Bahá'ís as "the privileged heirs and present successors of the heroes of the Primitive Age of our Faith," invokes the memory of Badasht to underline the quality of dedicated service required of the Bahá'í community for the achievement of the far-reaching goals of the teaching initiative, known as the Ten Year Crusade (1953–63). He calls for

> . . . a renewed dedication, at this critical hour in the fortunes of mankind, on the part of the entire company of my spiritual brethren in every continent of the globe, to the high ideals of the Cause they have espoused, as well as to the immediate accomplishment of the goals of the Crusade on which they have embarked, be they in active service or not, of either sex, young as well as old, rich or poor, whether veteran or newly enrolled—a dedication reminiscent of the pledges which the Dawn-breakers of an earlier Apostolic Age, assembled in conference at Badasht, and faced with issues of a different but equally challenging nature, willingly and solemnly made for the prosecution of the collective task with which they were confronted.[29]

While there is recognition that different circumstances require different responses, a number of parallel themes might be identified to highlight the qualities exemplified by the early Bábís of the Heroic Age and their spiritual descendants in the West who are following in their footsteps in surmounting the challenges to promote the teachings of the new day. As at Badasht, each member of the community is responsible for recognizing and accepting the new Messenger of God and for observing the ordinances associated with His revelation. It is insufficient just to proclaim one's belief. It is also vital to put the teachings of the religion into practice in one's daily life. The requirement to act is underscored by Bahá'u'lláh. Writing in His Book of Laws, He attests: "These twin duties are inseparable. Neither is acceptable without the other."[30]

Just as at Bada<u>sh</u>t, the continuing development of the Faith may well require a sudden and dramatic break with the past, a new way of serving the religion, and a demonstration of commitment to the implementation of its vision. From time to time, the pressing needs of the evolving Faith present its followers with opportunities to rededicate themselves to the promotion of its interests. When confronted with such opportunities, the individual members of the community are challenged to make a conscious decision to act in a decisive manner, and to adopt new and innovative approaches that answer the critical needs of the new situation. Examples of the heroic services of the American Bahá'ís at critical turning-points in the evolution of the Bahá'í Faith are plentiful. They are amply illustrated by their sacrificial efforts to raise the framework of the Bahá'í administrative system, to promote the worldwide expansion of the religion, to create a community that exemplifies the Bahá'í way of life, and to achieve the emancipation of their Faith. While retaining the guiding vision of the Faith, the pursuit of these various initiatives obviously requires frequent reflection and reassessment as to the appropriateness of the strategies used, and openness to the need for adjustment in light of changing conditions and circumstances.

The impact of the conference of Bada<u>sh</u>t was twofold. The assertion of independence, the expression of views that challenged the prevailing religious tradition, and the dramatic actions of Ṭáhirih that flew in the face of entrenched cultural practices initially aroused alarm among the Bábís. A few, feeling unable to accept the new ideas and adjust to the required changes in their way of life, decided to withdraw from the community. The conference also impacted the wider society. Threatened by the Bábís' radical break with the past, the civil and ecclesiastical leadership of Persia initiated a concerted program of attacks against the followers of the Báb, a program which, paradoxically, served to reinforce their determination to usher in the new Dispensation.

Similarly, in contemporary times, not every follower of the religion is able to rise to the challenge, and the behavior of the Bahá'ís may well attract opposition and social criticism. Writing on this theme Shoghi Effendi foreshadows the nature of the opposition that will confront the American Bahá'í community, and he offers the following encouragement to its members:

> Let not, however, the invincible army of Bahá'u'lláh, who in the West, and at one of its potential storm centers is to fight, in His name and for His sake, one of its fiercest and most glorious battles, be afraid of any criticism that might be directed against it. Let it not be deterred by any condemnation with which the tongue of the slanderer may seek to debase its motives. Let it not recoil before the threatening advance of the forces of fanaticism, of orthodoxy, of corruption, and of prejudice that may be leagued against it. The voice of criticism is a voice that indirectly reinforces the proclamation of its Cause. Unpopularity but serves to throw into greater relief the contrast between it and its adversaries, while ostracism is itself the magnetic power that must eventually win over to its camp the most vociferous and inveterate amongst its foes.[31]

Perhaps the most thought-provoking feature of the conference of Badasht is the extent to which it demonstrates the dramatic impact of historical circumstances on the life of the individual. At critical points in time, when confronted by the requirements of evolutionary change, individuals are faced with determining how to respond and challenged to take mature and decisive action. The seminal event at

Badasht, having set in train processes destined to emancipate the world from "the dark and embattled forces of fanaticism, of priestcraft, of religious orthodoxy and superstition,"[32] underscores the inescapability of individual responsibility at such critical junctures. It illustrates the responsibility of the individual believer to independently investigate spiritual truth, to free him or herself from superstition and fanaticism, to take stock of the needs of the religion he or she has adopted, to determine how best to serve its evolving interests, and, over the long-term, faithfully and joyously to persist in his or her chosen fields of activity despite the inevitable setbacks and challenges encountered along the way. Such is the legacy which the spiritual descendants of the dawn-breakers of the Formative Age aspire to uphold!

6

THE CRADLE AND STRONGHOLD OF THE BAHÁ'Í ADMINISTRATIVE ORDER

The highly challenging task of establishing the Bahá'í Administrative Order calls for the same qualities of spirit and character, and a level of heroism and self-sacrifice, that were demonstrated by the dawn-breakers of the Heroic Age as they struggled to ensure the survival of the new revelation. Writing to the American believers on this theme Shoghi Effendi states:

> The community of the organized promoters of the Faith of Bahá'u'lláh in the American continent—the spiritual descendants of the dawn-breakers of an heroic Age, who by their death proclaimed the birth of that Faith—must, in turn, usher in, not by their death but through living sacrifice, that promised World Order, the shell ordained to enshrine that priceless jewel, the world civilization, of which the Faith itself is the sole begetter . . . this community . . . is now busily engaged in laying the foundations and in fostering the growth of those institutions which are to herald the approach of the Age destined to witness the birth and rise of the World Order of Bahá'u'lláh.[1]

In this chapter we review some of the initial actions taken by the American Bahá'ís, "the first-born of the communities of the West" in their efforts to establish the foundation of the Bahá'í administrative system. We explore the implications of Shoghi Effendi's designation of the North American Bahá'í community as "the cradle and stronghold of the Administrative Order of Bahá'u'lláh."[2]

THE CHALLENGE

It is evident that the task of building the World Order of Bahá'u'lláh is exceedingly challenging and of long duration. It demands, and will continue to call for, the heroic efforts of Bahá'ís for many centuries to come. The work required to bring this Order into being requires the spirit of service and individual initiative, the establishment of the framework of the Bahá'í administrative system, and the gradual development of a faith community that is imbued with the teachings of the religion and serves as a harbinger of a future world civilization.

A number of unique and innovative provisions govern the organization of the Bahá'í community. Of particular significance is the fact that the Bahá'í Faith is a lay religion, devoid of a clerical class. Within the Bahá'í community there are no figures comparable to the rabbis, priests, ministers, or mullas who exercise individual authority over the mass of the faithful and enjoy rights and privileges not accorded to their fellow-believers. With the rigid hierarchical distinction between clergy and layman removed, each Bahá'í is expected to accept personal responsibility for his or her spiritual progress rather than depending on the instructions and ministrations of a priest.

Underlining the uniqueness of this provision in the Bahá'í Administrative Order, Shoghi Effendi refers to "The abolition of professional priesthood with its accompanying sacraments of baptism, of communion and of confession of sins, the laws requiring the election by universal suffrage of all local, national, and international Houses of Justice, the total absence of episcopal authority with its attendant privileges, corruptions and bureaucratic tendencies," and he indicates that such provisions constitute "evidences of the non-autocratic character of the Bahá'í Administrative Order and of its inclination to democratic methods in the administration of its affairs."[3]

Although the Bahá'í Faith has no priesthood and no ordained clerical class, it does assign responsibility for administrative actions to certain individuals. The affairs of the community are administered by a system of democratically elected Spiritual Assemblies, operating under the guidance of the head of the Faith, and assisted by individuals who are appointed to provide a counseling and educational function. The Bahá'ís who serve in these capacities, however, do not have episcopal authority over the other members of the community, nor do they constitute an inherently superior and privileged class.[4]

The approach to building the Bahá'í Administrative Order, the precursor of the World Order of Bahá'u'lláh is holistic, organic, and evolutionary. Multiple interrelated activities need to be undertaken simultaneously, especially as the influence of the new religion becomes progressively more widespread. In the first instance, for example, the Bahá'í Faith must be introduced to the people in a particular locality and attract a number of followers before a Bahá'í community can come into being. A sizeable and informed Bahá'í community must be raised up prior to the election of a Local Spiritual Assembly, and a sufficient number of local Assemblies must exist before a National Spiritual Assembly is elected. However, the election of the Spiritual Assembly is not an end in itself. Hence, Shoghi Effendi's advice: ". . . it behooves us to reflect on the animating purpose and the primary functions of these divinely established institutions, the sacred character and the universal efficacy of which can be demonstrated only by the spirit they diffuse and the work they actually achieve."[5] In brief, leadership of the Bahá'í community is vested in the elected

Spiritual Assembly. It serves as the point of authority and unity and the vehicle for directing the activities of the community. It ensures the ongoing promotion of the Bahá'í teachings within the community, and organizes educational activities to increase the understanding of the members—children, pre-youth, youth, and adults—about the history and teachings of the Faith they have embraced, and it fosters the practice of its laws and administrative principles. As the Spiritual Assembly grows in experience, programs of social and economic development and humanitarian projects are instituted. Hence growth and development in one area of Bahá'í activity tends to reinforce progress and mature activity in another; and the nature of the activities change in light of changing needs and circumstances and the increased availability of human and material resources.

Further, the existence of an elected Bahá'í Spiritual Assembly working in close collaboration with the members of the Bahá'í community, serves as the primary agency for the efficient and systematic prosecution of plans and activities that are designed to meet the needs of the evolving community. Indeed, the lack of an Assembly in an area has been cited as an obstacle to the development of the religion and may well constitute a barrier to its expansion. A brief sketch of the early years of the North American Bahá'í community will serve to illustrate some of the processes described above. It also highlights the vital need for a system of administration to guide and direct the affairs of the Bahá'í community and the importance of the community members' wholehearted support for the plans initiated by the Bahá'í administrative institutions.

THE ORIGINS OF THE NORTH AMERICAN BAHÁ'Í COMMUNITY

During the ministries of Bahá'u'lláh and 'Abdu'l-Bahá emphasis was placed on spreading information about the existence of the new revelation and endeavoring to increase its membership. In the North American continent this process received special impetus from the activities of American pilgrims who visited 'Abdu'l-Bahá in the Holy Land and returned to their homes, inspired to share the message of the new day with their fellow citizens. Shoghi Effendi captures the impact of their meeting with 'Abdu'l-Bahá and the importance of their services: "I can never pay sufficient tribute to that spirit of unyielding determination which the impact of a magnetic personality and the spell of a mighty utterance kindled in the entire company of these returning pilgrims, these consecrated heralds of the Covenant of God, at so decisive an epoch of their history."[6]

To facilitate the process of spreading the teachings of the religion, 'Abdu'l-Bahá dispatched teachers from the East to North America, and he addressed a constant stream of letters to his followers in that continent, "embodying in passionate and unequivocal language His instructions and counsels, His appeals and comments, His hopes and wishes, His fears and warnings."[7] His letters were translated, collected, published, and circulated within the community, and were, for a time, the only literature in English available to the American Bahá'ís. These letters served to formulate and clarify the basic tenets of the Faith. In due course the literature of the Faith was enriched with works by Bahá'í authors, and the Bahá'í Publishing Society and a number of periodicals were established as a means of providing information about the teachings of the religion to the general public.

The process of expansion was furthered by American Bahá'ís arising to teach their religion to their fellow citizens in other parts of the nation, and by some undertaking pioneer teaching efforts to a number of European countries including France, Great Britain, and Germany, and also to the Pacific islands and to China and Japan.

'Abdu'l-Bahá's travels in North America lent further impetus to the expansion of the Bahá'í Faith in that continent. In the United

States and Canada, he spoke about the teachings of the Faith before a large number of religious, humanitarian, and educational groups. His presentations served to clarify the vision of the Faith and its socially developmental mission.[8] 'Abdu'l-Bahá's presence in North America also helped the American Bahá'ís to gain a greater awareness of the need both to put the spiritual and social teachings of the religion into practice in their daily life, and to develop Bahá'í community life, incorporating its principles concerning social organization. These activities gave rise to the introduction of study classes and summer schools, aimed at increasing the general level of understanding of the religion and equipping individual members of the community to share the teachings of the Faith with others; classes were also instituted for the Bahá'í education of children. A regular community meeting, known as the Nineteen Day Feast, designed to enhance the spiritual, social, and administrative aspects of Bahá'í community life, gradually became an integral part of the life of the community.

As the community grew in size and the number of activities proliferated, the need increased for a system of organization, consonant with Bahá'í principles, to give direction to the work of the Cause. Committees and other designated groups were appointed or elected to take care of a wide range of functions, and the Bahá'í Temple Unity, which was to evolve into the National Spiritual Assembly of the Bahá'ís of the United States and Canada, was established for the all-important task of planning for the construction of the first Bahá'í House of Worship in the Western world. Nevertheless, there was no single designated administrative body with the necessary authority to direct all facets of the work of the small but rapidly diversifying North American Bahá'í community. In subsequent chapters we will describe the impact of the development of the Bahá'í Administrative Order on the expansion of the Faith's influence around the world and on the multiplication of its society-building and humanitarian functions.

At the time of the inception of the Formative Age in 1921, the Bahá'í administrative system existed, at best, in embryonic form. During 'Abdu'l-Bahá's lifetime a small number of embryonic consultative groups existed in the East and to a lesser extent in the West. However, there were no uniform procedures governing such features as how they were to be elected, the number of members, and even the title by which they were to be known.[9]

The Formative Age was ushered in by the passing of 'Abdu'l-Bahá and the disclosure of His Will and Testament, a document which, together with Bahá'u'lláh's Book of Laws, constitutes the charter of the New World Order and defines the major institutions that are to serve as the nucleus and pattern of this new Order. It was the role of Shoghi Effendi, the appointed Guardian of the Bahá'í Faith, to begin to translate into visible form the guidance set out in the writings of Bahá'u'lláh and 'Abdu'l-Bahá concerning the Bahá'í administrative structure.

Just as the American Bahá'í community responded with dedication, resourcefulness, and energy to spread the teachings of the new religion, so too, it immediately grasped the importance of the Bahá'í Administrative Order and arose to further its interests. Writing on this theme, Shoghi Effendi stresses the immediacy of this community's response. He compares their actions to those of the dawn-breakers of the Heroic Age of the Faith, and foreshadows the significance of the unique contribution this community is destined to make, by embracing the provisions of 'Abdu'l-Bahá's Will and Testament, to the development of the Administrative Order. He states:

With that self-same spontaneity which had characterized her response to the Message proclaimed by Bahá'u'lláh America had now arisen to espouse the cause of the Administration which the Will and Testament of His Son had unmistakably established. It was given to her, and to her alone, in the turbulent years following the revelation of so momentous a Document, to become the fearless champion of that Administration, the pivot of its new-born institutions and the leading promoter of its influence. To their Persian brethren, who in the heroic age of the Faith had won the crown of martyrdom, the American believers, forerunners of its golden age, were now worthily succeeding, bearing in their turn the palm of a hard-won victory. The unbroken record of their illustrious deeds had established beyond the shadow of a doubt their preponderating share in shaping the destinies of their Faith.[10]

And, in another passage Shoghi Effendi writes:

It was this community, the cradle and stronghold of the Administrative Order of the Faith of Bahá'u'lláh, which, on the morrow of 'Abdu'l-Bahá's ascension, was the first among all other Bahá'í communities in East and West to arise and champion the cause of that Order, to fix its pattern, to erect its fabric, to initiate its endowments, to establish and consolidate its subsidiary institutions, and to vindicate its aims and purposes.[11]

In the remainder of this chapter we will trace some of the actions taken by the American Bahá'ís in striving to carry out the tasks involved in establishing the Bahá'í administrative system from the earliest days of the Formative Age. We will also examine some of the implications of Shoghi Effendi's designation of the North American Bahá'í community as "the cradle and stronghold of the Administrative Order of Bahá'u'lláh."[12]

THE CRADLE AND STRONGHOLD

The response of the American Bahá'ís to the guidance from Shoghi
Effendi, the newly designated head of the Faith, concerning the establishment of the Bahá'í Administrative Order was immediate and
positive, though, inevitably, it required a period of adjustment.

The passing of 'Abdu'l-Bahá in November 1921, not only called for
the systematic introduction of elected institutions operating at local
and national levels of society as part of the development of the Bahá'í
Administrative Order, it also called for a change in leadership style—
i.e. from the charismatic, individualistic style of leadership associated
with 'Abdu'l-Bahá to a more institutional style, in which democratically
elected assemblies operated in close collaboration with the Guardian.
The Bahá'ís, as individuals, were accustomed to turning directly to
'Abdu'l-Bahá for counsel and advice. They cherished their personal
contact with such a spiritual and caring figure. It was 'Abdu'l-Bahá who
resolved difficulties, settled disputes, and soothed troubled hearts. Any
embryonic Bahá'í council that existed at the time had limited authority
and, in some instances, may well have been regarded as not constituting
an integral or even a necessary part of the religion itself.

The American Bahá'ís, however, willingly embraced the new stage in
the evolution of the Faith and endeavored to make the necessary adjust-
ments to their behavior. In addition to the their spiritual receptivity
and their evolving understanding of the special station conferred on
the North American Bahá'í community by 'Abdu'l-Bahá, it seems likely
that the existence of a democratic and republican form of government
in the United States might well have provided a receptive milieu for
the establishment of the Bahá'í system of social organization since the
general population, including the members of the Bahá'í community,
would have had a degree of familiarity with various governmental processes and with the actions required of the good citizen. No doubt,
they already had some experience with such Bahá'í Administrative

activities as voting by secret ballot, electing their leaders, and expressing their individual opinions about issues. They were also likely to be familiar with the operation of the principle of majority rule, and the importance of citizen participation in government. In addition, understanding concerning the purpose and function of a constitution as the legal basis for the operation of government permeated the society. The American constitution was prized as the document that established the structure and purposes of the government and the rights of its citizens; and, among other things, defined the powers of officers, how they are elected, and their term of office.

While the American Bahá'í community may have been somewhat practiced in the processes of governance, the provisions of the Bahá'í Administrative Order were unique and the implications of this uniqueness gradually became evident as they endeavored to put its procedures into practice. With the guidance of Shoghi Effendi's letters, many of which were addressed to their community, they embarked on a long learning process to understand the vision and purpose of the new Administrative Order, the uniqueness of its institutions—their fundamentally spiritual foundation and distinctiveness when compared with existing theocratic or secular forms of governance—and, the means by which they operated.[13]

Horace Holley, a long-serving secretary of the National Spiritual Assembly of the Bahá'ís of the United States, whose extraordinary contribution to the development of the Bahá'í administrative system in North America will be discussed below, comments on the role of organization in religion and illustrates some of the unique features of the Bahá'í Administrative Order, in the following description:

> It has been the general characteristic of religion that organization marks the interruption of the true spiritual influence and serves to prevent the original impulse from being carried into the world.

The organization has invariably become a substitute for religion
rather than a method or an instrument used to give the religion
effect. . . . Up to the present time, in fact, no Founder of a revealed
religion has explicitly laid down the principles that should guide
the administrative machinery of the Faith He has established.

In the Bahá'í Cause, the principles of world administration
were expressed by Bahá'u'lláh, and these principles were developed in the writings of 'Abdu'l-Bahá, more especially in His *Will
and Testament.*

The purpose of this organization is to make possible a true and
lasting unity among people of different races, classes, interests,
characters, and inherited creeds. A close and sympathetic study
of this aspect of the Bahá'í Cause will show that the purpose
and method of Bahá'í administration is so perfectly adapted to
the fundamental spirit of the Revelation that it bears to it the
same relationship as body to soul. In character, the principles of
Bahá'í administration represent the science of cooperation; in
application, they provide for a new and higher type of morality
worldwide in scope. In the clash and confusion of sectarian
prejudice, the Bahá'í Movement is impartial and sympathetic,
offering a foundation upon which reconciliation can be firmly
based. Amid the complex interrelations of governments, the
Movement stands absolutely neutral as to political purposes
and entirely obedient to all recognized authority. It will not be
overlooked by the student that Bahá'u'lláh is the only religious
teacher making obedience to just government and rulers a
definite spiritual command.[14]

Commenting further on the centrality of the Bahá'í Administrative
Order and the relationship between its spiritual foundation and the
achievement of unity, Mr. Holley states:

The Administrative aspect of the Bahá'í Cause is in reality no mere set of external regulations but the very fruit of its universal spirit. Bahá'í administration is nothing less than a worldwide ethics, the special characteristic of which is to transform subjective faith into positive cooperative action—unifying the whole being of each believer through his unity with his spiritual brothers. Its unbreakable foundation is the principle of consultation, which 'Abdu'l-Bahá declared to be the fulfillment of individual conscience in this new age.[15]

And, in relation to the "method of Bahá'í administration," Holley asserts that

. . . with its provision for local, national and international units, [it] is the most perfect plan of worldwide spiritual unity ever evolved. It is the confident faith of the Bahá'ís, however, that this plan is unworkable without the requisite spiritual basis— the sincere desire for true, organic unity raised above personal or group ambitions such as obtains only in a Cause possessing divine authority and evoking self-sacrifice among its adherents.[16]

Finally, Mr. Holley identifies the local Bahá'í group as the critical starting point not only for the evolution of the Administrative Order but also for the religion, itself. He writes:

It is the genius of the Bahá'í Cause that the principle underlying the administration of its affairs aims to improve the life and upbuild the character of the individual believer in his own local community . . . and not to enhance the prestige of those relatively few who, by election or appointment, hold positions of higher authority. . . . The local group, involving as it does men and women in all the normal activities and relations of life, is the foundation upon which rests the entire evolution of the Cause.[17]

The local Bahá'í community, characterized by Holley as "a unity of minds and hearts, an association of people entirely voluntary in character, established upon a common experience of devotion to the universal aims of Bahá'u'lláh and agreement as to the methods by which these aims can be advanced,"[18] is given official recognition only after its number of adult declared believers has become nine or more, at which time a nine-member Local Spiritual Assembly is elected from among the membership of the community. The responsibility for and supervision of local Bahá'í affairs is vested in this democratically elected body. Prior to the election of the Assembly, the community exists as a voluntary group of workers and students of the Cause. As will be seen from later discussion, great emphasis is placed on fostering the development of the local Bahá'í groups and increasing their membership to enable the election of Local Spiritual Assemblies.

The enormous task of building the Bahá'í Administrative Order from the grassroots of the Bahá'í community becomes evident when the statistical information concerning the North American Bahá'í community provided in *The Bahá'í Year Book*, volume 1 (April, 1925–April, 1926) is studied.[19] It reported that Local Spiritual Assemblies and Bahá'í Groups were to be found in only 26 states in the United States and in three provinces of Canada. The greatest concentrations of membership appear to have been on the East and West coasts, with the Bahá'í population being sparsely scattered throughout the rest of the continent.

SHOGHI EFFENDI THE MASTER-BUILDER

Shoghi Effendi initiated an intensive process of education for the Bahá'í community, the first stage of which extended over a twenty-

year period. Through his letters he patiently and progressively defined the procedures for the election and functioning of the Bahá'í
institutions. It was through his exchanges of correspondence with
the national governing body of the North American Bahá'ís and the
questions that body addressed to him that Shoghi Effendi trained and
educated the American Bahá'ís to accept the authority of the elected
institutions, to rely on the process of consultation, and to work in an
administrative manner.

In one of his earliest letters addressed to the American Bahá'ís,
Shoghi Effendi linked the realization of the mission of the Bahá'í
Faith to the formation of Local and National Spiritual Assemblies.
He placed primary emphasis on laying the foundation of the administrative structure by first establishing Local Assemblies, stressing "the
vital necessity of having a local spiritual Assembly in every locality
where the number of adult declared believers exceeds nine." Once
these local institutions were established, it would be possible to elect
"a Body that shall adequately represent the interests of all the friends
and Assemblies throughout the American Continent."[20]

In this same letter Shoghi Effendi describes "the duties and
functions of Spiritual Assemblies," institutions whose potential significance should not be underestimated, since they are "later to be
designated as the local Houses of Justice." He also calls attention to
"the sacredness of their nature, the wide scope of their activity, and
the grave responsibility which rests upon them."[21] In addition, Shoghi
Effendi stresses the importance of Bahá'í consultation in Assembly
decision-making. He offers guidance concerning the qualities of mind
and spirit to be manifested by Assembly members participating in the
consultation process, and he stresses the authority of the Assemblies
and the importance of the believers turning to them for guidance and
being willing to obey their directives. In this regard, Shoghi Effendi
cites the following advice of 'Abdu'l-Bahá:

It is incumbent upon every one not to take any step without consulting the Spiritual Assembly, and they must assuredly obey with heart and soul its bidding and be submissive to it, that things may be properly ordered and well arranged. Otherwise every person will act independently and after his own judgment, will follow his own desire, and do harm to the Cause.[22]

As a means of upholding the authority of the embryonic Spiritual Assemblies in the community and of ensuring the efficient completion of the manifold tasks undertaken by the community members, Shoghi Effendi issues an appeal for order and collaborative action within the community:

Full harmony . . . as well as cooperation among the various local assemblies and the members themselves, and particularly between each assembly and the national body, is of the utmost importance, for upon it depends the unity of the Cause of God, the solidarity of the friends, the full, speedy and efficient workings of the spiritual activities of His loved ones.[23]

He ends his letter by directing the National Spiritual Assembly to appoint committees from among the members of the community, to assist it with the planning and execution of aspects of its work relating to such areas as teaching, publishing, and the construction of the Bahá'í House of Worship.

Progressively, Shoghi Effendi elucidated the importance of centralizing authority in the hands of the elected institutions of the Faith, and he clarified the functions of the institutions of the Bahá'í administrative system. He explained the spiritual nature of Bahá'í elections and established procedures for the annual election of Local Spiritual Assemblies and the National Spiritual Assembly on the first day of the Riḍván festival (21 April). In Bahá'í elections any adult believer is eligible for election; there is no slate of candidates representing different parties, and no process of nomination. To assist those Bahá'ís who were called upon to elect the members of these institutions, Shoghi Effendi advised them "to consider without the least trace of passion and prejudice, and irrespective of any material consideration, the names of only those who can best combine the necessary qualities of unquestioned loyalty, of selfless devotion, of a well-trained mind, of recognized ability and mature experience."[24]

In addition, the Guardian defined the role of the delegates who served as the electors of the National Spiritual Assembly and the functions of the National Bahá'í Convention, at which the election of this institution took place, and he outlined the responsibilities of the elected representatives. Addressing the members of the National Spiritual Assembly, Shoghi Effendi calls attention to the high moral qualities they must endeavor to manifest. He counsels:

> Their function is not to dictate, but to consult. . . . They must regard themselves in no other light but that of chosen instruments for a more efficient and dignified presentation of the Cause of God. They should never be led to suppose that they are the central ornaments of the body of the Cause, intrinsically superior to others in capacity or merit. . . . They should approach their task with extreme humility, and endeavor, by their open-mindedness, their high sense of justice and duty, their candor, their modesty, their entire devotion to the welfare and interests of the friends, the Cause, and humanity, to win, not only the confidence and the genuine support and respect of those whom they serve, but also their esteem and real affection.[25]

During Riḍván 1923, the procedures outlined by Shoghi Effendi were implemented for the first time. The Local Spiritual Assemblies and the National Spiritual Assembly that were elected in that year embraced the functions of spiritual assemblies as we now recognize them in the East and West.[26] In 1925, the National Spiritual Assembly introduced a national Bahá'í newsletter, which became known as *Bahá'í News*. Its regular publication facilitated the process of educating the American Bahá'í community concerning the Administrative Order. It fostered a sense of Bahá'í identity and provided information about the activities of the Bahá'í community in North America and throughout the world. Writing to the National Assembly, Shoghi Effendi expressed satisfaction at this new initiative and, foreseeing its potential, offered the following guidance to further its development:

> That it may attain its object it must combine the essential qualities of accuracy, reliability, thoroughness, dignity and wisdom. It should become a great factor in promoting understanding, providing information on Bahá'í activity, both local and foreign, in stimulating interest, in combating evil influences, and in upholding and safeguarding the institutions of the Cause. It should be made as representative as possible, should be replete with news, up-to-date in its information, and should arouse the keenest interest among believers and admirers alike in every corner of the globe. I cherish the hope for its immediate future, and I trust you will devote your special attention to its development, and by devising well-conceived and worldwide measures transform this News Letter into what I hope will become the foremost Bahá'í Journal of the world.[27]

As the Bahá'í community gradually became somewhat familiar with the procedures for the operation of the Bahá'í administrative system, Shoghi Effendi turned his attention to fostering its efficient functioning in anticipation of its taking on a wider range of activities. For example, reminiscent of Quddús calling on Mullá Ḥusayn to count the number of defenders in the fort of Shaykh Ṭabarsí, Shoghi Effendi instructed the National Spiritual Assembly to maintain accurate membership rolls. Furthermore, cognizant of the difficult circumstances under which the administrators of the Cause were endeavoring to operate, Shoghi Effendi empathized with their current situation and offered the following encouragement:

> I am deeply conscious of the manifold and unavoidable difficulties that confront you in your labors for the administrative affairs of the Cause. Vast distances; personal professional preoccupations; insufficient number of capable and experienced teachers, unhampered by the necessity of earning their means of livelihood; the inadequacy of the means at your disposal, financial and otherwise; the prevailing tendencies in the general thought, sentiment, and manners of the people in whose midst you work—all these, though insuperable obstacles at present, will, if we stand steadfast and faithful, be one by one removed, and pave the way for the ultimate ascendancy of the Cause and the fruition and triumph of our labors.[28]

Calling for practical action, he stressed the importance of making a careful estimate of the available human and financial resources before embarking on a new project, in order to assess the viability of the project and to make the most efficient use of the limited resources. To this end he encouraged individual believers to consult with the

Spiritual Assembly before starting on any new initiative, as a means of avoiding unnecessary duplication of effort and ensuring that the projects undertaken could be sustained. While rejoicing in the exuberance of "the valiant warriors of the Cause," he cautioned lest "an undue multiplication of their activities, and the consequent dissipation of their forces, defeat the very purpose which animates them in the pursuit of their glorious task."[29]

THE ADMINISTRATIVE ORDER AS VEHICLE

By May 1926, Shoghi Effendi determined it was time to put the institutions of the embryonic administrative system to work. Writing to the National Spiritual Assembly he indicates that, "The administrative machinery of the Cause having now sufficiently evolved, its aims and object fairly well grasped and understood, and its method and working made more familiar to every believer, I feel the time is ripe when its should be fully and consciously utilized to further the purpose for which it has been created." He goes on to explain the "twofold purpose" it should be made to serve: "On the one hand, it should aim at a steady and gradual expansion of the Movement along lines that are at once broad, sound and universal; and on the other it should insure the internal consolidation of the work already achieved. It should both provide the impulse whereby the dynamic forces latent in the Faith can unfold, crystallize, and shape the lives and conduct of men, and serve as a medium for the interchange of thought and the coordination of activities among the divers elements that constitute the Bahá'í community."[30]

In setting into motion this process of systematic and goal-directed activity, Shoghi Effendi endorsed the Plan of Unified Action submitted by the National Assembly for his approval. The Assembly's Plan broke new ground since, in the words of the Guardian, it "combines, embodies, and serves the twofold purpose of the present-day Bahá'í administration in the United States and Canada, namely the promotion of the vitally needed teaching work, and the provision for the gradual completion of the Mashriqu'l-Adhkár [the Bahá'í House of Worship]."[31] Both these areas of activity continued to engage the minds and hearts of the Bahá'ís for many decades. Their exploits in relation to the systematic expansion of the Bahá'í Faith and the construction of the House of Worship in Wilmette will be described in subsequent chapters.

While retaining the Bahá'í community's primary focus on the twofold objectives of the Plan of Unified Action, Shoghi Effendi also gradually widened the scope of its teaching activities and sought to increase the level of participation in this all-important undertaking. In this regard, he called upon the National Assembly to "stimulate the spirit of enterprise among the believers in order to further the teaching as well as the administrative work of the Cause,"[32] and he encouraged the Assembly's continuing involvement in the area of interracial amity. Commenting on the critical importance of this issue not only for the developing Bahá'í community but to society at large, Shoghi Effendi states:

> As this problem, in the inevitable course of events, grows in acuteness and complexity, and as the number of faithful from both races multiplies, it will become increasingly evident that the future growth and prestige of the Cause are bound to be influenced to a very considerable degree by the manner in which the adherents of the Bahá'í Faith carry out, first among themselves and in their relations with their fellow-men, those high standards of inter-racial amity so widely proclaimed and so fearlessly exemplified to the American people by our Master 'Abdu'l-Bahá.[33]

Further, as a means of fostering "the attitude that should characterize the conduct of the members of the Bahá'í family," Shoghi
Effendi encouraged both the members of the National Assembly,
to whom he refers as "the Trustees of God's sacred Faith" and the
members of the Bahá'í community to participate in gatherings arranged at Green Acre, a venue for Bahá'í educational activities. He
expressed the hope that these gatherings "may serve as a testing
ground for the application of those ideals and standards that are
the distinguishing features of the Revelation of Bahá'u'lláh," and he
foreshadowed the far-reaching import of such occasions: "May the
assembled believers—now but a tiny nucleus of the Bahá'í Commonwealth of the future—so exemplify that spirit of universal love
and fellowship as to evoke in the minds of their associates the vision
of that future City of God which the almighty arm of Bahá'u'lláh
can alone establish."[34]

Shoghi Effendi also began to expand the American believers'
sense of responsibility for the progress of the Bahá'í Faith beyond
the confines of the North American continent. For example, when
the opportunity arose to further the promotion of Bahá'í educational
institutions in Iran, he asked the National Spiritual Assembly to
find two capable American teachers who were willing to spend an
extended period of time in Ţihrán and to assist with "the meritorious
work of fostering the cause of Bahá'í education, for both boys and
girls."[35] The task of selecting the two candidates was assigned to the
National Assembly.

From time to time, Shoghi Effendi also turned to the National
Spiritual Assembly of the United States and Canada for assistance in
relation to the defense of their oppressed and persecuted coreligionists
in Iran, Egypt, and the Soviet Union. Addressing the Western Bahá'ís
Shoghi Effendi writes:

It is to you . . . who are the standard-bearers of the emancipation and triumph of the Bahá'í Faith, that our afflicted brethren of the East have turned their expectant eyes, confident that the day cannot be far-distant when, in accordance with 'Abdu'l-Bahá's explicit utterance, the West will "seize the Cause" from Persian's fettered hands and lead it to glorious victory.[36]

Hence, the Spiritual Assemblies of the West, "on whom the almighty Providence has conferred the inestimable benefits of religious toleration and freedom" were called upon to devise ways to bring to the attention of people of influence the plight of the oppressed believers, and to secure the fullest publicity of the situations confronting the Bahá'ís in Iran and other Eastern countries. Describing a recent attack against the Persian Bahá'ís, the Guardian provided guidance concerning the approach to be adopted in this publicity campaign. He states that it should aim "to arouse by every means at our disposal the conscience of unheeding humanity, and to direct the attention of men of vision and authority to these incredibly odious acts which in their ferocity and frequency cannot but constitute in the eyes of every fair-minded observer the gravest challenge to all that is sacred and precious in our present-day civilization."[37]

FORGING THE ADMINISTRATIVE MACHINERY

Many Bahá'ís, from all walks of life, were actively involved in the work of laying the foundations of the Bahá'í administrative system and in establishing its institutions. While their self-sacrificing and devoted services are cherished, all too often their individual contributions have not been documented. To illustrate some of the processes involved in the early stages of forging the administrative machinery, we will examine the unique and outstanding contribution of Horace Holley, the long-serving secretary of the National Spiritual Assembly

of the United States and Canada. We also briefly consider the role
of the American National Assembly in framing and promulgating
the national Bahá'í constitution, and explore the implications of this
historic document for the legal recognition of the Bahá'í Faith and its
institutions throughout the world, and its emergence as an independent world religion

MR. HORACE HOLLEY

A New Englander by birth, Horace Holley has been described
as "one of the foremost exponents of Bahá'í administration in the
world." Commenting on his personal qualities, Rúḥíyyih Khánum,
the widow of Shoghi Effendi, the Guardian of the Bahá'í Faith, states
that he shared some of the typical characteristics of people who come
from New England, namely, "hardheaded, independent, humorous
and yet taciturn people, descendants of the first colonists of America,
who are renowned for their rugged individualism, who were largely
responsible for winning the United States its political independence
and who later played no small part in abolishing slavery from their
nation." His personality, she said, had two strongly defined aspects;
he possessed not only "a brilliant, analytical mind, but at the same
time he was a dreamer, idealist and mystic."[38]

No doubt his cultural background and the historical perspective it
embodied, together with his capacity for both visionary thinking and
critical analytical thought, prepared Mr. Holley for the role he was
to play in the development of the Bahá'í Administrative Order. It is
indeed an interesting paradox that such a rugged individualist should
have willingly committed himself to the task of constructing and
nurturing the administrative machinery of the religion! In an address
to a Bahá'í meeting, Mr. Holley shed some light on his motivation
for taking on this responsibility and on the approach he adopted.
According to the report,

Mr. Holley felt that the administrative aspects of the Faith were not developing fast enough, so he raised all kinds of questions with the Guardian, both as a member of the Local Spiritual Assembly of New York and as a member of the National Spiritual Assembly. As the answers came, he said, the pattern of the administrative order began to unfold. Every time a letter came from the Guardian giving answers to specific questions, it was shared with the local assemblies. Finally, Mr. Holley began to compile these answers, and *Bahá'í Administration* came into being.*

Mr. Holley pointed out that, as the Cause grew and the American Bahá'í community began to get responsibilities in other countries, the questions he had asked the Guardian helped to answer similar questions that came up in other areas . . . especially in the Western Hemisphere.[39]

Shoghi Effendi's answers to the questions addressed to him by Horace Holley, in his capacity as secretary of the National Spiritual Assembly, represent the exposition of fundamental Bahá'í administrative principles and served as the primary source of guidance to local and national Assemblies throughout their formative years.

The importance of the relationship between Horace Holley and Shoghi Effendi was critical to the development of the Administrative Order. Mr. Holley was first elected to the National Spiritual Assembly in 1923, and was a member of that institution for thirty-six years, serving as its secretary for thirty-four years. His clear vision of the

---

* A reference to a collection of letters written by Shoghi Effendi that were first published in 1928.

uniqueness and significance of this evolving Order and the practical experience he gained in implementing the guidance contained in the letters of Shoghi Effendi enabled him to interact with the young Guardian in a way that not only furthered but also accelerated the community's understanding of the administrative machinery.

Rúḥíyyih Khánum attests that Shoghi Effendi highly valued Mr. Holley's intellectual qualities and his immense capacity for work, and greatly appreciated the personal sacrifices he willingly made in discharging the many responsibilities he undertook in service to the Faith. Underlining the importance of the partnership between the Guardian and Mr. Holley, Rúḥíyyih Khánum observes that with the strengthening of the American National Spiritual Assembly and

> . . . with a man of Horace's calibre devoting his entire time and energy to its work, Shoghi Effendi found that he could set the forces of Bahá'í Administration in motion. Halfway across the world there was a collaborator who grasped the import of his instructions and interpretations of the Teachings and who, as the "indefatigable and distinguished" secretary of that Assembly, as Shoghi Effendi characterized him, in conjunction with its other eight members, and backed up by a devoted and enthusiastic Bahá'í community, not only saw they were implemented, but expounded and classified them.[40]

She cautions against underestimating this partnership, and comments on some of its features:

> That it worked so well, bore such fruit and survived the acid test of time, is a great compliment to the two people involved. For Shoghi Effendi was not dealing with a sycophant but a man of strong personality, views and capacity, and Horace was not deal-

ing with a mere leader but a divinely inspired, infallibly guided spiritual ruler. The execution of the tasks set by the Guardian for Horace was therefore not without its hazards. But the loyalty of Horace on the one hand and Shoghi Effendi's patience and tact on the other, avoided situations which in other circumstances might have led to difficulties.[41]

Rúhíyyih Khánum expresses the view that the letters addressed to Mr. Holley by Shoghi Effendi testify to the outstanding role he played in the early history of the Formative Age and illustrate how deeply the Guardian valued his services. To illustrate her point, she provides the following examples from the letters of Shoghi Effendi addressed to Horace:

"Your ready pen, your brilliant mind, your marvellous vigour and organizing ability, above all your unwavering loyalty are assets that I greatly value and for which I am deeply grateful" he wrote in 1931. In 1932 Shoghi Effendi wrote to him ". . . your active share in the administrative activities of the Cause, your splendid letters of appeal in connection with the Plan of Unified Action, your wise leadership of the New York Assembly—all testify to your marvellous efficiency and your high spiritual attainments." . . . And in 1943 Shoghi Effendi reiterates these sentiments in even warmer terms: "I greatly value, as you already know, your presentation of the various aspects of the Cause, for whose expansion, consolidation and defense you have, during so many years, laboured so indefatigably and served with such distinction. I will, I assure you, continue to pray for you and for your dear collaborator Mrs. Holley, that you may both enrich still further the record of your past services."[42]

The range of Mr. Holley's services was immense. In addition to the outstanding administrative function he performed, he was an able spokesman for the religion, addressing audiences on many aspects of the Faith not only in North America but also at international Bahá'í gatherings in different parts of the world. Furthermore, with the Guardian's approval, he also initiated publication of the American *Bahá'í News*. He made a major contribution to the preparation and publishing of *The Bahá'í World* volumes. He collected and published the writings of Bahá'u'lláh and 'Abdu'l-Bahá as well as the letters of guidance from Shoghi Effendi, ensuring thereby the circulation of authentic and reliable information about the teachings of the Faith and its vision for the transformation of human society. He enriched the literature on the Bahá'í Faith by his own books and the articles that appeared in Bahá'í periodicals. And, through the illuminating letters he wrote in his capacity as secretary of the National Assembly, he enhanced the understanding of the Bahá'í community of the social mission of Bahá'u'lláh and of the present-day administration of the Bahá'í Faith. In 1951 Mr. Holley was appointed to the high office of Hand of the Cause by Shoghi Effendi, a function he performed while continuing to serve as the secretary of the National Assembly. Following the death of Shoghi Effendi in 1957, Mr. Holley was asked by the Hands of the Cause in the Holy Land to transfer his residence to the World Center of the Bahá'í Faith in Haifa, Israel, where the last days of his life were spent assisting the Hands with the international administration of the Faith. He passed away in Haifa in July 1960.

In her moving and enlightening tribute to this great servant of the Faith, Rúḥíyyih Khánum attests: "He grasped, perhaps better than anyone else, just what the Guardian was constructing through the erection of the Administrative Order. He assisted in this through all the powers of his mind, giving, year after year, an unstinting service to its realization."[43]

THE BAHÁ'Í CONSTITUTION

The establishment of Local and National Spiritual Assemblies and the initial maturation of their functioning set the scene for a new stage in the evolution of the administrative machinery of the Cause, which had implications not only for the legal status of the Bahá'í community in North America but also contributed to "the unification of the Bahá'í world community and the consolidation of its Administrative Order."[44]

One critical element of this new phase of development was the formulation of local and national Bahá'í constitutions. Again, the North American Bahá'í community was the first to arise to play a vital role in this arena of service. Praised by Shoghi Effendi as "the formulator of the national Bahá'í constitution," and as "these privileged framers and custodians of the constitution of the Faith of Bahá'u'lláh,"[45] the elected members of the American National Spiritual Assembly set in motion the process of framing the constitution.

The National Assembly requested its Legal Committee to consider the issue of the legal recognition of the Bahá'í institutions. In presenting its findings, the Legal Committee commented on the challenges involved in endeavoring to find ways to reconcile the unique and essential requirements of the Bahá'í administrative concepts with existing legal statutes. The National Spiritual Assembly studied the Committee's recommendations and with the assistance of its Chairman, Mountford Mills, who was a legal expert, prepared the final draft of a document referred to by Shoghi Effendi as the Bahá'í constitution. In 1927 the National Spiritual Assembly adopted and promulgated a Bahá'í National constitution, which comprised a Declaration of Trust and a set of by-laws. This historic document was to have a major impact on the development of the Bahá'í Administrative Order throughout the world, in that its text, "with slight variations suited to national requirements" was to serve as "the charter" for all existing National Spiritual Assemblies.[46]

The Bahá'í national constitution, completed in 1927, represents the first systematic attempt to codify fundamental administrative principles and processes that underpin the operation of the Bahá'í administrative machinery. Describing the breadth of the contents of this document, Shoghi Effendi writes:

> The text of this national constitution comprises a Declaration of Trust, whose articles set forth the character and objects of the national Bahá'í community, establish the functions, designate the central office, and describe the official seal, of the body of its elected representatives, as well as a set of by-laws which define the status, the mode of election, the powers and duties of both local and national Assemblies, describe the relation of the National Assembly to the International House of Justice as well as to local Assemblies and individual believers, outline the rights and obligations of the National Convention and its relation to the National Assembly, disclose the character of Bahá'í elections, and lay down the requirements of voting membership in all Bahá'í communities.[47]

In presenting the constitution to the American Bahá'í community, Horace Holley, writing as secretary of the National Assembly commented on the task just completed and placed it into an historical perspective. He states:

> This task consisted in creating with the invaluable assistance of the Legal Committee a legal form which gives proper sub-

stance and substantial character to the administrative processes embodied in the Bahá'í Teachings. . . . The famous Covenant adopted by the Pilgrim Fathers on the Mayflower, the first legal document in American history, is of the same nature as the Declaration of Trust voted by the National Spiritual Assembly.[48]

The National Assembly secretary then offers the following explanation about the document and underlines its significance:

Careful examination of the Declaration and its By-Laws will reveal the fact that this document contains no arbitrary elements nor features new to the Bahá'í Cause. On the contrary, it represents a most conscientious effort to reflect those very administrative principles and elements already set forth in the letters of the Guardian and already determining the methods and relationships of our collective associations. . . .

The Declaration, in fact, is nothing more or less than a legal parallel of those moral and spiritual laws of unity inherent in the fullness of the Bahá'í Revelation and making it the fulfillment of the ideal of Religion in the social as well as spiritual realm. Because in the Bahá'í Faith this perfect correspondence exists between spiritual and social laws, let us ever bear in mind that administrative success, for Bahá'ís, is identical with moral success; and that nothing less than the true Bahá'í spirit of devotion and sacrifice can inspire with effective power the worldwide body of unity revealed by Bahá'u'lláh.[49]

Shoghi Effendi expressed his pleasure at this outstanding and historic achievement in the evolution of the Administrative Order. Describing the Declaration of Trust as being "Clear and concise in its wording, sound in principle, and complete in its affirmations of the fundamentals of Bahá'í administration," Shoghi Effendi affirmed that "it stands in its final form as a worthy and faithful exposition of the constitutional basis of Bahá'í communities in every land," and he stated that it foreshadowed "the final emergence of the world Bahá'í Commonwealth of the future." In a later letter, he praised the by-laws, attached to this document, as representing "this first and very creditable attempt at codifying the principles of general Bahá'í administration," and he anticipated that "it will contribute to pave the way for the elaboration of the beginnings of the constitution of the worldwide Bahá'í Community that will form the permanent basis upon which the blest and sanctified edifice of the first International House of Justice will securely rest and flourish." It is clear that Shoghi Effendi regarded this document as a model and prototype for all national Bahá'í constitutions and he instructed the National Spiritual Assemblies to endeavor to follow its provisions.

Once the Bahá'í national constitution was completed the American Bahá'í community immediately turned its attention to framing a similar document containing the by-laws of Bahá'í Local Assemblies. Thus, the document drafted in 1931 by the Local Spiritual Assembly of New York City became "a pattern for all local Bahá'í constitutions." Rejoicing in this unique accomplishment, Shoghi Effendi asks: "What other community can to its eternal credit claim to have been the first to frame its national and local constitutions, thereby laying down the fundamental lines of the twin charters designed to regulate the activities, define the functions, and safeguard the rights, of its institutions?"[50]

While the establishment of local and national constitutions constituted an important milestone in the unfoldment of the Administrative Order, these constitutions also opened the way for the next stages in its evolution, by providing the necessary foundation for the legal incorporation of Local and National Spiritual Assemblies in accordance with the civil statutes controlling religious or commercial bodies. Underscoring the importance of giving Spiritual Assemblies a legal standing, Shoghi Effendi explains that "this incorporation greatly consolidated their power and enlarged their capacity," and he calls attention to the unique contribution of the American Bahá'í community in this new field of activity. He observes that, "in this regard the achievement of the National Spiritual Assembly of the Bahá'ís of the United States and Canada and the Spiritual Assembly of the Bahá'ís of New York again set an example worthy of emulation by their sister Assemblies in both the East and the West."[51]

In May 1929, the American National Spiritual Assembly was incorporated as a voluntary Trust, a type of corporation recognized under the common law, which enabled it to enter into contracts, hold property, and receive bequests. The legal incorporation of the Local Spiritual Assembly of New York City took place in 1932, and was soon followed by the incorporation of a large number of local Assemblies, which "succeeded, gradually and after submitting the text of almost identical Bahá'í local constitutions to the civil authorities in their respective states or provinces, in constituting themselves into societies and corporations recognized by law, and protected by the civil statutes operating in their respective countries."[52] Before long, the initiatives taken in North America paved the way for the rest of the Bahá'í world. Local and National Spiritual Assemblies were progressively able to obtain incorporation or registration according to the law of the country in which they functioned.

The legal recognition accorded by the civil local and national authorities to the Bahá'í Local and National Spiritual Assemblies enabled these institutions to own and hold title to property. This paved the way for the establishment of local and national endowments—property belonging to the Faith in the form of land, national and local Bahá'í headquarters, historic sites, and in some cases Bahá'í

Houses of Worship. Once again, it was the American Bahá'í community who was the first to initiate what the Guardian referred to as "a historic undertaking."[53]

The efforts of the American Bahá'í community and its elected institutions to frame local and national Bahá'í constitutions and to pursue legal recognition not only enabled the Administrative Order to move to the next stage in its evolution, but they also involved strategic actions aimed at establishing the independence of the Bahá'í Faith and furthering the "full recognition of its position in history" and ensuring that it "be treated on an equal footing with other world religions."[54]

RELATIONSHIP OF BAHÁ'Í INSTITUTIONS TO GOVERNMENT

As the North American Bahá'í community continued to invest a great deal of its energy in establishing and expanding the functions of its democratically elected Local and National Spiritual Assemblies, institutions that are destined to evolve into future Bahá'í Houses of Justice, questions inevitably arose concerning the relationship between these Assemblies and the government of the land. And as the political climate of the world changed and the work of the Spiritual Assemblies began to focus on issues relating to the legal recognition of the administrative institutions and various actions taken to protect the Faith from criticism and persecution, the attitude of the Bahá'í community toward politics and the state came to the fore. The community therefore sought the guidance of the Guardian, Shoghi Effendi.

In response to these queries Shoghi Effendi reiterated two vital principles found in the writings of Bahá'u'lláh and 'Abdu'l-Bahá, which govern the interactions of the believers and their institutions with government, namely the principles of obedience to government and the noninvolvement in partisan political affairs. Shoghi Effendi states: "Theirs is the duty to demonstrate, on one hand, the non-political character of their Faith, and to assert, on the other, their unqualified loyalty and obedience to whatever is the considered judgment of their respective governments."[55]

Highlighting the uniqueness of the Bahá'í Faith and its administrative machinery, and the primary necessity of obedience to government, Shoghi Effendi's secretary, writing on his behalf states:

> At the outset it should be made indubitably clear that the Bahá'í Cause being essentially a religious movement of a spiritual character stands above every political party or group, and thus cannot and should not act in contravention to the principles, laws, and doctrines of any government. Obedience to the regulations and orders of the state is, indeed, the sacred obligation of every true and loyal Bahá'í. Both Bahá'u'lláh and 'Abdu'l-Bahá have urged us all to be submissive and loyal to the political authorities of our respective countries. . . . There is nothing more contrary to the spirit of the Cause than open rebellion against the governmental authorities of a country, specially if they do not interfere in and do not oppose the inner and sacred beliefs and religious convictions of the individual . . .[56]

Commenting further on the practical implications of the principle of loyalty to government, the Guardian's secretary sets the following vital limits to the requirement of obedience to the state:

> For whereas the friends should obey the government under which they live, even at the risk of sacrificing all their administrative affairs and interests, they should under no circumstances suffer their inner religious beliefs and convictions to be violated and

transgressed by any authority whatever. A distinction of a fundamental importance must, therefore, be made between spiritual and administrative matters. Whereas the former are sacred and inviolable and hence cannot be subject to compromise, the latter are secondary and can consequently be given up and even sacrificed for the sake of obedience to the laws and regulations of the government. Obedience to the state is so vital a principle of the Cause that should the authorities in . . . decide today to prevent Bahá'ís from holding any meeting or publishing any literature they should obey. . . . But, as already pointed out, such an allegiance is confined merely to administrative matters which if checked can only retard the progress of the Faith for some time. In matters of belief, however, no compromise whatever should be allowed, even though the outcome of it be death or expulsion.[57]

Finally, stressing this important distinction between obedience in relation to administrative matters and matters of belief, Shoghi Effendi invokes the memory of the martyrs of the Heroic Age who willingly laid down their lives rather than violate their deeply held beliefs.

To all administrative regulations which the civil authorities have issued from time to time, or will issue in the future . . . , the Bahá'í community, faithful to its sacred obligations towards its government, and conscious of its civic duties, has yielded, and will continue to yield implicit obedience. . . . To such orders, however, as are tantamount to a recantation of their faith by its members, or constitute an act of disloyalty to its spiritual, its basic and God-given principles and precepts, it will stubbornly refuse to bow, preferring imprisonment, deportation and all manner of persecution, including death—as already suffered by the twenty thousand martyrs that have laid down their lives in the path of its Founders—rather than follow the dictates of a temporal authority requiring it to renounce its allegiance to its cause.[58]

The second principle, the noninvolvement in partisan politics, articulated by Shoghi Effendi to guide the Bahá'í community has far-reaching implications. While the members of the Bahá'í community and its institutions are patriotic and supporters and well-wishers of the government and their fellow-citizens, they are, at the same time, called upon to "refrain from associating themselves, whether by word or by deed, with the political pursuits of their respective nations, with the policies of their governments and the schemes and programs of parties and factions."[59] Such partisanship would, undoubtedly, undermine the fundamental unity the community is striving so hard to build.

In stressing some of the potential dangers of political involvement, Shoghi Effendi anticipates that, at a future time, when the Bahá'í communities throughout the world are greatly expanded and "their power, as a social force, becomes increasingly apparent, they will no doubt find themselves increasingly subjected to the pressure which men of authority and influence, in the political domain, will exercise in the hope of obtaining the support they require for the advancement of their aims."[60] He also warns the Bahá'ís to guard against unwittingly compromising their spiritual ideals and principles in their eagerness to further the aims of their Faith and its institutions. He sets out the following standard of behavior:

Let them proclaim that in whatever country they reside, and however advanced their institutions, or profound their desire to enforce the laws, and apply the principles, enunciated by Bahá'u'lláh, they will, unhesitatingly, subordinate the operation of such laws and the application of such principles to the requirements and legal enactments of their respective governments. Theirs is not the purpose, while endeavoring to conduct and perfect the administrative affairs of their Faith, to violate, under any circumstances, the provisions of their country's constitution, much less to allow the machinery of their administration to supersede the government of their respective countries.[61]

Some of the implications of the principles that govern the relationship between the Bahá'í Administrative Order and the state will be further explored in the chapter dealing with the role of the American Bahá'í community in the emancipation of the Bahá'í Faith.

A NOBLE RECORD OF SERVICE

Shoghi Effendi described the American Bahá'í community as the "fearless champion"[62] of the Bahá'í Administrative Order. Within the North American continent this community successfully laid the foundation of the administrative structure, established local and national institutions, and ensured their legal recognition and protection. These Local and National Assemblies were later mobilized by Shoghi Effendi to serve as effective instruments for the expansion of the Faith throughout the world, ushering in a new phase in the implementation of America's God-given mandate, and creating the conditions necessary for the ultimate election of the supreme governing body, the Universal House of Justice.

The establishment of the Universal House of Justice, however, could not take place until the framework of the administrative structure had been raised throughout the world. Therefore, the American

Bahá'ís were called upon to lend active assistance to the global expansion of the Faith—first in Central and South America, then in Europe, and later in the rest of the world. The challenge was not only to form Local Spiritual Assemblies but progressively to establish National Spiritual Assemblies in the various goal countries, which would serve as "the pillars" supporting the Universal House of Justice, "the final unit crowning the entire edifice."[63] The formation of National Spiritual Assemblies was crucial since it is the prerogative of the members of the National Assemblies to elect the membership of the Universal House of Justice.

As will be seen in a subsequent chapter, Shoghi Effendi guided the efforts of the American Bahá'í community through a series of regional and global teaching Plans, whose objectives were designed to extend the influence of the Faith and foster the establishment of its institutions. When Shoghi Effendi passed away suddenly in 1957, the Hands of the Cause of God, an institution with the function of promoting and protecting the Bahá'í Cause, whose members were designated by Shoghi Effendi as the "chief stewards" of the Faith,[64] provided leadership to the community for an interim period. Judging that the administrative basis of the community was sufficiently well established, the Hands of the Cause set in motion the necessary processes that would culminate in the election of the Universal House of Justice, the international governing body of the Faith whose establishment was foreshadowed in the seminal writings of Bahá'u'lláh, Himself. In April 1963, the members of the fifty-six Bahá'í National Assemblies, which had been established by that time, convened in Haifa, Israel, to participate in the first historic election of this Institution. Following the example of Shoghi Effendi, the Universal House of Justice continues to issue Plans to the Bahá'ís of the world, which are designed to promote the life-transforming teachings of Bahá'u'lláh, and to foster the next stages in the evolution of the Bahá'í community. As in the

time of Shoghi Effendi, the House of Justice relies on the members of
the American Bahá'í community to assume major responsibility for
the expansion and consolidation of the Faith.

The role of the North American Bahá'í community, the "champion-builders" of the Administrative Order, is without a doubt unique.
With an astonishingly clear vision, this youthful community was,
in the words of Shoghi Effendi, "the first to grasp the implications,
evolve the pattern, and lay the basis, of the structure of the Bahá'í
Administrative Order in the entire Bahá'í world." Not only did it
understand the vision and purpose of the administrative machinery,
but its members exerted heroic efforts to bring it into being. Shoghi
Effendi underlines this community's outstanding contribution, at-
testing that it was "chiefly responsible . . . for the fixing of the pattern,
the elaboration of the national constitution, and the erection of the
basic institutions, of a divinely conceived Administrative Order."[65]

Such accomplishments by the spiritual descendants of the dawn-
breakers of the Heroic Age call for qualities of spirit and character
that are reminiscent of those exemplified by their spiritual forebears.
Extolling the deeds of the American Bahá'ís, Shoghi Effendi asks:
"What other community has been capable of demonstrating, with
such consistency, the resourcefulness, the discipline, the iron determination, the zeal and perseverance, the devotion and fidelity, so
indispensable to the erection and the continued expansion of the
framework within which those nascent institutions can alone multi-
ply and mature?"[66]

While the unique contribution of Horace Holley serves to illustrate the nature of the involvement of the North American Bahá'í
community to laying the foundations of the Administrative Order of
the Faith, it is also evident that the establishment, nurturance, and
development of its nascent administrative institutions, and the efforts
exerted to obtain their legal recognition and protection, required the

self-sacrificing efforts of the rank and file of the membership, women and men, alike. Indeed, whether acting alone, or serving as a member of a Bahá'í institution, or simply by being a member of a local Bahá'í community, it is the individual believer who is called upon to shoulder the multiplicity of tasks involved. Referring to the mighty challenge facing the individual believer "on whom, in the last resort, depends the fate of the entire community," Shoghi Effendi writes:

This challenge, so severe and insistent, and yet so glorious, faces no doubt primarily the individual believer on whom, in the last resort, depends the fate of the entire community. He it is who constitutes the warp and woof on which the quality and pattern of the whole fabric must depend. He it is who acts as one of the countless links in the mighty chain that now girdles the globe. He it is who serves as one of the multitude of bricks which support the structure and insure the stability of the administrative edifice now being raised in every part of the world. Without his support, at once whole-hearted, continuous and generous, every measure adopted, and every plan formulated, by the body which acts as the national representative of the community to which he belongs, is foredoomed to failure. The World Center of the Faith itself is paralyzed if such a support on the part of the rank and file of the community is denied it. The Author of the Divine Plan Himself is impeded in His purpose if the proper instruments for the execution of His design are lacking. The sustaining strength of Bahá'u'lláh Himself, the Founder of the Faith, will be withheld from every and each individual who fails in the long run to arise and play his part.[67]

7

CHIEF EXECUTOR AND CUSTODIAN OF 'ABDU'L-BAHÁ'S DIVINE PLAN

At the midpoint of his ministry 'Abdu'l-Bahá undertook an historic journey to the West. During his prolonged visit to North America in 1912, he nurtured and trained the embryonic American Bahá'í community, and worked tirelessly to unfurl the standard of Bahá'u'lláh in the heart of that vast continent. 'Abdu'l-Bahá's love and appreciation for the potential of this community is further confirmed by his revelation, in the evening of his life, of a set of fourteen documents, which together form the Tablets of the Divine Plan. These tablets invested his American followers with "a mandate to plant the banner of His Father's Faith, as He had planted it in their own land, in all the continents, the countries and islands of the globe." Addressing the North American Bahá'ís, 'Abdu'l-Bahá attests that their mission is "unspeakably glorious," and foreshadows, that should success crown their enterprise, "America will assuredly evolve into a center from which waves of spiritual power will emanate, and the throne of the Kingdom of God, will in the plenitude of its majesty and glory, be firmly established."[1] He makes the following dramatic affirmation:

The moment this Divine Message is carried forward by the American believers from the shores of America, and is propagated through the continents of Europe, of Asia, of Africa and of Australasia, and as far as the islands of the Pacific, this community will find itself securely established upon the throne of everlasting dominion. Then will all the peoples of the world witness that this community is spiritually illumined and divinely guided. Then will the whole earth resound with the praises of its majesty and greatness.[2]

The historic Tablets of the Divine Plan were written during World War I. However, due to the disruptions caused by the war years, many of the tablets did not arrive in North America until the cessation of hostilities. Even after their arrival, the full-scale implementation of this mandate had to be held in abeyance for almost twenty years, until the machinery of the Administrative Order had been devised and forged under the guidance of the Guardian, Shoghi Effendi, and until the elected Local and National Spiritual Assemblies more clearly understood their purpose and functions and had acquired the necessary experience to discharge their responsibilities in an efficient manner. Shoghi Effendi's secretary, writing on his behalf, underlines the vital role of the Spiritual Assemblies in furthering the development of the religion at this transitional stage:

Now that they have erected the administrative machinery of the Cause they must put it to its real use—serving only as an instrument to facilitate the flow of the spirit of the Faith out in the world. Just as the muscles enable the body to carry out the will of the individual, all Assemblies and Committees must enable the believers to carry forth the Message of God to the waiting public, the love of Bahá'u'lláh, and the healing laws and principles of the Faith to all men.[3]

The Spiritual Assemblies were now called upon to become the instruments that gave leadership and direction to the systematic implementation of 'Abdu'l-Bahá's Divine Plan.

The execution of the Divine Plan ushered in a new stage in the unfoldment of the Formative Age of the Faith. This stage is marked by the mobilization of the Bahá'í community by the Spiritual Assemblies in a series of collective enterprises of ever-widening scope, aimed at introducing the teachings of the religion to specific geographic areas, in a systematic and planned manner. The outcome of this initiative was not only an increase in the membership of the community, but it also served to strengthen and expand the foundations of its administrative structure in the newly opened geographic areas.

In this chapter we examine the nature of the mandate contained in 'Abdu'l-Bahá's Divine Plan and the response of the North American Bahá'í community. We describe the contents of the tablets that form the charter of the Divine Plan and discuss the stages of its unfoldment through a series of plans devised, initially, by the National Spiritual Assembly of the United States and Canada, and subsequently also by the National Spiritual Assembly of Canada, following its formation in 1948. These plans derive their inspiration from 'Abdu'l-Bahá's master plan for the global expansion of the Faith. They also give direction to the progressive development of the Bahá'í Administrative Order through the establishment of new Local and National Spiritual Assemblies throughout the five continents of the globe. The achievement of the plans called for sustained effort and a high degree of sacrifice on the part of the members of the Bahá'í community—an effort that was in many instances made more challenging by the force of historical circumstances, including war, economic and social up-heavals, and changes on the world political scene. Finally, we reflect on the challenges faced by the Spiritual Assemblies and the members of the community in their determination to achieve the goals of these plans, and draw parallels between the processes of expansion in the time of the dawn-breakers of the Heroic Age of the Faith and the strategies employed by the North American Bahá'ís, the community singled out by 'Abdu'l-Bahá to be "the principal custodian and chief executor"4 of the systematic plan for the spread of the Bahá'í Faith to all parts of the globe.

THE TABLETS OF THE DIVINE PLAN— THE MANDATE

The inspiration for 'Abdu'l-Bahá's Plan can be traced beyond his visit to the West to the seminal statements of Bahá'u'lláh in His book of laws, the Kitáb-i-Aqdas. Shoghi Effendi attests that "The Divine Plan . . . may be said to have derived its inspiration from, and been dimly foreshadowed in, the injunction so significantly addressed by Bahá'u'lláh to the Chief Magistrates of the American continent." The fourteen tablets addressed to the Bahá'ís of the United States and Canada during World War I set out his transformative vision for the spiritual conquest of the globe, and unfolded to the eyes of his dearly loved North American Bahá'ís "His conception of their spiritual destiny, His Plan for the mission He wished them to undertake."5

The first eight tablets were revealed between 26 March and 22 April 1916. They include 'Abdu'l-Bahá's messages to each of five separate regions of the United States and Canada—Canada and Greenland, and the Northeastern, the Southern, the Central, and the Western States of the United States—and three general letters addressed collectively to the believers in North America, which embodied his mandate to diffuse "the fame of the Cause of God . . . throughout the East and the West" and to proclaim "the advent of the Kingdom of the Lord of Hosts . . . in all the five continents of the globe." The first of the general tablets named the republics, territories, and islands of the Western Hemisphere, and called upon the Bahá'ís to arise to open these regions to the Faith of Bahá'u'lláh. The second was a call to propagate the religion "through the continents of Europe, of Asia, of Africa, and of Australasia, and as far as the islands of the Pacific." And, in the third, 'Abdu'l-Bahá addressed the believers as "Apostles of Bahá'u'lláh" and he specified the conditions on which the attainment of this special station depends.[6]

Six additional tablets were revealed between 2 February and 8 March 1917, in five of which 'Abdu'l-Bahá elaborated and reinforced his guidance to the five regions of the United States and Canada. His final general tablet described the nature of collective centers and the power of unity, and contained a renewed appeal to the believers to travel throughout the Western Hemisphere.[7]

In all, 120 territories and islands are mentioned by name in these tablets. Particular importance is attached to teaching the Eskimos and other indigenous Americans, and to establishing the religion in Alaska; Greenland; Mexico; Panama; and in Bahia (Salvador), Brazil. The tablets also include a number of prayers, specific guidance to teachers, and practical advice concerning the organization of teaching activities.

As mentioned above, the delivery of these historic documents was interrupted and delayed by the war. It is reported that five of the tablets revealed in 1916

. . . had actually reached America and been published in the September 8, 1916, issue of *Star of the West*. After that all communication with the Holy Land was severed, . . . the remainder of the Tablets were kept in a vault in the Shrine of the Báb on

Mt. Carmel for the duration of the war. They were dispatched to America at the end of the war where they were unveiled in befitting ceremonies during the "Convention of the Covenant" held at Hotel McAlpin in New York City on April 26–30, 1919.[8]

INITIAL RESPONSE

At first "a handful of men and women . . . arose to carry out the mandate which 'Abdu'l-Bahá had issued." "Forsaking home, kindred, friends and position" these "enterprising ambassadors of the Message of Bahá'u'lláh" were instrumental in spreading the Bahá'í Faith to the far corners of the earth. The first to arise in response to the call contained in the Tablets of the Divine Plan was Miss Martha Root, the intrepid star-servant of the Cause of Bahá'u'lláh. In 1919 she embarked on the first of four historic world-encircling journeys in the initial phase of which she visited many of the important cities in South America. Two years later Leonora Holsapple Armstrong settled in the Brazilian town of Bahia (Salvador).[9]

In 1920, a new continent was opened to the Faith when John and Clara Hyde-Dunn, then in their late middle-age, left the United States and settled as Bahá'í pioneers in Australia. Despite limited means they succeeded not only in carrying "the Message to no less than seven hundred towns throughout that Commonwealth," but they also made a significant contribution to the establishment of the Bahá'í community in New Zealand. In that same year, Miss Fanny Knobloch arrived in Cape Town and became the first Bahá'í teacher to visit South Africa. She spent the next two years traveling to many parts of the country to teach the Faith and to nurture the embryonic Bahá'í communities.[10]

John and Louise Bosch, a Swiss couple living in California, were attracted by 'Abdu'l-Bahá's call to take the Faith to the islands of Polynesia in the Pacific Ocean. Eager to assist in this enterprise, and being fluent in the French language, they chose as their post, Tahiti in the Society Islands. In 1920 they taught for five months in the capital, Papeete, and also visited the island of Moorea. Though confronted by many challenges, including lack of adequate accommodation, illness, the rigors of the tropical climate, and communication difficulties, they were enchanted by the local Tahitians and the exquisite beauty of the islands, and they were able to introduce the Faith to several people including a young woman and an elderly Tahitian minister, who later thanked 'Abdu'l-Bahá for sending these emissaries to his people. On one memorable occasion this cultured, highly refined, middle-aged, and most venturesome couple set out in a small motorboat for Moorea Island to visit a leading personage named Madame Tepori. When they were five kilometers out in the open ocean, the engine of the boat died! After reaching the home of Madame Tepori, they spoke with her in French and told her about 'Abdu'l-Bahá. She was so happy she continually praised God! John Bosch described the colorful scene when they came to leave Moorea: "When we returned to Papeete, the first passenger on the little boat was an immense pig—the second was the minister—then some Chinese—then we followed." He described how Madame Tepori "stood at the pier, tears streaming, with out-stretched arms—in white against the dark, wooded mountains, two doves flying over her head."[11]

As the day of their departure from Tahiti approached, the islanders showered John and Louise Bosch with gifts, and bestowed new names on them, it being a Tahitian custom to bestow names and titles upon departing friends. The extent of the islanders' esteem and gratitude is evident from the title Mr. Bosch received. It had the meaning: "First king of the great family of Bahá'ís arrived among us."[12]

In 1921 when visiting Haifa, Louise and John Bosch were able to display an image of the people of Tahiti in 'Abdu'l-Bahá's presence on almost the last day of his life. Louise recounts what happened:

I laid the photograph of an old full-blooded Tahitian lady of several generations back at 'Abdu'l-Bahá's place at the table. He took it up and looked at it, asking whose it was. I told Him it was the picture of the wife of a native chief whose present-day descendants had listened to the Message we had taken to them. His reply was: "She was a good tree, she has borne good fruit!"[13]

The brief examples mentioned above serve to illustrate the exploits of the small band of individuals whose response to the Tablets of the Divine Plan was immediate. Shoghi Effendi attests to the importance of the heroic and exemplary services of these early believers who, "fired with a zeal and confidence which no human agency can kindle, arose to carry out the mandate which 'Abdu'l-Bahá had issued." The accomplishments of "these intrepid heralds of the Faith of Bahá'u'lláh," he states are "unique and eternal," and he provides the following tribute:

> In the face of almost insurmountable obstacles they have succeeded in most of the countries through which they have passed or in which they have resided, in proclaiming the teachings of their Faith, in circulating its literature, in defending its cause, in laying the basis of its institutions and in reinforcing the number of its declared supporters. It would be impossible for me to unfold in this short compass the tale of such heroic actions. Nor can any tribute of mine do justice to the spirit which has enabled these standard-bearers of the Religion of God to win such laurels and to confer such distinction on the generation to which they belong.[14]

INITIATION OF COLLECTIVE ACTION

The Divine Plan of 'Abdu'l-Bahá "underwent a period of incubation, after His ascension, while the machinery of a divinely appointed

Administrative Order was being laboriously devised and its processes set in motion." Once the administrative institutions were functioning with some degree of efficiency and unity, Shoghi Effendi directed the North American Bahá'ís assembled at the 1936 National Bahá'í Convention to devise and inaugurate a systematic campaign to begin to implement systematically the provisions of 'Abdu'l-Bahá's Divine Plan. Calling attention to the deepening gloom of the world situation and the healing potential of the message of Bahá'u'lláh to alleviate the ills of a declining age, the Bahá'ís were encouraged to open to the Faith every state within North America and every republic in the American continent and to establish the structural basis of its administrative structure before the end of the first Bahá'í century in 1944.[15] Commenting on the significance and scope of such an enterprise, and its potential impact, Shoghi Effendi writes:

> The promulgation of the Divine Plan . . . is the Key which Providence has placed in the hands of the American believers whereby to unlock the doors leading them to fulfill their unimaginably glorious Destiny. As the proclamation of the Message reverberates throughout the land, as its resistless march gathers momentum, as the field of its operation widens and the numbers of its upholders and champions multiply, its potentialities will correspondingly unfold, exerting a beneficial influence, not only on every community throughout the Bahá'í world, but on the immediate fortunes of a travailing society.[16]

The full implementation of the Divine Plan of 'Abdu'l-Bahá was formally launched in 1937 when Shoghi Effendi conferred on the North American Bahá'í community the mission of the First Seven Year Plan (1937–44), the first of a series of plans designed to carry out its provisions to increasingly fuller degrees. The charter and motivating force of the First Seven Year Plan and of all subsequent future plans are 'Abdu'l-Bahá's Tablets of the Divine Plan, since these "epoch-making Tablets" call for the American Bahá'ís to carry the banner of the Faith "to the utmost ends of the earth" and to "lay an unassailable basis for the administrative structure of the Faith of Bahá'u'lláh."[17]

FIRST SEVEN YEAR PLAN—1937–44

The major objectives of the First Seven Year Plan were to establish the foundations of the Faith in the states and provinces of North America and in all the republics of Central and South America, and to complete the exterior ornamentation of the Bahá'í House of Worship in Wilmette.

In response to the enlargement of their teaching responsibility, the National Spiritual Assembly of the United States and Canada appointed an Inter-America Committee in 1936 to initiate and supervise activities in Central and South America and the islands of the Caribbean area, and to ensure the most efficient use of human resources. This committee provided orientation and continuing moral support to those who arose as pioneers, and coordinated the flow of travel teachers. It provided practical guidance about resettlement in Latin America, assisted with travel arrangements, and initiated the work of translating Bahá'í literature into Spanish. In addition, to achieve the goals of the Plan within North America, the National Assembly appointed Regional Teaching Committees to intensify the systematic expansion of the Bahá'í Faith. And, in 1937, to ensure the completion of the external ornamentation of the Bahá'í House of Worship within the seven year period, the National Spiritual Assembly adopted a schedule of successive contracts that would allow the construction to be completed on time.[18]

The far-reaching tasks to which this small and scattered North American Bahá'í community was called, were undertaken against the backdrop of a period of economic uncertainty and financial stringency confronting the nation and the inexorable approach of the war in Europe that was later to engulf North America. The Plan called for a large number of dedicated Bahá'ís to enter the pioneering field by moving to a new country or city for the purpose of introducing the Bahá'í Faith to the people of that area.

The Latin American cultural environment was unfamiliar to the Americans who ventured south. The Latin nations differed widely from each other, socially and politically. There were extremes of wealth and poverty, of culture and ignorance. At the same time, traditionally, the Latin Americans harbored a suspicion of friendly overtures coming from their North American neighbors, due in large part to a history of commercial exploitation and the condescending attitudes of many businessmen and tourists. Reflecting on the cultural challenges involved, Garreta Busey observed: "That this Faith should be destined to come to them from the United States and Canada was a severe test of the purity of their vision and their ability to overcome prejudice. . . . It is a glowing proof of the potency and universality of Bahá'u'lláh's Faith that, having chosen as the bearers to the South and Central American countries servants from a nation most suspect, it should have been so readily, so heartily received by a few people in every nation."[19]

In relation to the call for pioneers, it should be noted that the Bahá'í Faith is a lay religion. It has no clergy and no professional missionaries trained to teach the religion and to minister to its community. The role of the intrepid Bahá'í pioneers was unique. Leaving the comfort of their homes, the fellowship of family and friends, and the familiarity of their culture, and armed with deep faith and a desire to share the Bahá'í message, they ventured into the unknown. They grappled with such practical problems as obtaining entry permits, finding employment and a place to live, endeavoring to understand a new culture, and struggling to make friends and to learn a new language. Many experienced loneliness, discouragement, illness, and anxiety. Yet, while dealing with the struggles of everyday life, the pioneers ceaselessly endeavored to find creative ways to introduce the teachings of Bahá'u'lláh to the local, and often skeptical, population. Out of a sense of devotion to the Divine, the pioneer willingly assumed responsibility for sharing his or her Faith with others, presenting it as one would offer a gift to a king.

Conscious of the immense challenges involved in achieving the goals of the First Seven Year Plan, Shoghi Effendi, addressing the American believers, "the spiritual descendants of the heroes of God's Cause," assured them that if carried out in its entirety, "this dual enterprise would shed on the closing years of this first century of the Bahá'í Era a luster no less brilliant that the immortal deeds which have signalized its birth in the Heroic Age of our Faith."[20]

The implementation of the Seven Year Plan not only called for heroic sacrifice on the part of individuals but also demanded increased levels of administrative maturity and collaboration on the part of Local Spiritual Assemblies and the National Assembly and their committees. Local Spiritual Assemblies had to learn how to function as instruments of teaching in their area of jurisdiction, and to engage in extensive teaching activities. The phased construction work on the House of Worship was a continuing drain on the financial resources of the small community and, in the first two years of the Plan, tended to divert attention from the vital task of teaching. Early in 1939, Shoghi Effendi expressed concern about the slow progress in the expansion of the Faith in North America, which he viewed as a precondition to the inauguration of the planned systematic teaching campaign in

Central and South America. To remedy the situation he called for "nine holy souls" to arise and each one to settle in one of the nine states and provinces that had no resident Bahá'ís. To facilitate this project, Shoghi Effendi contributed the sum of 900 pounds sterling.[21]

While the story of the nine individuals who responded to the Guardian's call remains to be told, one example will serve to illustrate the caliber of their actions. Miss Honor Kempton, a refined woman of English background, in her late forties, volunteered immediately to go to Alaska, which was at the time a wild frontier place. When she communicated her offer to Shoghi Effendi, he expressed his great pleasure at the news and addressed to her the following words of encouragement, in a letter written in March 1939:

How proud I feel of the spirit that so powerfully animated you. My prayers will, I assure you, accompany you on your great and historic adventure. Persevere no matter how great the obstacles in your way. Future generations will glorify your deeds and emulate your example.[22]

She reached Juneau, Alaska on 18 April 1939 and two months later moved to Anchorage where she established the town's first bookstore, which was later described by a former governor of the state as "the cultural center of Alaska." After several months her teaching efforts were rewarded when an Alaskan woman accepted the Faith. Before long additional pioneers arrived, new believers joined the community, and in 1943, the first Local Spiritual Assembly was formed. During World War II, Miss Kempton became an American citizen and continued to find new ways to introduce people to the religion. It is reported that in exchange for book reviews she prepared for a radio station, she was given an opportunity to present a weekly radio broadcast on the Faith. In 1944, she attended the National Bahá'í Convention as

Alaska's first delegate. Miss Kempton remained in Alaska until 1946 when, with the approval of Shoghi Effendi, she pioneered to serve the Bahá'í Faith in Luxemburg, where she remained until the end of her life. At the time of her passing she was designated by the Universal House of Justice as the "mother" of both the Alaskan and Luxemburg Bahá'í communities.[23]

By the time of the Bahá'í National Convention in April 1939, every state and province in North America had been opened to the Faith, and a Local Spiritual Assembly had been established in Mexico, setting the stage for the next step in its "progressive systematic penetration" into Latin America. The methodical strategy suggested by Shoghi Effendi called for an initial and immediate focus on the "unexplored territories" of Central America. He challenged "all believers, white and Negro alike" to arise, and he assured them that "inestimable prizes" might well be won by "audacious adventurers in the path of Bahá'í service." Furthermore, in light of 'Abdu'l-Bahá's emphasis on the spiritual and geographic significance of the Republic of Panama in the Tablets of the Divine Plan, the Guardian instructed the National Spiritual Assembly and its Inter-America Teaching Committee to encourage "all would-be pioneers" to give preference to "this privileged Republic," while at the same time, exerting every effort to introduce the Faith, "however tentatively," to the other Central American countries.[24]

Without delay, the National Spiritual Assembly and the Inter-America Teaching Committee formulated and set in motion a plan to introduce the Bahá'í Faith into a number of Central American countries, including Panama. When informed of this initiative Shoghi Effendi underlined its historic significance by announcing the official inauguration of the world mission conferred on the North American Bahá'ís by 'Abdu'l-Bahá and he outlined some of the immediate implications and challenges associated with this new phase for the work of the community. His cable reads:

> NEWLY LAUNCHED CENTRAL AMERICAN CAMPAIGN MARKS OFFI-
> CIAL INAUGURATION LONG-DEFERRED WORLD MISSION CONSTI-
> TUTING 'ABDU'L-BAHÁ'S DISTINCTIVE LEGACY BAHÁ'Í COMMU-
> NITY NORTH AMERICA. CHOSEN COMMUNITY BROADENING ITS
> BASIS GAINING STATURE DEEPENING CONSECRATION. ITS VAN-
> GUARD NOW ENTERING ARENA MONOPOLIZED ENTRENCHED
> FORCES CHRISTENDOM'S MIGHTIEST ECCLESIASTICAL INSTITU-
> TIONS. LABORING AMIDST RACE FOREIGN IN LANGUAGE CUSTOM
> TEMPERAMENT EMBRACING VAST PROPORTION NEW WORLD'S
> ETHNIC ELEMENTS. AMERICAN BELIEVERS ISOLATED OVERSEAS
> TEACHING ENTERPRISES HITHERTO TENTATIVE INTERMITTENT
> NOW AT END. NEW EPOCH OPENING DEMANDING EXERTIONS
> INCOMPARABLE MORE STRENUOUS UNFLINCHINGLY SUSTAINED
> CENTRALLY DIRECTED SYSTEMATICALLY ORGANIZED EFFI-
> CIENTLY CONDUCTED. UPON ALACRITY TENACITY FEARLESSNESS
> PRESENT PROSECUTORS UNFOLDING MISSION DEPENDS SPEEDY
> FULLEST REVELATION IN FIRST SECOND CENTURIES POTENTI-
> ALITIES BIRTHRIGHT DIVINELY CONFERRED NORTH AMERICAN
> BELIEVERS.[25]

The Bahá'ís responded instantly to the new opportunities for service. At the end of the National Convention, Mr. Matthew Kaszab, without waiting for direction, immediately set out for Panama. During his short stay in Panama, before moving on to his assigned pioneering post in Nicaragua, he initiated teaching activity, succeeding in teaching the Faith to a receptive soul who became the first Bahá'í in Panama. He also gave a number of radio broadcasts and had articles published on the Bahá'í Faith. In October 1939, the first resident teacher, Mrs. Louise Caswell arrived, followed shortly after by Mrs. Cora Oliver. At the time of their arrival there was but one local Panamanian Bahá'í and the Faith was virtually unknown. By taking courses at the university the two women not only learned the Spanish language but also met many people who were interested in new ideas. To expand their field of contacts they attended public functions, made personal calls, befriended students at the University, and associated with people from all walks of life. They slowly became known as Bahá'ís and when the occasion presented itself they spoke about the Faith and distributed literature. They soon listed among their acquaintances professional and business people, humanitarians, and students who were invited to regular classes in their home as they tried continually to extend their efforts. They participated in the Women's College Clubs in Panama City and the Canal Zone, and lamented the lack of male Bahá'í pioneers who could more easily present the Faith to men. Mrs. Caswell began to divide her time between the capital and the Canal Zone, where she also established classes on the Faith. Their tireless efforts were reinforced by traveling teachers from the United States and Canada, and several other pioneers arrived during the course of the Seven Year Plan. Nevertheless, the work in Panama proceeded slowly and it was not until 1945 that the first Local Spiritual Assembly was formed.[26] When news of this historic accomplishment was conveyed to Shoghi Effendi, his secretary, responding on his behalf, wrote the following acknowledgement to Mrs. Caswell:

> The formation of this very important Assembly was a source of deep joy for him, and he feels that your persevering efforts, and those of Mrs. Oliver and all the other dear friends, have at last borne fruits in a worthy form; he hopes that the believers there will go forward, with the greatest love and unity, to the ac-

complishment of the many tasks that lie ahead, such as increasing the community's members, holding regular public meetings, teaching the Indians, etc.

He very greatly appreciates your own constant labors in this small but significant Republic . . .[27]

While the work was proceeding in Panama and in other countries in Latin America, the National Spiritual Assembly and the Inter-America Committee set in motion systematic plans to raise a band of pioneers and travel teachers to take the Faith to the remaining republics in Central and South America. Mrs. Frances Benedict Stewart was entrusted with the task of opening the doors of South America. A native Spanish speaker originally from Chile, Mrs. Stewart sailed from New York landing in Buenos Aires twenty days later. She found a ready receptivity to the Bahá'í teachings among the leading families of Argentina and soon attracted a group of intellectuals, scientists, and professors to her study classes. Urged by the National Spiritual Assembly to extend her activities to Uruguay, Mrs. Stewart arrived in Montevideo armed with letters of introduction from her new friends in Buenos Aires. Before long, she was able to establish a study class consisting of nine serious students of the Faith. Her next stop was Chile, where with her letters of introduction, she received a warm welcome. After spending time in Valparaiso, where she delivered a series of lectures on the Faith and established a study class, she proceeded to Santiago, arriving just before the major earthquake that devastated a neighboring city. It was Mrs. Stewart who was asked to speak on short wave radio, that reached as far as the United States and Europe, to raise the alarm and call for aid![28]

The work of the Seven Year Plan was greatly complicated by the deterioration of the world situation, which culminated in the outbreak of war in Europe in August 1939. Nevertheless, Shoghi Effendi appealed to the pioneers to refuse to abandon their posts and implored them not to surrender the responsibilities they assumed in pursuance of the mandate conferred on the North American Bahá'í community by 'Abdu'l-Bahá. By the end of the third year of the Plan, the teaching campaign embraced the whole of Central America and all but two countries in South America.[29]

As the continent of Europe, much of Africa, parts of Asia, and even the site of the World Center of the Faith itself were swept up in the turmoil of the war, the freedom of the embryonic Bahá'í communities to operate in those regions was severely restricted. In his communications with the North American Bahá'ís at that time Shoghi Effendi provided them with a framework within which to understand contemporary political events. He characterized the war and the resulting immense sufferings as a purifying process in the struggle of the world to attain to its stage of spiritual and social maturity, and he contrasted the declining fortunes of the old world with the slow but steady consolidation of the small but vibrant Bahá'í community. In addition, Shoghi Effendi sought to expand the American believers' understanding of the enterprise in which they were engaged—the Seven Year Plan not only aimed to expand the Bahá'í community and reinforce its administrative structure, but more fundamentally, the spread of the influence of the Faith and its teachings addressed the needs of a suffering humanity. It was in this spirit that Shoghi Effendi turned to the "new world champions" of the "New World Order [of] Bahá'u'lláh" to "stand fast," to "close ranks," and to pursue the "INCOMPARABLY SUBLIME TASK WHOSE OPERATION MUST HASTEN, WHOSE CONSUMMATION WILL SYNCHRONIZE, BOTH TRIUMPHANT ASCENDANCY BELOVED CAUSE SPIRITUAL REDEMPTION RECONSTRUCTED MANKIND."[30]

Once a foothold had been established in all the Latin American republics, Shoghi Effendi called upon the American National Spiritual

Assembly to carefully consolidate and train the new communities so they could, in the immediate future, function as independent entities. To achieve this end, he placed particular emphasis on the urgent need for administrative development. Hence he instructed the National Assembly:

> To nurse these tender plants of the Vineyard of God, to foster their growth, to direct their development, to accord them the necessary recognition, to help resolve their problems, to familiarize them, with gentleness, patience and fidelity, with the processes of the Administrative Order and thus enable them to assume independently the conduct of future local and national Bahá'í activities . . .[31]

Once this call was raised, a band of knowledgeable Bahá'ís experienced in the Bahá'í Administrative Order arose to carry out this vital educational process and within a relatively short period of time, the new fledgling communities began to assume responsibility for the advancement and consolidation of the Faith in their areas. They gradually matured in their administrative functioning and widened the scope of their activities to focus on such things as the translation of Bahá'í literature into Spanish and Portuguese, and the education of children and youth.

In December 1941, the United States entered the war. The challenges confronting the American Bahá'ís and their institutions multiplied tremendously. The economic situation and the shortages of materials resulting from the conduct of the war particularly impacted the work on the exterior ornamentation of the House of Worship. The manpower of the community was stretched to its limits. There were restrictions on both domestic and foreign travel, and even when travel was permitted it was frequently difficult to secure transportation. Given the severity of the situation and, with the approach of the final year of the Plan, which was scheduled to coincide with the centenary of the Declaration of the Báb, Shoghi Effendi reminded the American believers of the example of the dawn-breakers of the Heroic Age who willingly sacrificed their lives for the Faith. Aware as he was of the difficulties they faced, he challenged them with the following rhetorical question: "CAN SACRIFICE HOME POSSESSIONS COMFORT SECURITY BY . . . CHAMPION BUILDERS FORMATIVE AGE BE DEEMED TOO GREAT FOR SAKE PLAN . . . ?" To support their efforts and to ease the burden, Shoghi Effendi also provided the funds to deputize five members of the community who were willing to pioneer to priority locations.[32]

While the progress of the Plan had been steady, the remaining tasks to be accomplished during the last two years of the First Seven Year Plan, that "gigantic enterprise which the American believers are pledged to consummate," were breathtaking in scope, and their completion called for "an intensification of Bahá'í activity throughout the entire Western Hemisphere,"[33] at a time when the world was preoccupied with the forces of war. Writing to the American Bahá'ís in August 1942, Shoghi Effendi set before them their outstanding tasks and the qualities they must needs manifest in arising to carry them out:

An unprecedented multiplication in the number of pioneer teachers and settlers; an unexampled flow of material resources for their maintenance and the extension of their labors; a still wider dissemination of Bahá'í literature, to aid and support them in their presentation of the Faith to Latin American peoples; an immediate increase in the number of groups and Assemblies in the states and provinces of North America; an increased aware-ness on the part of all believers, whether in the North or in the South, whether newly enrolled or of old standing in the

Faith, that every one of them shares, vitally and directly and without any exception, in the responsibility for the successful prosecution of the Plan; a still firmer resolution not to allow a world-convulsing conflict, with its attendant miseries, perils, dislocations, and anxieties, to deflect them from their course or distract their attention; these are the crying needs of this critical, this challenging, this swiftly passing hour. To exploit its possibilities, to meet its challenge, to grasp its implications, is the manifest, the inescapable and urgent duty of every member of the Bahá'í communities now laboring so assiduously in the Western Hemisphere.[34]

The immediate audacious and sacrificial response of the American Bahá'ís to filling the unfinished tasks of the Plan earned the praise and gratitude of Shoghi Effendi. As 1943, the final year of the First Seven Year Plan dawned, he expressed his delight at the completion of the external ornamentation of the Bahá'í House of Worship, and he directed the attention of the National Spiritual Assembly to the work of planning a befitting event and a nationwide publicity campaign to mark the centenary of the birth of the Bahá'í Faith. To this end, he called upon the National Assembly to convene in May 1944, an All-American Convention comprising representatives from every republic in Central and South America as well as from all states and provinces in North America. This gathering was to celebrate not only the hundredth anniversary of the declaration of the Báb and the birth of the Bahá'í Faith, but also to mark the fiftieth anniversary of the establishment of the Faith in the western world and the completion of the exterior ornamentation of the first Bahá'í House of Worship in the western world.[35]

The exploits of the American believers served as an inspiration to their coreligionists in the East. Shoghi Effendi reported that, emulating the example of the Americans, ninety-five Persian Bahá'í families left Iran to pioneer to surrounding countries. Similarly in Egypt, Iraq, and India the Bahá'ís were able to make considerable advances. He stressed the need for the believers everywhere to ensure that the victories won, with such great effort, be carefully safeguarded.[36]

As the final months of the Plan slipped by, Shoghi Effendi called upon the stalwart American believers to make one final push to accomplish the remaining goals. He issued the following words of encouragement:

Whoever will arise, in these concluding, fast-fleeting months of the last year of the first Bahá'í Century, to fill the remaining posts, and thereby set the seal of total victory on a Plan so pregnant with promise, will earn the lasting gratitude of the present generation of believers in both the East and the West, will merit the acclaim of posterity, will be vouchsafed the special benediction of the Concourse on High, and be made the recipient of the imperishable bounties of Him Who is the Divine Author of the Plan itself. Whoever will rush forth, at this eleventh hour, and cast his weight into the scales, and contribute his decisive share to so gigantic, so sacred and historic an undertaking, will have not only helped to seal the triumph of the Plan itself but will also have notably participated in the fulfillment of what may be regarded as the crowning act of an entire century. The opportunity that presents itself at this crucial hour is precious beyond expression. The blessings destined to flow from a victory so near at hand are rich beyond example. One final surge of that indomitable spirit that has carried the American Bahá'í community to such heights is all that is required, as the first Bahá'í Century speeds to a close, to release the flow of those blessings that must signalize the termination of the first, and usher in the dawn of the second, Bahá'í Century.[37]

The intensity of the response to the Guardian's appeal was immediate, energetic, and widespread. Believers contributed to a newly established deputization fund enabling new pioneers to depart for the field. The tenor of the final flurry of activity that led to the culmination of the Plan is captured by the following fragmentary report:

> Flora Hottes, who had been awaiting transportation, flew down to Bolivia to take up the work begun by Eleanor Smith (Adler). . . . Mr. and Mrs. C.E. Hamilton went to reside in Cristobal and so gave help to those steadfast pioneers in Panama, Louise Caswell and Cora Oliver, who were further reinforced a little later by Julia Regal. Mr. Malcolm King of Milwaukee prepared to return to Jamaica, his native land, to teach the Faith. Clarence Iverson in San Salvador, was joined by his mother. Gertrude Eisenberg went to Brazil and Virginia Orbison to Chile. . . . Ruth Shook, bound for Colombia, rather than wait for air transportation, went by rail to Mexico City and then by way of Guatemala and San Salvador. John Eichenauer, now in Guatemala, had with him his brother Marshall. And Philip Sprague planned another teaching trip which took him through Panama, Colombia, Ecuador, Peru, and Chile. That winter also, Winifred Baker sailed for Colombia, Gwen Sholtis went to Venezuela, and Mrs. Barton visited Wilfred in Montevideo. Later Etta Mae Lawrence went down to Buenos Aires to work with the youth group there.

The stories of these pioneers and of those who preceded them are tissues woven of the darkness of discouragement and the shining threads of victory. The recounting of the many small miracles by which human hearts were changed and the light of Bahá'u'lláh was spread must be left to the men and women who helped to bring them about. They will constitute a glorious chapter in the history of mankind.[38]

The last remaining teaching goal of the First Seven Year Plan, namely the establishment of a Local Spiritual Assembly in every state and province of North America, was finally achieved on 28 March 1944, when three Spiritual Assemblies were elected in Canada, thereby completing the structural basis of the Administrative Order in the continent of America.[39]

At the beginning of the Plan in 1937, there were 72 Local Spiritual Assemblies in 26 states and provinces in North America. In 1944, at the end of the Plan, there were 136 Local Assemblies, 126 in the United States and 10 in Canada, and Bahá'ís had established their residence in some 78 countries around the world.[40]

Reviewing the major accomplishments of the First Seven Year Plan, Shoghi Effendi rejoiced in the actions of the "champion-builders" of Bahá'u'lláh's World Order, the American Bahá'í community, in laying the structural basis of the Bahá'í Administrative Order throughout North America, and in introducing the Bahá'í Faith in each of the republics of Central and South America. Indeed, their exploits surpassed the goals of the Plan! They also succeeded in establishing Spiritual Assemblies in "thirteen republics of Latin America, as well as in two dependencies in the West Indies." These far-reaching achievements were made possible by the sacrificial participation of several hundred rank and file Bahá'ís, including many women, who arose to pioneer and to serve as travel teachers in North and South America. Their names and fields of service, abroad and on the home front, have been recorded in *The Bahá'í World*, volume IX. Finally, to such stellar victories in the arena of teaching and administration was added the completion of the external ornamentation of the Bahá'í House of Worship in Wilmette.[41]

While statistically the record is compelling, the significance of the First Seven Year Plan far exceeds any quantitative analysis. Shoghi Effendi characterizes the Plan as the "greatest collective enterprise ever launched by the Western followers of Bahá'u'lláh, and indeed ever undertaken by any Bahá'í community in the course of an entire century." He attests that it has "shed imperishable luster on the immortal records of His Faith during the first hundred years of its existence," and envisages that it will be acclaimed by posterity "as one of the most brilliant episodes in the history of the Formative Age of the Faith of Bahá'u'lláh, as well as one of the most momentous enterprises undertaken during the entire course of the first century of the Bahá'í Era."[42]

Shoghi Effendi pays eloquent testimony to the members of the American Bahá'í community, who exemplified "so remarkable a spirit of heroism and self-sacrifice,"[43] and he underlines the historic significance of the qualities they manifested in their exertions and the scope of their services by comparing them with the dramatic exploits of the dawn-breakers of the Heroic Age. He writes:

> To the band of pioneers, whether settlers or itinerant teachers, who have forsaken their homes, who have scattered far and wide, who have willingly sacrificed their comfort, their health and even their lives for the prosecution of this Plan; to the several committees and their auxiliary agencies that have been entrusted with special and direct responsibility for its efficient and orderly development and who have discharged their high responsibilities with exemplary vigor, courage and fidelity; to the national representatives of the community itself, who have vigilantly and tirelessly supervised, directed and coordinated the

unfolding processes of this vast undertaking ever since its inception; to all those who, though not in the forefront of battle, have, through their financial assistance and through the instrumentality of their deputies, contributed to the expansion and consolidation of the Plan, I myself, as well as the entire Bahá'í world, owe a debt of gratitude that no one can measure or describe. To the sacrifices they have made, to the courage they have so consistently shown, to the fidelity they have so remarkably displayed, to the resourcefulness, the discipline, the constancy and devotion they have so abundantly demonstrated future generations, viewing the magnitude of their labors in their proper perspective, will no doubt pay adequate tribute—a tribute no less ardent and well-deserved than the recognition extended by the present-day builders of the World Order of Bahá'u'lláh to the Dawn-Breakers, whose shining deeds have signalized the birth of the Heroic Age of His Faith.[44]

The stage was now set for the gathering of "the elected representatives of all the Bahá'í communities in the New World" to assemble beneath "the Dome of the Mother Temple of the West" to mark the centenary of the birth of the Bahá'í Faith, the hundredth anniversary of the birth of 'Abdu'l-Bahá, the fiftieth anniversary of the founding of the Bahá'í Faith in the Western Hemisphere, and the completion of the exterior ornamentation of the first Bahá'í House of Worship of the West.[45]

TWO YEAR RESPITE—1944–46

The consummation of the First Seven Year Plan prepared the way for the opening of a new phase in the implementation of the provisions of 'Abdu'l-Bahá's Tablets of the Divine Plan, a phase that was destined to carry the Bahá'í Faith beyond the Western Hemisphere to the continent of Europe. However, while the war continued in Europe and in parts of Asia and the Pacific, it was not possible to launch a systematic campaign of teaching in Europe. Shoghi Effendi, therefore, focused the attention of the Bahá'ís on the no less pressing need to make strenuous efforts to consolidate the victories that had been achieved in North and South America during the Seven Year Plan. They were called upon to intensify efforts to teach the Bahá'í Faith, to introduce its ideas to leaders of thought, to arrange for the widespread dissemination of its literature, and to strengthen the foundations of its Administrative Order by the formation of new Spiritual Assemblies in the Western hemisphere. Indeed, the strengthening of the home front in North America and of the communities in Central and South America were specified as a necessary prerequisite for embarking on the next stage of the implementation of the Divine Plan. Writing on this theme to the American Bahá'ís in 1945, Shoghi Effendi affirms:

Not until, however, normal conditions are fully restored and the world situation is stabilized, and, above all, the prizes won through the operation of the Seven Year Plan are adequately safeguarded and the basis of the newly established Administrative Order sufficiently consolidated throughout the Western Hemisphere, can the ambassadors of the Faith of Bahá'u'lláh, carrying aloft the banner of His Name in the American continent, be called upon to undertake unitedly and systematically, collective responsibility for the diffusion of His Message, and for the erection of the fabric of His Administrative Order, amidst the sorrow-stricken, war-lacerated, sorely bewildered nations and peoples of the European continent.

The sooner the home tasks are fully discharged and newly fledged Assemblies in Central and South America enabled to function adequately and vigorously, the sooner will the stalwart members of the American Bahá'í community, who, during so brief a period, and despite the prevailing darkness, achieved such wonders throughout the Americas, extend the healing influence of their Faith, on a scale as yet unprecedented, to the waiting masses of that agitated continent.[46]

The cessation of hostilities in Asia and the Pacific in August 1945, and the gradual return to normality in the war-torn areas of the world, opened the way for the launching of the Second Seven Year Plan at Riḍván 1946.

SECOND SEVEN YEAR PLAN (1946–53)

After a respite of two years a Second Seven Year Plan was given to the North American Bahá'ís by Shoghi Effendi. Commencing in April 1946, the conclusion of the new Plan was scheduled to coincide with the Centenary of the Birth of Bahá'u'lláh's Revelation in 1953. The Second Seven Year Plan represented the next stage in the unfoldment of 'Abdu'l-Bahá's Divine Plan. As expected, it drew its inspiration and direction from the historic tablets addressed to this privileged community by 'Abdu'l-Bahá.

In his visionary cable announcing the Plan, Shoghi Effendi summoned the North American Bahá'ís to arise collectively to achieve exploits that were destined to far outweigh what had been achieved during the First Seven Year Plan. Recognizing the proven capacity of the American Bahá'ís, a community designated as the "vanguard of the Dawn-breakers in the West," the "champion-builders of Bahá'u'lláh's Order," the "torchbearers of world civilization," and the "executors of 'Abdu'l-Bahá's mandate," the Guardian now called upon them to strive to accomplish the tasks set out in the new Plan. He outlined the four major objectives of the Second Seven Year Plan as follows: the consolidation and multiplication of Bahá'í centers throughout the Americas, and the bolder proclamation of the Faith to the masses; the completion of the interior ornamentation of the Bahá'í House of Worship in Wilmette; the formation of three National Spiritual Assemblies, one in Canada, one in Central America, and one in South America; and the implementation of a new teaching initiative in Western Europe involving the formation of at least one Spiritual Assembly in each of ten countries—Belgium, Netherlands, Norway, Denmark, Sweden, Luxemburg, Switzerland, Italy, Portugal, and Spain. And, in a later cable, a supplementary goal was added, namely to raise the number of Local Spiritual Assemblies in North America to 175 by 21 April 1948, through the establishment of thirty new Local Spiritual Assemblies.[47]

While simultaneous work on all the objectives of the Second Seven Year Plan was immediately initiated, Shoghi Effendi called for special urgent attention to be given to devising systematic efforts to introduce the Faith to Western Europe. He underlined the urgency of "extending the ramifications of the Divine Plan to a continent which . . . stands in dire need of the ennobling, the reinvigorating, and spiritualizing influence of a world-redeeming Faith." And, linking the significance of this important venture to the future exploits of the American community, Shoghi Effendi attested that it "must serve as a stepping-stone to the spiritual conquest of the vast and numerous territories, lying as yet beyond the scope of the Plan, in both the Asiatic and African continents, and which must, in the course of successive epochs, be warmed and illuminated by the rays of Bahá'u'lláh's Revelation as prescribed in the Tablets revealed by the Center of His Covenant and the Authorized Interpreter of His teachings." The unique importance and critical nature of the European project is further emphasized by

Shoghi Effendi. He affirms that it not only heralded the spiritual re-generation of the continent, but it also serves as the "pivot" on which the success of the Second Seven Year Plan was hinged.[48]

Given the importance accorded to the European mission, the activities undertaken in pursuit of this objective will be described in more detail below. However, in order to gain an appreciation of the scope and nature of the activities in which the Bahá'ís and their institutions engaged, it is necessary, in the first instance, to comment briefly on some of the actions they pursued in relation to the other three objectives of the Second Seven Year Plan.

Concerning the objective of the consolidation of the American home front and the more focused proclamation of the Faith to the leaders of thought and the masses, the National Spiritual Assembly and its teaching committees set in motion plans for a series of nationwide public meetings that were held in local Bahá'í communities. These meetings were supplemented by study classes for interested inquirers, while individual members of the community held fireside meetings in their homes and in local Bahá'í meeting places. In parallel to the public meetings and study groups, the National Assembly inaugurated a public relations program, which publicized the Faith through press and radio. In order to increase the human resources of the Bahá'í community a new approach to community education, combining spiritual devotion, discussion, and study, was developed. The method had for its aim the self-education of a Bahá'í community by mutual participation, since as one report indicated "the era of the proficient teacher able to travel from community to community appears to have closed." The rapid expansion of the administrative structure of the Faith called for in the first years of the Plan, resulted in 135 American Bahá'ís arising as pioneers to make their homes in new cities and towns where Local Spiritual Assemblies were needed. By the end of the Plan, there were 168 Local Spiritual Assemblies in the United States and 16 in Canada, and Bahá'ís had established their residence in over 1300 localities in North America.[49]

The objective of the Second Seven Year Plan calling for the completion of the Bahá'í House of Worship in Wilmette constituted a major challenge for the Bahá'í community for the duration of the Plan. Not only was there a great deal of work to be done to complete the building—contracts for the ornamentation, utilities and furnishings of the interior and for the landscaping of the grounds all had to be executed prior to the end of the Plan—there were also a number of other urgent calls on the limited financial resources, especially in relation to the dispatch of pioneers to Europe and to reinforce the work in Latin America. Nevertheless, the interior of the House of Worship was completed by the spring of 1951, and the landscaping was ready in time for the much anticipated public dedication held on 2 May, 1953.[50]

The third major objective of the Second Seven Year Plan called for the establishment of three National Spiritual Assemblies, one in Canada and one each in Central and South America. From the early days of the Bahá'í Faith in the West, the Bahá'ís of the United States and Canada shared a common history and their destinies were intertwined. They formed one administrative community and elected one National Spiritual Assembly, and both shared the experience gained in the work of prosecuting the first Seven Year Plan. Nevertheless, the time had now come for their separation. The National Spiritual Assembly of Canada was elected in Montreal in April 1948. The new institution immediately formulated for the Canadian Bahá'í community a Five Year Plan (1948–53). Included among its objectives were the legal incorporation of the National Assembly, the establishment of a national endowment, and the diversification of the community by the enrollment of Eskimos and Native Americans. The Plan also called for the number of Local Spiritual Assemblies in Canada to be raised to thirty. All these objectives were accomplished by the end of the Plan, and the teaching and administrative work of the Faith were organized and placed on a firm foundation.[51]

While the Canadian Bahá'í community had been relatively well established with a body of informed and administratively experienced members and the existence of a number of Local Spiritual Assemblies, the situation in Central and South America was much different. By 1946 some countries already had more than one Local Assembly; in others the fledgling institutions were very weak. In addition, there was a need to expand the size and to diversify the composition of the membership of the community, to develop an active sense of community among the Bahá'ís in each international area through a series of conferences and Bahá'í schools, to train the new members of the community in the processes of administrative functioning, and in due course to emancipate them from reliance on the services of pioneers. The Inter-America Committee appointed by the National Spiritual Assembly of North America, therefore, set in motion a number of initiatives to assure the formation of a National Spiritual Assembly in Central America and another in South America before 1953. A report written at the end of the Second Seven Year Plan summarizes the strategy adopted:

Since the delegates who would elect the members of these Assemblies would be representative of the local Bahá'í Assemblies in existence at the time, an energetic teaching plan was inaugurated by the National Spiritual Assembly of the United States to develop at least one Assembly in each country. The activities of the Teaching Committee appointed to carry out the plan included the appointment of regional teaching committees, and the holding of annual conferences and Bahá'í Schools, each designed to prepare the Latin American Bahá'ís for the responsibilities they would ultimately assume as independent Bahá'í communities.[52]

The fruition of the strenuous efforts made by the Bahá'ís in Latin America, in concert with their coreligionists in the North, resulted in the holding of two historic conventions for the election of the new regional National Spiritual Assemblies of Central America and of South America in April 1951. The National Spiritual Assembly of the Bahá'ís of South America was elected in Lima, Peru; and the election of the National Spiritual Assembly of Central America was held in Panama City, Panama. Representatives of the National Spiritual Assembly of the United States and its Inter-America Committee were on hand to congratulate the new Assemblies and to rejoice with them in the dawning of a new stage in the evolution of the Administrative Order in Latin America.[53]

THE EUROPEAN CAMPAIGN

The European mission is characterized by Shoghi Effendi as "by far the most momentous, the most arduous, the most challenging task to be carried out under the Second Seven Year Plan."[54] In setting out his vision of this new initiative, the Guardian not only highlighted the significance of this venture as "constituting a stepping-stone on the road leading to the redemption of the Old World," but he also called attention to some of the difficulties the Bahá'ís could expect to encounter in the course of implementing the Plan. Referring to challenges and opportunities inherent in "this transatlantic field of service," he writes:

Its challenge is overwhelming and its potentialities unfathomable. Its hazards, rigors and pitfalls are numerous, its field immense, the number of its promoters as yet utterly inadequate, the resources required for its effective prosecution barely tapped. The races, nations and classes included within its orbit are numerous and highly diversified, and the prizes to be won by its victors incalculably great. The hatreds that inflame, the rivalries that agitate, the controversies that confuse, the miseries that afflict, these races, nations, and classes are bitter and of long standing. The influence and fanaticism, whether ecclesiastical or political, of potentially hostile organizations, firmly entrenched within their ancestral strongholds, are formidable.

The members of the North American Bahá'í Community, to whose care the immediate destinies of this fate-laden crusade have been entrusted, are standing at a new crossroads.[55]

Stressing the urgency of this undertaking, in a cable addressed to the American National Spiritual Assembly immediately after the announcement of the new Plan, Shoghi Effendi urged the National Assembly to devote special attention to the requirements of the plan for the European continent at its June 1946 meeting, and he set out a number of specific steps to be taken to inaugurate the project.[56]

Before describing the actions undertaken by the American Bahá'ís in fulfillment of the objectives of the Second Seven Year Plan to establish the Bahá'í Faith in the heart of the European continent, it is useful to consider the extent of the spread of the Faith in Europe prior to the beginning of the Plan in 1946.

The systematic expansion of the Bahá'í Faith and its administrative institutions in Europe did not begin until the inception of the Second Seven Year Plan. Embryonic Bahá'í communities were established in England, France, and Germany during the lifetime of 'Abdu'l-Bahá, and intrepid Bahá'í traveling teachers had crisscrossed Western and Central Europe during the 1930s, leaving in their wake scattered groups of believers in a number of countries. Local Spiritual Assemblies were progressively established in England and Germany, and in 1923 a National Spiritual Assembly was formed in the British Isles and another in Germany and Austria. However, the progress of the development of the administrative institutions of the Faith was interrupted when the government of Nazi Germany banned the Bahá'í Faith and the operation of the Local and National Spiritual Assemblies in May, 1937. As a result of this order the archives of the Bahá'í administrative institutions in Germany were confiscated, Bahá'í books were seized, the publication of Bahá'í books was prohibited, and the Bahá'ís were forbidden to meet in large groups. Some members of the community were called in for interrogation, some were falsely accused of political involvement and put on trial, and others were sent to concentration camps. Despite the persecutions and the rigors of war, the German Bahá'ís endeavored to keep the light of their faith alive. With the cessation of hostilities, this most difficult period of testing came to an end. In August 1945, the American Army of Occupation issued a permit authorizing the German Bahá'í community to resume practice of their religion. Publication of Bahá'í literature was resumed despite severe paper supply restrictions; public gatherings were arranged, and by early April 1946 it was possible to hold a national convention in the American zone to elect a National Spiritual Assembly for the first time since 1937.[57]

The development of the Bahá'í Faith outside the ten goal countries assigned by Shoghi Effendi to the American Bahá'í community, was largely directed by the National Spiritual Assembly of the British Isles and the newly restored National Spiritual Assembly of Germany and Austria. The former adopted a Six Year Plan (1944–50) with the primary goal of establishing a total of nineteen Local Spiritual Assemblies in England, Wales, Scotland, Northern Ireland, and the

Republic of Eire, while the German National Assembly formulated a Five Year Plan in 1949 aimed at consolidating the community and strengthening its administrative structure.[58]

To ensure that the European campaign was speedily and befittingly inaugurated, Shoghi Effendi urged the prompt dispatch of nine competent pioneers to as many of the ten goal countries as possible for the purpose of initiating systematic teaching activities, to begin the process of settlement, and to promote the dissemination of Bahá'í literature. To give direction and concentrated attention to this new field of service, the Guardian also encouraged the American National Spiritual Assembly to establish a European Teaching Committee. A branch office of the Committee was set up in Geneva in order to foster the development of Spiritual Assemblies in the goal countries.

The driving force behind the European Teaching Committee was Miss Edna True, who served as its chairman for an extended period of time. At the time of her death in 1988, the Universal House of Justice characterized her as a "single-minded, energetic, [and] resourceful promoter [of the] European Bahá'í community whose rise after [the] Second World War is forever linked with her extensive activities for seventeen years [on] behalf [of the] European Teaching Committee." For some time, Miss True operated a prestigious travel bureau north of Chicago. She made available the facilities of her business to secure travel arrangements for many pioneers at a time when the means for travel were difficult to come by, due to the restrictions associated with war and the lack of facilities that resulted from the conflict. Following her election to the National Spiritual Assembly of the United States and Canada in 1946, Miss True was immediately appointed to the European Teaching Committee. The duties associated with her membership of the committee took her to Europe at least once a year where she assessed firsthand the needs and opportunities of the teaching work, oversaw the activities of the Geneva branch of the committee, and played a major role in the organization of a number of conferences and schools aimed at increasing a sense of Bahá'í identity among the newly declared European Bahá'ís, and preparing them to take responsibility for the development of the administrative structure of the Faith in Western Europe.[59]

At the outset, the European Teaching Committee determined that the settlement of Bahá'í pioneers in Western Europe would be accelerated if, as far as possible, the initial pioneers were natives of the country in which they were to serve. The following report lists the names of the twenty-five Bahá'í pioneers who entered the field of service during the first year of the Second Seven Year Plan. It illustrates both the cultural diversity of the American Bahá'í community at the time, and the eagerness of these pioneers to introduce the teachings of the Bahá'í Faith to the citizens of the countries in which they were born:

The first pioneer, Mrs. Solveig Corbit, departed on September 3, 1946, for her mission in Norway. In order to survey the Bahá'í activities, and the supply of literature in the several native languages, Mrs. Etty Graeffe was dispatched on the same boat. During 1946–1947, two pioneers departed for Holland, Miss Rita Van Sombeek and Mrs. Jetty Straub, two pioneers for Denmark, Mr. and Mrs. Anders Nielsen, Miss Honor Kempton went to Luxembourg, Miss Virginia Orbison proceeded to Spain, Mrs. Madeline Humbert settled in Belgium, Mr. and Mrs. Ugo Giachery in Italy, Mrs. Alice Dudley in Sweden, Mr. and Mrs. John Shurcliff in Belgium, Miss Sally Sanor and Miss Anita Ioas in Luxembourg, John Carre in Netherlands, Mrs. Jennie Anderson in Sweden, Miss Elsa Steinmetz and Miss Fritzi

Shaver in Switzerland, Miss Charlotte Stirratt in Netherlands, Mr. and Mrs. Philip Marangella in Italy, Miss Dagmar Dole in Denmark and Mrs Elinore Gregory in Norway.[60]

The strategic evolutionary approach and the complexity and nature of the tasks spearheaded by the European Teaching Committee in the course of implementing the goals of the European campaign are highlighted as follows:

The organic plan developed for the successful prosecution of this vast project rested upon the pioneers who gradually developed the nucleus of a Bahá'í community, visits from travelling teachers, the distribution of teaching and news bulletins, the publication of literature in the language of the country, contact and correspondence maintained through the Geneva office, and an annual Conference and School bringing together representatives from every local group. For this organism of spiritual influence an efficient and devoted committee supplied energy, plans and materials, the American Bahá'í community supplied funds exceeding those provided for teaching in America itself, and overall the Guardian of the Faith maintained vigilant watch and released inspiration and guidance for each stage of the momentous task.[61]

During the first two years of the Plan eight Spiritual Assemblies were established in seven of the ten goal countries. In the following two years, the number had risen to twelve. Commenting on some of the challenges involved, one of the members of the committee wrote:

What was accomplished in these two years can be stated in the brief factual report given here, but *how* it was accomplished would furnish material for an entire volume. Uncharted seas for the Committee, strange and unknown lands for many of our pioneers, new languages to learn, new customs to become adjusted to, alone and often lonely, armed at first with perhaps one book and one pamphlet; these were the outward circumstances of their lives. But within the pioneers burned that deep conviction, inspired by the Guardian's assurance that Europe was ready to receive the redeeming Faith of Bahá'u'lláh, and that they, the pioneers, must be the pure channels through which these suffering and disillusioned peoples must receive God's Message. Their abiding help came from the certain knowledge that they were accompanied by the Hosts of the Supreme Concourse and were sustained by the Author of the Divine Plan Himself.[62]

One of the critical ingredients of the campaign was the convening, under the auspices of the European Teaching Committee, of a series of large Bahá'í teaching conferences in a number of goal cities. These conferences proved to be the source of inspiration and encouragement, as well as a means of retaining a clear focus on the goals. They provided the opportunity for evaluating the progress of the work, for sharing experiences, for rejoicing in what had been accomplished, and for fostering an enlarged sense of community. In addition, the conferences directly served the teaching efforts. The program of each conference included a public meeting held at a prestigious venue, with the aim of increasing awareness of the Faith among leaders of society. They also provided the opportunity to undertake special proclamation activities. For example, in connection with the conference held in Holland in 1951, the Dutch Bahá'ís were able to acquaint Queen Juliana in a dignified way with the Bahá'í teachings and to present her with Bahá'í literature that had recently been translated into the Dutch language.[63]

The progress of the European teaching campaign continued at a steady pace. In November 1951, Shoghi Effendi expressed his delight that the campaign had "not only achieved its original aims, but exceeded all expectations through the formation of a local spiritual assembly in the capital city of each of the ten goal countries included within its scope." At the end of the Second Seven Year Plan, a total of eighteen Local Spiritual Assemblies had been established in the goal countries opened to the Faith by the American Bahá'í community, and Bahá'ís resided in no fewer than fifty localities throughout these countries. The administrative structure of the region was further reinforced by the formation of the National Spiritual Assembly of Italy and Switzerland in 1953. Although not originally designated as an objective of the Plan, in 1952 Shoghi Effendi announced that the development of the Faith in these two countries warranted the election of the national administrative body. Described by the Guardian as "the fairest fruit" of the "mighty" European mission, the new National Assembly was elected in the city of Florence. Included among the guests at the convention were the chairman of the National Spiritual Assembly of the United States, together with Miss Edna True, chairman of the European Teaching Committee, and Dr. Ugo Giachery, a recently appointed Hand of the Cause, who with his wife, were part of the first wave of pioneers to arise and settle in Italy during the European Campaign. In addressing the gathering, Miss True expressed the pride of both the American and European Bahá'ís in the remarkable progress of the Faith in Italy and Switzerland in the seven short years since the inauguration of the Second Seven Year Plan. Reflecting on this outstanding accomplishment and the responsibilities that must necessarily accompany it, Dr. Giachery, the chairman of the newly elected National Assembly, remarked: "Six years ago who would have dreamed that we should meet in Florence, today; that our two countries would be joined in an undertaking whose vastness leaves us aghast? Let each one of us take inventory and realize what his share in effort, dedication and sacrifice must be!"[64]

The first phase of the European Teaching campaign was thus concluded in 1953 with the end of the Second Seven Year Plan. With the beginning of the last year of the Plan, Shoghi Effendi focused the attention of the members of the American National Assembly on "the three outstanding functions" that had yet to be completed, namely, the dedication of the Bahá'í House of Worship, the convocation in Wilmette of the first of a series of intercontinental conferences and the holding of the annual Bahá'í convention, and the "effective participation of the members of the American Bahá'í Community, both officially and unofficially, in the three other historic Inter-continental Conferences to be convened successively in Kampala, Stockholm, and New Delhi." All these historic events were scheduled to coincide with the centenary of Bahá'u'lláh's imprisonment in the Síyáh-Chál in Ṭihrán. All the remaining tasks were successfully completed, and the dedication of the Bahá'í House of Worship not only gave rise to a great deal of positive publicity for the Faith, but it marked the end of fifty years of heroic struggle by the members of the community to raise the funds necessary for its construction! The four intercontinental conferences constituted "the highlights of the centenary celebrations," and served as the launching pads for the new teaching plans that derived their authority and direction from 'Abdu'l-Bahá's Tablets of the Divine Plan, plans that were designed to promote the next stage in the evolution of the worldwide Bahá'í community.[65]

THE TEN YEAR SPIRITUAL CRUSADE (1953–63)

In October 1952, six months before the end of the Second Seven Year Plan, Shoghi Effendi formally announced the projected inauguration of the World Bahá'í Crusade, which was to be launched on the occasion of the convocation of four intercontinental conferences, to be held successively during the final months of the Plan and prior to the end of the Holy Year, on four continents of the globe—in Wilmette, Kampala, Stockholm, and New Delhi. Described as "the fate-laden, soul-stirring, decade-long, world-embracing Spiritual Crusade," the new plan was to involve the participation of the existing twelve National Spiritual Assemblies through the "simultaneous initiation of twelve national Ten Year Plans," all of which derived their inspiration and direction from 'Abdu'l-Bahá's Tablets of the Divine Plan. The Plan's overall aim was "the immediate extension of Bahá'u'lláh's spiritual dominion as well as the eventual establishment of the structure of His administrative order in all remaining Sovereign States, Principal Dependencies comprising Principalities, Sultanates, Emirates, Shaykhdoms, Protectorates, Trust Territories, and Crown Colonies scattered over the surface of the entire planet." Four major objectives underpinned the multitude of goals that were assigned to the participating National Assemblies. They were the "development of the institutions at the World Center of the Faith in the Holy Land;" the "consolidation, through carefully devised measures on the home front of the twelve territories destined to serve as administrative bases for the operations of the twelve National Plans;" the "consolidation of all territories already opened to the Faith;" and "the opening of the remaining chief virgin territories on the planet through specific allotments to each National Assembly functioning in the Bahá'í world." The culmination of the global Plan in 1963 was scheduled to coincide with the hundredth anniversary of Bahá'u'lláh's historic Declaration. The "Centenary of the Ascension of Bahá'u'lláh to the Throne of His Sovereignty," and "the world-wide celebrations of the Most Great Jubilee," were to be marked by the convocation of a "World Bahá'í Congress."[66]

In a message addressed to the American Inter-continental Conference in May 1953, Shoghi Effendi provides the following visionary assessment of the purpose of the Ten Year Plan. He stresses the underlying spiritual nature of the enterprise, spells out the unprecedented scope and the inherent complexity of the Plan, describes the significant role to be played by the Bahá'í institutions and individual believers alike, in particular, the members of the American Bahá'í community, and he links the outcome of the Plan with the emergence of the Bahá'í international governing body, the Universal House of Justice. Shoghi Effendi attests:

> Let there be no mistake. The avowed, the primary aim of this Spiritual Crusade is none other than the conquest of the citadels of men's hearts. The theater of its operations is the entire planet. Its duration a whole decade. . . . The agencies assisting in its conduct are the nascent administrative institutions of a steadily evolving divinely appointed order. Its driving force is the energizing influence generated by the Revelation heralded by the Báb and proclaimed by Bahá'u'lláh. Its Marshal is none other than the Author of the Divine Plan. Its standard-bearers are the Hands of the Cause of God appointed in every continent of the globe. Its generals are the twelve national spiritual assemblies participating in the execution of its design. Its vanguard is the chief executors of 'Abdu'l-Bahá's master plan, their allies and associates. Its legions are the rank and file of believers standing behind these same twelve national assemblies and sharing in the global task embracing the American, the European, the African, the Asiatic and Australian fronts. The charter directing its course is the immortal Tablets that have flowed from the pen of the Center of the Covenant Himself. The armor with which its onrushing hosts have been invested is the glad tidings of God's own message in this day, the principles underlying the order proclaimed by His Messenger, and the laws and ordinances

governing His Dispensation. The battle cry animating its heroes and heroines is the cry of Yá-Bahá'u'l-Abhá, Yá 'Alíyyu'l-A'lá.

So vast, so momentous and challenging a crusade that will, God willing, . . . pave the way for, and constitute the prelude to, the initiation of the laborious and tremendously long process of establishing in the course of subsequent crusades in all the newly opened sovereign states, dependencies and islands of the planet, as well as in all the remaining territories of the globe, the framework of the Administrative Order of the Faith, with all its attendant agencies, and of eventually erecting in these territories still more pillars to share in sustaining the weight and in broadening the foundation of the Universal House of Justice.[67]

The American Bahá'í community was called upon to assume a preponderating share in the prosecution of the Ten Year Plan. In all, twenty-four specific goals were assigned to this community. A message addressed to the United States Bahá'í National Convention in 1953 outlines the prodigious scope and range of activities allocated to the American Bahá'ís. Beyond that, in addition to their allotted tasks, as the "chief executors of 'Abdu'l-Bahá's Divine Plan," and because of "the primacy" conferred upon them in his Tablets, this community was also "accorded the prerogative" of dispatching "pioneers to the virgin territories allocated to their sister communities [in the] East and West."[68]

The Ten Year Plan included a number of challenging objectives aimed at the worldwide expansion and consolidation of the Bahá'í community and the development and strengthening of its administrative system. The American Bahá'í community was invited to assume the lion's share of the work! For example, the Plan called for doubling the number of countries where Bahá'ís resided and quadrupling the number of elected National Spiritual Assemblies throughout the world. Of the 131 new countries to be opened to the Bahá'í Faith in the course of the Plan, twenty-nine countries in four continents were assigned to the American Bahá'í community. Of the forty-eight new Regional and National Spiritual Assemblies to be elected during the ten year period, the National Spiritual Assembly of the United States was responsible for thirty-six, comprising one in Africa, twenty-one in the Americas, two in Asia, and twelve in Europe. In addition, the American National Assembly was assigned the task of consolidating twenty-three territories that had been previously opened to the Faith, but which required major reinforcement. This included twelve coun-tries in Europe, six in Asia, three in the Americas, and two in Africa. To facilitate and coordinate the teaching activities in the newly as-signed Asian countries, the National Assembly was requested to form an Asian Teaching Committee. Working alongside the existing Inter-American and European Teaching Committees, this new committee would provide the necessary focus on Asia.[69]

Within the United States itself, the Plan contained a number of specific goals aimed at expanding and strengthening the foundations of the American Bahá'í community. For example, the community was called upon to raise the number of Local Spiritual Assemblies to three hundred, to diversify its membership by the conversion to the Faith of members of the leading Indian tribes, and to engage in active proclamation of the Faith through the press and radio throughout the Unties States.[70]

Shoghi Effendi rallied the members of the American Bahá'í commu-nity by invoking the memory of the dawn-breakers of the Heroic Age of the Bahá'í Faith, and by calling attention to the responsibilities that must necessarily accompany the community's special status. He writes:

> May this community—the spiritual descendants of the
> dawn-breakers of the Heroic Age of the Bahá'í Faith, the chief

repository of the immortal Tablets of 'Abdu'l-Bahá's Divine Plan, the foremost executors of the Mandate issued by the Center of Bahá'u'lláh's Covenant, the champion-builders of a divinely conceived Administrative Order, the standard-bearers of the all-conquering army of the Lord of Hosts, the torchbearers of a future divinely inspired world civilization—arise, in the course of the momentous decade . . . to secure, as befits its rank, the lion's share in the prosecution of a global crusade designed to diffuse the light of God's revelation over the surface of the entire planet.[71]

The immediate priority was the dispersal of pioneers to the designated unopened territories of the planet. Shoghi Effendi designated the Bahá'ís who were the first pioneers to arrive in lands where no Bahá'í had previously resided as "Knights of Bahá'u'lláh." To record the historic and sacrificial services of these believers, he announced his intention of establishing "an illuminated Roll of Honor" in which he would inscribe the names of these "spiritual conquerors."[72]

The response of the members of the venturesome American Bahá'í community to the call for pioneers was instantaneous. Bahá'ís, veterans and newly declared alike, arose by the hundreds to carry the message of Bahá'u'lláh to every corner of the globe. During the first year of the Plan, 157 pioneers, including five members of the United States National Spiritual Assembly, left the comfort of their homes to serve the Faith in designated goal areas, while during the second year, a further 125 settled in areas assigned to the American Bahá'í community. This great outflow of pioneers continued until all accessible goals were settled.[73] In April 1957, Shoghi Effendi announced to the Bahá'í world that:

Every single territory of the hundred and twenty, mentioned by the Author of the Divine Plan in His memorable Tablets, is now opened to His Father's Faith, proclaiming the exemplary fidelity of His followers to the dearest wishes expressed by the Center of the Covenant in those Tablets.[74]

It should be noted that the territorial goals of the Ten Year Plan were broader and more inclusive than the geographical areas listed in 'Abdu'l-Bahá's Tablets of the Divine Plan. Nevertheless, it is evident that Shoghi Effendi took great pleasure in this accomplishment and he was moved to pay tribute to "the fidelity" of the Bahá'ís to 'Abdu'l-Bahá's wish to see the Faith spread throughout the length and breadth of the earth.

Beyond the statistical accounting, there are myriad human stories of personal commitment, challenge, sacrifice, and service. The stories of the pioneers are legion and it is only possible to recount here a few to give the flavor of this remarkable group of spiritually motivated souls. Matthew W. Bullock (1881–1972) was one of the first African American Bahá'ís to respond to Shoghi Effendi's call for pioneers during the Ten Year Plan. Mr. Bullock was one of the five members of the United States National Spiritual Assembly to resign their positions in order to go pioneering. In 1953, at the age of seventy-two, he went to the Dutch West Indies, where he helped to establish the first Local Spiritual Assembly. For a period of seven years, he traveled throughout the West Indies, teaching people about the Bahá'í Faith and forming and strengthening Local Spiritual Assemblies. Shoghi Effendi designated Mr. Bullock a Knight of Bahá'u'lláh for his services in the Dutch West Indies. He remained at his pioneering post until 1960, when due to advanced age and frailty, he returned to the United States.[75]

Gertrude and Alvin Blum, Bahá'ís of Jewish background from the East Coast of the United States were named Knights of Bahá'u'lláh for arising to introduce the Bahá'í Faith to the Solomon Islands in the South Pacific in March 1954.[76] Alvin Blum served in the United States Army Medical Corps during the Second World War. In 1945, Mr. Blum was onboard a troop ship en route to the Philippine Islands. The ship stopped briefly at the Solomon Islands, which had for three years been the scene of bitter fighting, most notably during the long struggle on Guadalcanal. This brief encounter made a deep impression on him. At the end of the war, Mr. and Mrs. Blum served as home-front pioneers before arising to assist the development of the Faith in New Zealand. When Shoghi Effendi announced the goals of the Ten Year Plan, the Blums and their infant daughter chose the Solomon Islands, one of the virgin areas in the Pacific, as their field of service. They traveled on a small cargo ship and were brought ashore at Honiara, the capital, in a small dinghy on 1 March 1954. They made their home in the Solomons, and spent the rest of their lives at their pioneering post.

Alvin Blum was an extremely resourceful and energetic man. At the behest of Shoghi Effendi he engaged in business and quietly sought out individuals who were receptive to the Bahá'í teachings. In the early years, many difficulties were encountered. Eventually the way was opened when a government employee, who was a highly respected chief, accepted the Faith, and he introduced the Bahá'í teachings to his fellow citizens. Both Mr. and Mrs. Blum worked ceaselessly for the establishment and expansion of the Faith throughout the Pacific, and served as members of its elected institutions. They also made an outstanding contribution to the development of the Solomon Islands. At the time of Alvin's passing in 1968, Mrs. Blum described some of his accomplishments:

He . . . made a significant contribution to the public welfare by putting in badly needed service industries, by accepting the appointment by the High Commissioner to serve as a charter member of the Honiara Town Council, by serving as chairman of the Medical Board, by helping to found the Chamber of Commerce and the Scout Movement, and by acting as financial adviser to the Young Farmers Club. He was known everywhere for his constant activity and lively presence.[77]

Gertrude Blum remained at her post until the time of her passing in June 1993. She dedicated almost forty years of her life to nurturing both the Bahá'í community in the Solomon Islands and to enhancing the quality of life in this small Pacific nation. Her services to the Bahá'í Faith and the wider community were recognized by Queen Elizabeth II, who honored Mrs. Blum by bestowing on her an M.B.E. (Membership of the British Empire) award.[78]

Another of the venturesome souls who arose to pioneer was Mrs. Maude Elizabeth Todd Fisher, who in her youth had driven her own covered wagon across the plains and on into the mountain country of the United States. Mrs. Fisher became a member of the Bahá'í Faith in 1927. She was an active teacher and served on a number of Local Spiritual Assemblies. At the age of eighty-two, following the Bahá'í Intercontinental Conference in Chicago in 1953, she made plans to pioneer to Africa. She was to accompany her daughter and son-in-law, Valera and John Allen, to Swaziland. Though her departure had to be postponed because of her ill-health, she resolutely continued with her plans and finally arrived in Johannesburg, South Africa, from where she made the final journey overland to Swaziland with members of her family.

On arrival in Swaziland, Mrs. Fisher immediately began teaching. The Africans she met found her good humor and her simple and practical way of speaking, very attractive. In no time, she was regarded as a grandmother to them all. Despite advanced age and recurrent bouts of poor health, she made teaching trips to Mozambique, Southern and Northern Rhodesia, and South Africa. She helped to establish and she served on the first Local Spiritual Assembly in Swaziland. Her courage, indifference to fatigue, and dedication to the work of the Faith were an inspiration to all. Mrs. Fisher died at her post. At her funeral, one of the African Bahá'ís uttered the following eloquent farewell, which captured the unifying spirit inherent in the teachings of Bahá'u'lláh: "Go well, mother of us all. We love you very much."[79]

After surveying the progress of the Plan in 1957, Shoghi Effendi was moved to pay "a special tribute . . . to the heroic band of pioneers, and particularly to the company of the Knights of Bahá'u'lláh." Extolling their services, he attests that:

> . . . as a result of their indomitable spirit, courage, steadfastness, and self-abnegation, [they] have achieved in the course of four brief years, in so many of the virgin territories newly opened to His Faith, a measure of success so far exceeding the most sanguine expectations. Such a success, reflected in both the numerical strength of these territories and the range and solidity of the achievements of the Bahá'í crusaders responsible for their opening and development, has surpassed to an unbelievable extent the goals set for them under the Ten-Year Plan.[80]

It is interesting to consider that these outstanding accomplishments were achieved against the backdrop of a decline in the political, economic, and social conditions of the world. The Ten Year Plan coincided with the confluence of such world-shaping events as the lowering of the Iron Curtain onto Europe, the rise of the Cold War, the outbreak of hostilities on the Korean Peninsula, and the rise of opposition to colonial powers in Africa and parts of Asia. In addition, there was a renewed outbreak of persecutions against the Bahá'í in Iran in 1955, which, for a time hindered the progress of the Plan in that land.

As the new Bahá'í communities grew in size and strength, priority attention was focused on the establishment of Local Spiritual Assemblies, which were to form the structural basis for the election of the National Assemblies destined to emerge in each of the designated areas. Stressing the importance and scope of this activity and its relationship to the eventual formation of the Bahá'í international governing body, the Universal House of Justice, Shoghi Effendi states:

> Above all, an effort unprecedented in its range and intensity, must be exerted for the speedy multiplication of local spiritual assemblies in all the territories where National Spiritual Assemblies, whether independent or regional, provisional of permanent, are to be established, for the purpose of broadening and strengthening the foundations on which these potent national institutions—the pillars of the future Universal House of Justice—must rest.[81]

To ensure unity of vision and a clear focus on the remaining goals of the Ten Year Plan, in October 1957, Shoghi Effendi announced the convocation of a series of five intercontinental conferences to take place between January and September 1958, at the midpoint of the Plan, and he further clarified the functions of the Hands of the Cause, an action which was to have enormous consequences for the uninterrupted development of the Faith. The conferences were "to be held successively in Kampala, Uganda, in the heart of the African continent; in the city of Sydney, the oldest Bahá'í center established in the Antipodes; in Chicago, where the name of Bahá'u'lláh was publicly mentioned for the first time in the western world; in the city of Frankfurt, in the heart of the European continent; and in Djakarta, the capital city of the Republic of Indonesia." Their purpose was five-fold: to offer "humble thanksgiving" to Bahá'u'lláh; to review and celebrate "the series of signal victories won so rapidly"; to consult on ways and means to ensure the "triumphant consummation" of the Plan; and to give impetus to the construction of the three Houses of Worship—in Europe, Australia, and Africa. The Guardian expressed the hope that "the deliberations and resolutions of the attendants at these forthcoming Conferences" would result in "an upsurge of enthusiasm and consecration" and lead to exploits that would far outshine what had so far been achieved.[82]

To buttress the formulation and implementation of the specific plans and strategies, slated to emerge from these conferences, Shoghi Effendi named a number of the Hands of the Cause, designated by him as "the high-ranking officers of a fast evolving World Administrative Order," and the "Chief Stewards of Bahá'u'lláh's embryonic World Commonwealth," to attend these gatherings as his representatives. He also instructed the Hands to collaborate actively with the Spiritual Assemblies and individual believers in their prosecution of the Plan.[83]

This fateful message of October 1957 proved to be the last major communication Shoghi Effendi addressed to the Bahá'ís of the world. On 4 November 1957, Shoghi Effendi passed away suddenly and unexpectedly while in London, England. Though grieving for their beloved Guardian, the Bahá'ís rallied around the institutions of their Faith and, led by their National Spiritual Assemblies, turned for direction and advice to the Hands of the Cause, in their capacity of the "Chief Stewards" of the Faith. The body of Hands residing in the Holy Land was empowered to deal with problems of protecting the Faith, correspond with Hands who resided in other parts of the world and with National Spiritual Assemblies, and to assist National Assemblies in administrative matters. The Hands of the Cause also deliberated on ways to set in motion the processes that would culminate in the election of the international governing body, the Universal House of Justice, in 1963.

The five intercontinental conferences consolidated the unity of the Bahá'í community, sharpened its vision, and stimulated sustained and dedicated efforts to complete the remaining goals of the Plan.[84] The wise stewardship of the Hands of the Cause and the leadership of the National Spiritual Assemblies brought the global Ten Year Plan to a successful conclusion. It is interesting to note that Shoghi Effendi testified to the extraordinary character of the victories achieved during the course of the Plan. Alluding to the scope and historical significance of the anticipated outcomes of the Plan in his letter of October 1957 to the Bahá'ís of the world, he wrote:

The phenomenal advances made since the inception of this globe-girdling Crusade, in the brief space of less than five years, eclipses—if we pause to ponder the scope and significance of recent developments—in both the number and quality of the feats achieved by its prosecutors, any previous collective enterprise undertaken by the followers of the Faith, at any time and in any part of the world, since the close of the initial and most turbulent epoch of the Heroic Age of the Bahá'í Dispensation.[85]

A brief selection of some of the noteworthy achievements of the Plan, which pertain to the expansion of the Faith and the establishment of its administrative structure, are as follows: The number of countries opened to the Faith was more than doubled. In 1963, there were 259 countries and territories where Bahá'ís resided. The Faith was now truly a global religion and the diversity of its membership was dramatically enhanced by the inclusion of Bahá'ís from a multitude of different races and tribal backgrounds. Indeed, in the United States, alone, no fewer than twenty-five Indian tribes were represented in the American Bahá'í community. Forty-four new National and Regional Spiritual Assemblies were established during the ten year period, bringing the total number for the world to fifty-six. In April 1963, there were still 388 adult American pioneers in foreign fields of service, who were willing to continue at their posts as long as there was a need.[86]

On the American home front, the goals of the Plan had also been surpassed. Rather than 300 Local Spiritual Assemblies, 331 were established, and 111 Spiritual Assemblies were legally incorporated, instead of the 100 called for in the Plan. Bahá'ís now lived in over 1700 different localities scattered throughout the country.

The Ten Year Plan was the first systematic global teaching and consolidation plan undertaken by the Bahá'í community. It drew its inspiration from 'Abdu'l-Bahá's Tablets of the Divine Plan. Shoghi Effendi formulated its overall objectives and guided its implementation. The execution of the Plan required the active collaboration of twelve National Spiritual Assemblies in existence in 1953, with the American National Assembly being called upon to assume major responsibility.

The outstanding contribution of the American Bahá'í community to the execution of the Ten Year Plan might well be highlighted by reference to the last major letter Shoghi Effendi addressed to the American Bahá'í community in September 1957, written less than two months before his death. In it the Guardian expressed his appreciation for the qualities exemplified by the members of this community. In particular, he referred to its "striking display, and a remarkable combination of American Bahá'í initiative, resourcefulness, generosity, fidelity and perseverance."[87] Anticipating that the American Bahá'í community had the capacity to complete the task it had undertaken, he wrote:

A prodigious expenditure of effort, a stupendous flow of material resources, an unprecedented dispersal of pioneers, embracing so vast a section of the globe, and bringing in their wake the rise, the multiplication and consolidation of so many institutions, so divers in character, so potent and full of promise, already stand to their credit, and augur well for a befitting consummation of a decade-long task in the years immediately ahead.[88]

Indeed, Shoghi Effendi attests that the Ten Year Plan was to constitute but "the first stage of their world-encompassing mission," a God-given mission that continues to be reflected in all subsequent Plans on which the worldwide Bahá'í community has been called upon to embark. The "privileged champion builders of the World Order of Baha'u'llah," the members of the American Bahá'í community are, therefore, invested with the responsibility for spreading the Bahá'í Faith throughout the world. However, as the newer Bahá'í communities mature, their resources grow, and their institutions develop, the kinds of assistance the Americans will be called upon to provide their coreligionists will change and diversify according to the needs of the maturing global Faith.[89]

Two historic events marked the conclusion of the Ten Year Plan. The first involved the participation of the members of the fifty-six National and Regional Spiritual Assemblies who assembled at the First International Bahá'í Convention held in the Holy Land on 21–23 April 1963, for the purpose of electing the first Universal House of Justice. The second was the gathering held in London, England, on 28 April–2 May 1963, of more than six thousand Bahá'ís from all over the world to celebrate the hundredth anniversary of the Declaration of Bahá'u'lláh's prophetic mission. The Universal House of Justice in one of its early letters captured the excitement and the sense of celebration mixed with relief, which pervaded the gathering in London. It wrote:

. . . this greatest gathering of Bahá'ís ever held in one place was permeated by a spirit of such bliss as could only have come from the outpourings of the Abhá Kingdom. The review of the progress of the Cause, the presentation of believers from the new races and countries of the world brought within the pale of the Faith during the Beloved Guardian's Ten Year Crusade, of the Knights of Bahá'u'lláh, those valiant souls who carried the banner of Bahá'u'lláh to the unopened and often inhospitable regions of the earth, the spontaneous outbursts of singing of "Alláh-u-Abhá," the informal gatherings, the constant greetings of Bahá'u'lláh's warriors known to each other only by name and service, the youth gatherings, the unprecedented publicity in the press, on radio and television, the daily stream of visitors to the beloved Guardian's resting-place,[90] the radiant faces and heightened awareness of the true and real brotherhood of the human race within the Kingdom of the Everlasting Father, are among the outstanding events of this supreme occasion, the crowning victory of the lifework of Shoghi Effendi.[91]

PATTERNS OF EXPANSION—THE HEROIC AGE AND THE FORMATIVE AGE

Shoghi Effendi's designation of the American Bahá'ís as the "spiritual descendants of the dawn-breakers" has implications not only for the functions they are called upon to assume, but also for the qualities of sacrifice and service they must demonstrate in carrying out these functions. In one of his letters, Shoghi Effendi writes:

The community of the organized promoters of the Faith of Bahá'u'lláh in the American continent—the spiritual descendants of the dawn-breakers of an heroic Age, who by their death proclaimed the birth of that Faith—must, in turn, usher in, not by their death but through living sacrifice, that promised World Order, the shell ordained to enshrine that priceless jewel, the world civilization, of which the Faith itself is the sole begetter . . . this community, preserved by the immutable decrees of the omnipotent Ordainer and deriving continual sustenance from the mandate with which the Tablets of the Divine Plan have invested it, is now busily engaged in laying the foundations and in fostering the growth of those institutions which are to herald the approach of the Age destined to witness the birth and rise of the World Order of Bahá'u'lláh.[92]

It is evident that the task of "laying the foundations" of the administrative structure of the Faith is inextricably linked to the implementation of the mission, outlined in 'Abdu'l-Bahá's Tablets of the Divine Plan, of raising the banner of the Faith throughout all the countries in the East and West. The activities, described above, undertaken by the American Bahá'ís in pursuit of the goals of the Plans, clearly illustrate the relationship between teaching the Faith and administrative development. Hence, to consolidate and ensure the continued evolution of new Bahá'í communities, it is necessary to establish and foster the growth of Spiritual Assemblies. It is the role of the Spiritual Assembly to plan the next stage in the expansion and consolidation of the Bahá'í community, thereby sustaining a culture of growth.

The goals of the three Plans assigned to the American Bahá'í community were exceedingly challenging and, indeed, daunting. Numerically small and lacking human and financial resources, the community was called upon to act during times of war and periods of political, social, and economic upheaval, as well as of persecution. Nevertheless, sustained by a deep conviction of the power of divine assistance, and guided by a clearly articulated vision and a strategic plan of action, the members of this community marshaled their personal and collective strengths and demonstrated the heroic qualities of character that enabled them to overcome obstacles and to accomplish their objectives.

The strategic approach to the expansion of the religion adopted by the American Bahá'ís is reminiscent of some of the actions taken by the Báb and His early followers, in the face of violent opposition, to introduce and ensure the continuity of the new revelation in the land of its birth. In the earliest days of His ministry, the Báb convened a gathering of the Letters of the Living, the first group of individuals who accepted the new religion. During this meeting, the Báb articulated His vision of the important role His chosen followers, who numbered fewer than twenty, were to play in the unfoldment of the new revelation, and He foreshadowed some of the difficulties and challenges they were bound to experience. He set out certain general objectives and assigned to each a special task in a particular geographical area. He also instructed His followers to maintain records of their activities and to provide Him with detailed reports. In later years, the followers of the Báb engaged in systematic collective actions in their efforts to defend the new religion against persecution and threats to wipe it out of existence.

Similarly, the Plans adopted by the American Bahá'ís were strategic and progressively focused on specific geographical areas. Laboring in the face of enormous difficulties, this numerically small enterprising community willingly embraced every challenge. With courage, a sense of consecration, and dogged tenacity, they brought to bear their great organizing ability, outstanding resourcefulness, and ingenuity in executing their mission. The scale of their operations continued to expand as the human and material resources were developed, and the administrative structure of the Faith was laid. With the formation of Spiritual Assemblies it became possible to marshal and use the available resources in an efficient and systematic manner, and to coordinate projects requiring the collaboration of a number of Bahá'í communities. Indeed, the Ten Year Plan provided the American Bahá'í community with the challenge of engaging in activities in collaboration with their coreligionists in all parts of the globe. Referring to the high level of responsibility laid upon this community during the Ten Year Plan, Shoghi Effendi attests that this Plan was "the third and greatest collective enterprise embarked upon in American Bahá'í history," and he indicates that "their admiring and expectant sister communities throughout the world" were counting on them to arise to the challenge and to come to their assistance.[93]

The Plans formulated by Shoghi Effendi evoke a consciousness of the history of the Heroic Age of the Bahá'í Faith and an identification with and an appreciation for the sacrificial exploits of the early Persian believers. The Guardian's Plans challenge the American Bahá'ís, living during the period of the Faith's Formative Age, to arise to play their part in the current stage of the evolution of the Bahá'í community, and they provide the means whereby the believers can understand their role in this ongoing historical process. These visionary Plans not only foster a sense of identity with the dawn-breakers of the Heroic Age, but they also foreshadow the future Golden Age of the Faith, which is destined to emerge in the centuries ahead. Shoghi Effendi links the actions of the American Bahá'í community, the dawn-breakers of the Formative Age, to the emergence of the Golden Age. He, thus, raises their awareness of the significance of their current services by conceptualizing them within the context of laying "a firm foundation for the country's future role in ushering in the Golden Age of the Cause of Bahá'u'lláh."[94]

8

LAYING THE FOUNDATIONS
OF WORLD CIVILIZATION

The heroic exploits of the members of the North American Bahá'í community, "the chosen trustees"[1] of 'Abdu'l-Bahá's Divine Plan, resulted in the gradual and systematic spread of the Bahá'í Faith to the four corners of the globe and the establishment of the institutions of the Faith's Administrative Order. Simultaneous with this outward thrust, the community has, from its earliest years, been engaged in laying the foundations of Bahá'í community life. To this end, it has initiated programs and activities aimed at enhancing the spiritual, educational, and social aspects of the lives of its members, and at increasing the capacity of its embryonic institutions to devise and execute plans of action aimed at building the world civilization envisaged in the writings of Bahá'u'lláh.

This chapter explores some of the implications of Shoghi Effendi's designation of the American Bahá'í community as "the torchbearers of a future divinely inspired world civilization." It considers the symbolism of the Bahá'í House of Worship and its relationship to the Mashriqu'l-Adhkár, which is described as a "Harbinger of an as yet unborn civilization," and examines the seminal actions of 'Abdu'l-Bahá during his visit to North America as well as the activities subsequently undertaken by the American Bahá'ís and their elected Assemblies to set in motion the processes of civilization building.²

THE MASHRIQU'L-ADHKÁR

The term Mashriqu'l-Adhkár, literally "the Dawning place of the Praise of God," refers to the Bahá'í House of Worship and its dependencies or related institutions, which are dedicated to social, administrative, humanitarian, educational, and scientific affairs. The House of Worship forms the central edifice of the Mashriqu'l-Adhkár. As this complex unfolds and develops, it is slated to include "a hospital, a drug dispensary, a traveler's hospice, a school for orphans, and a university for advanced studies."³ It is envisaged that, in the future, Bahá'í Houses of Worship will be constructed in every town and village throughout the world.

The dramatic story of the construction of the American Bahá'í House of Worship, "the symbol and precursor of a future world civilization," has been told in detail elsewhere. Suffice it to say, that the ambitious project, undertaken by a small and struggling community, received the active support and encouragement of 'Abdu'l-Bahá. During his travels in North America in 1912, 'Abdu'l-Bahá laid the foundation stone of the "Mother Temple" of the West. Indeed, such was the importance of this venture, 'Abdu'l-Bahá asserted: "Out of this Mashriqu'l-Adhkár, without doubt, thousands of Mashriqu'l-Adhkárs will be born."⁴

Half a century was to elapse from the time of its inception in 1903, until its public dedication in 1953. During this time the Bahá'ís faced a multitude of challenges. Not only did the community lack human and financial resources, but the goals of the Plans were multi-focal —calling for attention to be given to the expansion of the Faith and the establishment of its administrative structure, as well as for ensuring the ongoing work necessary for the eventual completion of the

House of Worship. In addition, the financial crises resulting from the Great Depression of the 1930s and the disruptions associated with the Second World War impacted the efforts of the Bahá'ís, increasing the level of challenge and the need for sacrificial behavior. Shoghi Effendi compares the high degree of self-sacrifice and the level of concerted effort demonstrated by the American Bahá'ís in their efforts to erect the House of Worship in Wilmette, with the exploits of the dawn-breakers of the Heroic Age. He calls attention to the underlying significance of this historic undertaking, referring to it as "a collective enterprise that, by the range and quality of the sacrifice it entailed, deserves to be ranked among the most outstanding examples of Bahá'í solidarity ever since those deeds of brilliant heroism immortalized the memory of the heroes of Nayríz, of Zanján, and of Ṭabarsí."[5]

Further, with the approach of the centenary of the martyrdom of the Báb in 1950, the American Bahá'ís were struggling valiantly to complete a particular phase of the construction of the House of Worship and also to further the expansion of the Faith. Shoghi Effendi again took the opportunity to highlight the unparalleled degree of sacrifice required. In the following passage, he challenges the members of the community to reach new levels of self-sacrifice, stresses the uniqueness of the American Bahá'í House of Worship, and foreshadows its future significant role in Bahá'í history:

> The sacrifice demanded is such as to have no parallel, whatsoever, in the history of that community. The manifold issues inextricably interwoven with the campaign audaciously launched for the achievement of this high objective, are of such a weighty character as to overshadow every enterprise embarked upon, through the organized efforts of its members, in either the concluding years of the Heroic Age of the Faith or the first Epoch of the Age which succeeded it. . . . How meritorious, indeed,

are the self-denying acts which this supremely challenging hour now calls forth, amidst the perplexities and confusion which present-day society is now experiencing! And yet how trifling in comparison with the self-immolation of the most distinguished and the most precious heroes and saints of the primitive Age of our glorious Faith! An outpouring of treasure, no less copious than the blood shed so lavishly in the Apostolic Age of the Faith by those who in the heart of the Asiatic continent proclaimed its birth to the world, can befit their spiritual descendants, who, in the present Formative Age of the Bahá'í Dispensation, have championed the Cause, and assumed so preponderating a share in the erection, of its Administrative Order, and are now engaged in the final stage of the building of the House that incarnates the soul of that Faith in the American continent. No sacrifice can be deemed too great to ensure the completion of such an Edifice—the most holy House of Worship ever to be associated with the Faith of the Most Great Name—an Edifice whose inception has shed such a lustre on the closing years of the Heroic Age of the Bahá'í Dispensation, which has assumed a concrete shape in the present Formative Stage in the evolution of our beloved Faith, whose Dependencies must spring into existence in the course of successive epochs of this same Age, and whose fairest fruits will be garnered in the Age that is to come, the last, the Golden Age of the initial and brightest Dispensation of the five-thousand-century Bahá'í Cycle.[6]

THE SYMBOL OF THE MASHRIQU'L-ADHKÁR

Throughout religious history, it has been customary for the faithful to expend precious resources on the construction and beautification of houses of worship—churches, mosques, temples, and the like—that are dedicated to the worship of the Creator. The Bahá'í Faith follows in this tradition. Indeed, the institution of the Mashriqu'l-Adhkár is ordained by Bahá'u'lláh in His Book of Laws, the Kitáb-i-Aqdas. He calls for the construction of houses of worship "throughout the lands," in which individuals will gather "to listen to the verses of God."[7]

'Abdu'l-Bahá stresses the spiritual significance of the Mashriqu'l-Adhkár and the impact it has on "men's souls" and on life in general. He attests:

> Although to outward seeming the Mashriqu'l-Adhkár is a material structure, yet it hath a spiritual effect. It forgeth bonds of unity from heart to heart; it is a collective centre for men's souls. Every city in which, during the days of the Manifestation, a temple was raised up, hath created security and constancy and peace, for such buildings were given over to the perpetual glorification of God, and only in the remembrance of God can the heart find rest. Gracious God! The edifice of the House of Worship hath a powerful influence on every phase of life.[8]

Continuing with this theme, 'Abdu'l-Bahá states: "The Mashriqu'l-Adhkár is one of the most vital institutions in the world." He describes the connection and important relationship between the Bahá'í House of Worship, the central building of the complex, and the surrounding dependencies, and affirms: "The Temple is not only a place of worship; rather, in every respect is it complete and whole." Furthermore, anticipating the future development of this institution, Shoghi Effendi characterizes the dependencies that will cluster around the House of Worship as "institutions of social service," and he envisages that their functions will include affording "relief to the suffering, sustenance to the poor, shelter to the wayfarer, solace to the bereaved, and education to the ignorant."[9]

The institutions that are associated with the Mashriqu'l-Adhkár are intimately linked to the operation of the Bahá'í Administrative Order. Shoghi Effendi indicates that they will constitute the "seat" round which the "spiritual," "humanitarian and administrative activities" of this Order will "cluster."[10] Might not these activities be considered critical building blocks necessary for laying the foundation of a future world civilization?

To enlarge the vision of the American Bahá'ís concerning the purpose of the Mashriqu'l-Adhkár and its future role in the regeneration of human society, Shoghi Effendi explains in detail the significance of this institution and the dynamic interplay among the spiritual, administrative, and humanitarian activities that are destined to take place in the environs of the Mashriqu'l-Adhkár complex. In addition, he stresses the indispensability of these three elements to the effective functioning of that institution and to the evolution of the organic life of the Bahá'í community.

Beginning with a discussion of the spiritual component—the gathering of the Bahá'ís in the "serenely spiritual atmosphere" of the House of Worship to hear the Word of God in the form of readings from the Scriptures of the Divine Messengers—Shoghi Effendi describes the impact of this experience on those who participate in such gatherings. "To them," he states, "will the Mashriqu'l-Adhkár symbolize the fundamental verity underlying the Bahá'í Faith, that religious truth is not absolute but relative, that Divine Revelation is not final but progressive." He further avows that, being cognizant of the message of Bahá'u'lláh, the worshippers will be moved to express their gratitude to the Almighty, Who, "from time immemorial even unto our day," has sent forth Messengers and Prophets to guide the steps of humankind.[11]

Having established the exalted conception of Bahá'í worship, Shoghi Effendi now calls attention to the complex interactions between the spiritual, humanitarian, and administrative aspects of the Mashriqu'l-Adhkár, and he illustrates how they are designed both to operate in unison and to reinforce each other. In this regard, he writes:

> Divorced from the social, humanitarian, educational and scientific pursuits centering around the Dependencies of the Mashriqu'l-Adhkár, Bahá'í worship, however exalted in its conception, however passionate in fervor, can never hope to achieve beyond the meager and often transitory results produced by the contemplations of the ascetic or the communion of the passive worshiper.[12]

He highlights the inherent limitations to both the individual and society of focusing exclusively on the spiritual, cautioning that worship alone, "cannot afford lasting satisfaction and benefit to the worshiper himself, much less to humanity in general, unless and until translated and transfused into that dynamic and disinterested service to the cause of humanity," which is facilitated and promoted by the dependencies of the Mashriqu'l-Adhkár. He, likewise, calls attention to the essential link between administrative and spiritual activities, stating that the efforts of "those who within the precincts of the Mashriqu'l-Adhkár will be engaged in administering the affairs of the future Bahá'í Commonwealth" will fail to "fructify and prosper unless they are brought into close and daily communion with those spiritual agencies centering in and radiating from the central Shrine of the Mashriqu'l-Adhkár."[13]

Shoghi Effendi concludes his analysis by reiterating the importance of the spiritual, administrative, and humanitarian activities to the future regeneration of the world. He states:

> Nothing short of direct and constant interaction between the spiritual forces emanating from this House of Worship centering

in the spiritual heart of the Mashriqu'l-Adhkár, and the energies consciously displayed by those who administer its affairs in their service to humanity can possibly provide the necessary agency capable of removing the ills that have so long and so grievously afflicted humanity. For it is assuredly upon the consciousness of the efficacy of the Revelation of Bahá'u'lláh, reinforced on the one hand by spiritual communion with His Spirit, and on the other by the intelligent application and the faithful execution of the principles and laws He revealed, that the salvation of a world in travail must ultimately depend. And of all the institutions that stand associated with His Holy Name, surely none save the institution of the Mashriqu'l-Adhkár can most adequately provide the essentials of Bahá'í worship and service, both so vital to the regeneration of the world. Therein lies the secret of its loftiness, of the potency, of the unique position of the Mashriqu'l-Adhkár as one of the outstanding institutions conceived by Bahá'u'lláh.[14]

PROCESSES OF CIVILIZATION BUILDING

Shoghi Effendi's visionary depiction of "the true purpose and essential character of the Mashriqu'l-Adhkár" paints a vivid picture of both the processes by which it operates and of the role it is to play in the transformation of society as its functions progressively evolve and unfold. The rate at which these functions evolve is inextricably linked to the progress and maturation of the Bahá'í community and its Administrative Order. When, for example, the National Spiritual Assembly of the United States and Canada decided to establish its national headquarters in the vicinity of the slowly rising Mashriqu'l-Adhkár in Wilmette, Shoghi Effendi called attention to the highly important practical and spiritual implications associated with this decision, observing that it symbolizes, "in a befitting manner, the ideal of service animating the Bahá'í community in its relation alike to the Faith and to mankind in general," and, further, that it "signalizes the launching of yet another phase in the slow and imperceptible emergence . . . of a model Bahá'í community—a community divinely ordained, organically united, clear-visioned, vibrant with life, and whose very purpose is regulated by the twin directing principles of the worship of God and of service to one's fellow-men."[15]

Not only is the emergence of "a model Bahá'í community" linked to the interaction between these institutions, but their functions are destined to evolve at a pace commensurate with the rate of evolution of the Bahá'í community itself. Writing in December 1938, for example, the Guardian set out the functions to be performed both by the first American Bahá'í House of Worship of the West and the Spiritual Assemblies, functions that were appropriate to the particular stage of development of the embryonic Bahá'í community. Hence, in relation to the House of Worship, he specified that "it should be regarded, at the present time, as no more than an instrument for a more effective propagation of the Cause and a wider diffusion of its teachings." And, he indicated that "In this respect it should be viewed in the same light as the administrative institutions of the Faith which are designed as vehicles for the proper dissemination of its ideals, its tenets, and its verities."[16]

In this section, we examine some of the actions taken by the American Bahá'í community and its administrative institutions to establish the pattern of Bahá'í life among its members, to enhance the maturity of its functioning, and to minister to the needs of humanity in a travailing age.

In addition to bestowing a unique mandate on the North American Bahá'ís through the Tablets of the Divine Plan, 'Abdu'l-Bahá made a major contribution to laying the foundations of Bahá'í community life in that continent. He educated, nurtured, and trained the

early believers through the constant flow of guidance contained in his
Tablets, through his loving encouragement, and through his historic
travels in the West during which he not only explained in detail the
teachings of the Faith and demonstrated their application in his daily
life, but he also performed a number of seminal acts that gave impetus to the processes of community and administrative development.
Shoghi Effendi provides the following list of some of the most significant of these functions performed by the Master, and he highlights
their importance to the future functioning of the community and its
institutions:

> The laying, with His own hands, of the dedication stone of
> the Mashriqu'l-Adhkár, by the shore of Lake Michigan, in the
> vicinity of Chicago . . . ; the dynamic affirmation by Him of the
> implications of the Covenant instituted by Bahá'u'lláh, follow-
> ing the reading of the newly translated Tablet of the Branch,
> in a general assembly of His followers in New York, designated
> henceforth as the "City of the Covenant"; . . . the symbolic
> Feast He Himself offered to a large gathering of His disciples
> assembled in the open air, and in the green setting of a June day
> at West Englewood, in New Jersey; the blessing He bestowed on
> the Open Forum at Green Acre, in Maine, on the banks of the
> Piscataqua River, where many of His followers had gathered,
> and which was to evolve into one of the first Bahá'í summer
> schools of the Western Hemisphere and be recognized as one of
> the earliest endowments established in the American continent;
> His address to an audience of several hundred attending the last
> session of the newly-founded Bahá'í Temple Unity held in Chi-
> cago; and, last but not least, the exemplary act He performed
> by uniting in wedlock two of His followers of different nation-
> alities, one of the white, the other of the Negro race—these

must rank among the outstanding functions associated with His visit to the community of the American believers, functions designed to pave the way for the erection of their central House of Worship, to fortify them against the tests they were soon to endure, to cement their unity, and to bless the beginnings of that Administrative Order which they were soon to initiate and champion.[17]

The processes set in motion by 'Abdu'l-Bahá were nurtured by the guidance contained in the letters of Shoghi Effendi, and received impetus from the establishment of embryonic Spiritual Assemblies. The role of these administrative institutions in the systematic expansion of the Bahá'í Faith throughout the world has been described in an earlier chapter. In this chapter, the focus of the discussion is the role of Spiritual Assemblies and their subsidiary institutions as vehicles for the promotion of the practice of Bahá'í teachings and values within the Bahá'í community. First, however, it is necessary to consider the basic organizing principle of social organization.

THE ONENESS OF HUMANKIND—
THE ORGANIZING PRINCIPLE

The Bahá'í conception of the oneness of humanity might well be considered as the organizing principle of social organization. Indeed, the concept of social and economic development is enshrined in the sacred literature of the Bahá'í Faith. Writing on this theme, the Universal House of Justice states:

> From the beginning of His stupendous mission, Bahá'u'lláh urged upon the attention of nations the necessity of ordering human affairs in such a way as to bring into being a world unified in all the essential aspects of its life. In unnumbered verses

and tablets He repeatedly and variously declared the "progress of the world" and the "development of nations" as being among the ordinances of God for this day. The oneness of mankind, which is at once the operating principle and ultimate goal of His Revelation, implies the achievement of a dynamic coherence between the spiritual and practical requirements of life on earth. The indispensability of this coherence is unmistakably illustrated in His ordination of the Mashriqu'l-Adhkár, the spiritual centre of every Bahá'í community round which must flourish dependencies dedicated to the social, humanitarian, educational and scientific advancement of mankind.[18]

Commenting on the implications of this "pivotal principle" of Bahá'u'lláh's revelation for Bahá'í community life and for the responsibilities of Spiritual Assemblies, the Universal House of Justice writes:

Unity of mankind is the pivotal principle of His Revelation; Bahá'í communities must therefore become renowned for their demonstration of this unity. In a world becoming daily more divided by factionalism and group interests, the Bahá'í community must be distinguished by the concord and harmony of its relationships. The coming of age of the human race must be foreshadowed by the mature, responsible understanding of human problems and the wise administration of their affairs by these same Bahá'í communities. The practice and development of such Bahá'í characteristics are the responsibility alike of individual Bahá'ís and administrative institutions, although the greatest opportunity to foster their growth rests with the Local Spiritual Assemblies.

The divinely ordained institution of the Local Spiritual Assembly operates at the first levels of human society and is the basic administrative unit of Bahá'u'lláh's World Order. It is concerned with individuals and families whom it must constantly encourage to unite in a distinctive Bahá'í society, vitalized and guarded by the laws, ordinances and principles of Bahá'u'lláh's Revelation. It protects the Cause of God; it acts as the loving shepherd of the Bahá'í flock.[19]

THE ROLE OF SPIRITUAL ASSEMBLIES

From the earliest years of his ministry, Shoghi Effendi called attention to the significant role to be played by Spiritual Assemblies working in collaboration with the members of the American Bahá'í community in demonstrating the efficacy of the teachings of the Bahá'í Faith, and thereby setting in motion processes that would have a positive impact on the course of future civilization. The elements critical to this collaborative enterprise are set out in the following extract from a letter addressed to the Local Spiritual Assembly of New York in 1923. Shoghi Effendi writes:

> May the combined and enlightened efforts of the friends in New York, assisted by the vigilant care and the energetic direction of the servants of the Cause, the members of the Spiritual Assembly, and inspired by the undying example of our Master's life, make of that metropolis of the New World a model City, exemplifying to the East and to the West not only the principles of spiritual administration and progress, but also the beauty and power of the lives of its Bahá'í citizens.[20]

Shoghi Effendi helped the Bahá'ís to understand that participation in Bahá'í community life served as a "testing ground for the application of those ideals and standards that are the distinguishing features of the Revelation of Bahá'u'lláh."[21] He calls attention to the transforming power of exemplary behavior manifested by a small group of people, who are dedicated to high ideals, on social evolution:

> May the assembled believers—now but a tiny nucleus of the Bahá'í Commonwealth of the future—so exemplify that spirit of universal love and fellowship as to evoke in the minds of their associates the vision of that future City of God which the almighty arm of Bahá'u'lláh can alone establish.
>
> Not by merely imitating the excesses and laxity of the extravagant age they live in; not by the idle neglect of the sacred responsibilities it is their privilege to shoulder; not by the silent compromise of the principles dearly cherished by 'Abdu'l-Bahá; not by their fear of unpopularity or their dread of censure can they hope to rouse society from its spiritual lethargy, and serve as a model to a civilization the foundations of which the corrosion of prejudice has well-nigh undermined. By the sublimity of their principles, the warmth of their love, the spotless purity of their character, and the depth of their devoutness and piety, let them demonstrate to their fellow-countrymen the ennobling reality of a power that shall weld a disrupted world.[22]

To translate this visionary statement into a practical reality calls for specific actions that set in motion and, indeed, potentially magnify the processes of social change. Writing on his behalf, the Guardian's secretary not only emphasizes the importance of the individual member's active involvement in both the teaching and administrative fields of Bahá'í activity, but also stresses the importance of the Bahá'í community as a "laboratory" that provides the individual with opportunities to develop the skills and qualities necessary for effective service to the needs of the Cause. The letter offers the following guidance:

His brotherly advice to you, and to all loyal and ardent young believers like you, is that you should deepen your knowledge of the history and of the tenets of the Faith, not merely by means of careful and thorough study, but also through active, whole-hearted and continued participation in all the activities, whether administrative or otherwise, of your community. The Bahá'í community life provides you with an indispensable laboratory, where you can translate into living and constructive action the principles which you imbibe from the Teachings. By becoming a real part of that living organism you can catch the real spirit which runs throughout the Bahá'í Teachings. To study the principles, and to try to live according to them, are, therefore, the two essential mediums through which you can ensure the development and progress of your inner spiritual life and of your outer existence as well.[23]

The functions assigned to the Spiritual Assemblies in the writings of the religion are designed to foster the organic development of the Bahá'í community and to enhance its potential for healing the ills of society. In a letter written in March 1923, Shoghi Effendi sets out some of "the most outstanding obligations of the members of every Spiritual Assembly."[24] The functions pertain to the preservation of the unity of the community, engagement in humanitarian activities, the fostering of education, the provision of Bahá'í literature, the development of a Bahá'í identity through increasing communication with coreligionists throughout the world and through encouraging participation in activities that foster the spiritual, social, and intellectual aspects of Bahá'í community life. Addressing the members of the Assemblies, the letter states:

It is incumbent upon them to be vigilant and cautious, discreet and watchful, and protect at all times the Temple of the Cause from the dart of the mischief-maker and the onslaught of the enemy.

They must endeavor to promote amity and concord amongst the friends, efface every lingering trace of distrust, coolness and estrangement from every heart, and secure in its stead an active and whole-hearted cooperation for the service of the Cause.

They must do their utmost to extend at all times the helping hand to the poor, the sick, the disabled, the orphan, the widow, irrespective of color, caste and creed.

They must promote by every means in their power the material as well as the spiritual enlightenment of youth, the means for the education of children, institute, whenever possible, Bahá'í educational institutions, organize and supervise their work and provide the best means for their progress and development.

They must make an effort to maintain official, regular, and frequent correspondence with the various Bahá'í centers throughout the world, report to them their activities, and share the glad-tidings they receive with all their fellow-workers in the Cause.

They must encourage and stimulate by every means at their command, through subscription, reports and articles, the development of the various Bahá'í magazines, such as the "Star of the West" and the "Magazine of the Children of the Kingdom" in the United States of America. . . .

They must undertake the arrangement of the regular meetings of the friends, the feasts and the anniversaries, as well as the special gatherings designed to serve and promote the social, intellectual and spiritual interests of their fellow-men.

They must supervise in these days when the Cause is still in its infancy all Bahá'í publications and translations, and provide in general for a dignified and accurate presentation of all Bahá'í literature and its distribution to the general public.[25]

The functions of Spiritual Assemblies outlined by Shoghi Effendi are wide-ranging, and clearly appear to anticipate the maturation of these institutions and the availability of vastly increased human resources. Nevertheless, consistent with the evolutionary nature of development, Shoghi Effendi called for the progressive implementation of these functions. Clearly aware that the ability of the Assemblies to undertake these functions was dependent on the strength and level of functioning of the community, he instructed the Assemblies to begin to implement their prescribed duties. To give impetus to this process, and as a means of augmenting the level of administrative competence, the Guardian called for the appointment of committees to carry out aspects of the Assembly's work. "In whatever locality the Cause has sufficiently expanded," he writes, "and in order to insure efficiency and avoid confusion, each of these manifold functions will have to be referred to a special Committee, responsible to that Assembly, elected by it from among the friends in that locality, and upon whose work the Assembly will have to exercise constant and general supervision."[26]

The concluding sections of this chapter illustrate some of the actions taken by the American Spiritual Assemblies and their appointed agencies and committees to foster the processes of civilization building through the initiation of activities and programs designed to enhance the spiritual, social, and intellectual development of the members of the community. These actions not only implement the guidance of Shoghi Effendi but they are also a conscious extension of the seminal processes set in motion by 'Abdu'l-Bahá. Three specific examples are examined—systematic efforts to embed the practice of the Bahá'í Nineteen Day Feast in the life of the community; initiatives to diversify the membership of the Bahá'í community; and a range of educational programs designed to meet the needs of various sectors of the membership.

THE NINETEEN DAY FEAST

Each of the great religions of the world and the civilizations to which they gave rise has had its own unique calendar, including among others, the Jewish calendar, the Gregorian calendar (currently in use throughout much of the world), and the Muslim calendar. A calendar is not only a way of dating events and reckoning time for the practical operation of society—for defining the day of rest and giving focus to commercial and agricultural activities, etc.—but it is also linked to the determination of the timing of events of significance for the religion. The religious calendar is of great importance to the community of believers. It specifies the time of worship, stipulates the date for the beginning of the New Year, defines the period of fasting, and sets the order of the holy days and festivals, which are frequently allied with events associated with the life of the Founder and the history of the community. It also gives the community a sense of perspective in relation to both the past and the future.

The Bahá'í Faith uses a calendar that was established by the Báb, and confirmed by Bahá'u'lláh. Its calendar dates the Bahá'í Era from the Declaration of the Báb in 1844. The calendar specifies the timing of New Year's Day and the length and number of the months, as well as listing the schedule of Bahá'í anniversaries and annual feasts. While these occasions are typically linked to significant events in the life of the Founders, some, like the twelve-day Feast of Riḍván, also have important administrative implications. The Feast of Riḍván serves not only as a commemoration of the time period in which Bahá'u'lláh declared His mission, but is also the designated period for the annual election of Spiritual Assemblies.[27]

In the Bahá'í calendar, the first day of the year coincides with the spring equinox in the northern hemisphere, which usually occurs on 21 March. The year is divided into nineteen months of nineteen days each, with the addition of four intercalary days (five in a leap year). Each day is deemed to start at sunset. A Nineteen Day Feast is normally held on the first day of each Bahá'í month. Each month bears the name of one of the attributes of God.

The Nineteen Day Feast is the centerpiece of Bahá'í community life. From the very beginning of the religion, the Báb called upon His followers to gather together once every nineteen days to show hospitality and fellowship. Likewise, in the Most Holy Book, Bahá'u'lláh stresses the unifying role of such gatherings. The concept of the Feast has evolved in accord with the progressive development of the Faith. Thus the Universal House of Justice affirms:

At its earliest stage in Iran, the individual friends, in response to Bahá'u'lláh's injunctions, hosted gatherings in their homes to show hospitality once every nineteen days and derived inspiration from the reading and discussion of the Teachings. As the community grew, 'Abdu'l-Bahá delineated and emphasized the devotional and social character of the event. After the establishment of Local Spiritual Assemblies, Shoghi Effendi introduced the administrative portion and acquainted the community with the idea of the Nineteen Day Feast as an institution. It was as if a symphony, in three movements, had now been completed.[28]

THE EXAMPLE OF 'ABDU'L-BAHÁ

'Abdu'l-Bahá fostered the development of the Feast through the guidance contained in the tablets he addressed to the members of the Bahá'í community. He explained its significance and the transforming power of such gatherings, and he expressed his joy and happiness when the believers made a systematic effort to hold the Feast on a regular basis. In addition, "the symbolic Feast"[29] that 'Abdu'l-Bahá offered to his American followers in West Englewood left an indelible impression on the minds of those who were privileged to attend. Mirzá Maḥmúd, the diarist who accompanied 'Abdu'l-Bahá on his travels to the West, left an illuminating account of this historic gathering which took place on 29 June 1912 in the vicinity of the Wilhelm home in New Jersey. He indicated that 'Abdu'l-Bahá had invited the Bahá'ís and their friends in New York to attend this Unity Feast in New Jersey. He described what transpired:

> . . . the friends began to arrive from the surrounding areas and gathered on the lawn adjoining the house. The meeting was arranged in a circle under the trees, with almost two hundred people seated at table and being served by the Bahá'ís. Everyone enjoyed the delicacies and was extremely happy.
>
> The green lawn under the shady trees was strewn with flowers so that it seemed as if an embroidered carpet had been spread. . . . To see the Master walking in this green flower-covered garden, with a gentle breeze blowing, the purity of the air, the cleanliness of the surroundings and the rejoicing of the friends, was most pleasing; all seemed to vie with one another to please the Master.[30]

According to Maḥmúd, 'Abdu'l-Bahá entered the circle and began to address the gathering. He spoke about the greatness of the Cause and the importance of the meetings of the friends. Commenting on the significance and uniqueness of the occasion, he stated: "Such gatherings as this have no equal or likeness in the world of mankind, where people are drawn together by physical motives of furtherance of materials interests, for this meeting is a prototype of that inner and complete spiritual association in the eternal world of being." Elaborating on this theme, 'Abdu'l-Bahá affirmed: "True Bahá'í meetings are the mirrors of the Kingdom wherein images of the Supreme Concourse are reflected."[31]

'Abdu'l-Bahá proceeded to explain that those individuals who were privileged to hear of the teachings of the new day were called upon "to uplift the cause of unity among the nations of the earth," and he outlined specific actions that needed to be taken in order to fulfill this heavy responsibility. The actions he described were profoundly spiritual and calculated to radically transform individual behavior and social relations and, indeed, to set in train the necessary community building processes that would ultimately lead to the rise of a new, highly refined kind of civilization. Thus He instructed the assembled friends:

> First, you must become united and agreed among yourselves. You must be exceedingly kind and loving toward each other, willing to forfeit life in the pathway of another's happiness. You must be ready to sacrifice your possessions in another's behalf. The rich among you must show compassion toward the poor, and the well-to-do must look after those in distress. . . . Your utmost desire must be to confer happiness upon each other. Each one must be the servant of the others, thoughtful of their comfort and welfare. In the path of God one must forget himself entirely. He must not consider his own pleasure but seek the pleasure of others. He must not desire glory nor gifts of bounty

for himself but seek these gifts and blessings for his brothers and sisters. It is my hope that you may become like this, that you may attain to the supreme bestowal and be imbued with such spiritual qualities as to forget yourselves entirely and with heart and soul offer yourselves as sacrifices for the Blessed Perfection. You should have neither will nor desire of your own but seek everything for the beloved of God and live together in complete love and fellowship. May the favors of Bahá'u'lláh surround you from all directions. This is the greatest bestowal and supreme bounty. These are the infinite favors of God.[32]

After the talk, 'Abdu'l-Bahá strolled in the rose garden, and a number of photographs were taken. Later in the afternoon, when the friends were seated at the table, 'Abdu'l-Bahá anointed each one with attar of roses, a highly perfumed fragrance. Reflecting on the significance of the Master's action, Maḥmúd writes: "He thus made them the anointed of the Court of Servitude and the recipients of the spirit of devotion to the Threshold of God, for the bounties of the Holy Spirit had descended and the favors of God encompassed all." And, he characterized the reaction of those who were fortunate to be present at this historic gathering, a meeting which 'Abdu'l-Bahá, himself, described in his talk as a "prototype":[33]

That the friends were ecstatic today need not be stated, since their Host was the Beloved of the Covenant, their meeting was an assembly of love and amity, and the surroundings were green and verdant with trees in full bloom perfuming the air. There was a pilaf, a very delicious Persian dish that had been prepared for the occasion, sherbet, a Persian drink and many sweets. Everyone was happy at the unity of the gathering.[34]

Maḥmúd concludes his account of the Unity Feast by summarizing 'Abdu'l-Bahá's own evaluation of the significance of the event. He paraphrases the words of the Master thus: "This meeting will be productive of great results. It will be the cause of attracting a new bounty. This day in which we have come together is a new day, and this hour a new hour. These meetings will be mentioned in the future and their results will be everlasting in all the divine worlds."[35]

Both 'Abdu'l-Bahá and Shoghi Effendi gradually disclosed the institutional significance of the Nineteen Day Feast. While 'Abdu'l-Bahá emphasized the importance of its spiritual and devotional character, Shoghi Effendi not only elaborated the devotional and social aspects of the Feast, but he also developed the administrative element of these gatherings, and encouraged the Bahá'ís and their elected Spiritual Assemblies to establish the Feast within their communities.

ESTABLISHING THE INSTITUTION
OF THE NINETEEN DAY FEAST

The World Order of Bahá'u'lláh integrates the spiritual, administrative, and social aspects of life, and its institutions serve as vehicles for promoting these critical elements in the life of the community and for laying the foundations of a new civilization. The institution of the Nineteen Day Feast, operating at the very base of society—in villages, towns, and cities—is described by Shoghi Effendi as "the foundation of the new World Order."[36] Through actively and strategically giving attention to the spiritual, social, and administrative elements of individual and community life, the Nineteen Day Feast is the ideal medium for promoting unity, for enhancing a sense of Bahá'í identity and an awareness of the civic responsibilities associated with membership in society, for strengthening the democratic aspects of governance, and for stimulating progress.

Traditional worship services held in churches, synagogues, and mosques, are conducted by a member of the clergy. In contrast, the Bahá'í Nineteen Day Feast may be held in a variety of locations, including in a private home and out of doors; and the gathering is presided over by an elected member, usually the chairperson, of the Local Spiritual Assembly. Open to children and adults, the Nineteen Day Feast is the regular meeting that promotes and reinforces the unity of the local Bahá'í community. The term "Feast" is used purely in a symbolic way. The simple refreshments that are served represent an outward symbol of the spiritual bond existing between the members of the community. Noting that "the Feast is rooted in hospitality, with all its implications of friendliness, courtesy, service, generosity and conviviality," the Universal House of Justice comments on the society-building implications of the Feast:

> The very idea of hospitality as the sustaining spirit of so significant an institution introduces a revolutionary new attitude to the conduct of human affairs at all levels, an attitude which is critical to that world unity which the Central Figures of our Faith labored so long and suffered so much cruelty to bring into being.[37]

The program of the Feast has three distinct parts that are interrelated—the devotional, the administrative, and the social. It is nevertheless flexible and may be adapted to a variety of cultural and social settings. The three components of the Feast have been described as follows:

> The first entails the recitation of prayers and reading from the Holy Texts. The second is a general meeting where the Local Spiritual Assembly reports its activities, plans and problems

to the community, shares news and messages from the World Centre and the National Assembly, and receives the thoughts and recommendations of the friends through a process of consultation. The third involves the partaking of refreshments and engaging in other activities meant to foster fellowship in a culturally determined diversity of forms which do not violate principles of the Faith or the essential character of the Feast.[38]

As previously mentioned, the Bahá'í Faith has no class of professional clergy, such as rabbis, ministers, priests, and mullahs to lead the community and conduct worship services. The Bahá'í community is administered by democratically elected councils or Spiritual Assemblies. The functions of these bodies and their appointed committees include arranging the Nineteen Day Feast. Shoghi Effendi called for the systematic institution of the Feast in the heart of the Bahá'í community. So important was this activity, that he characterized it as one of the critical factors promoting the development and consolidation of the Administrative Order. To stimulate this process, he encouraged the embryonic Spiritual Assemblies to hold the Nineteen Day Feast in their local areas on a regular basis, and he counseled them to give special attention to the administrative component of the Feast. In the absence of a clerical class and in a community whose direction and organization depended on the active participation of the individual members, Shoghi Effendi gave attention to educating the Bahá'ís concerning the potential of the Feast to serve as an important training ground for the members of the Bahá'í community in the principles and methods of Bahá'í administration.

As part of this educational process, Shoghi Effendi in his letters explained in detail the purpose of the administrative component of the Feast. He highlighted the responsibilities and function of the individual and the Spiritual Assembly and described the way in which the Feast was not only the basis of Bahá'í community life in the local area but also served as a link with all levels of the Bahá'í administrative structure.

Central to the operation of the Bahá'í Administrative Order is the process of consultation, a process of collaborative decision-making, involving all members of the community. The Nineteen Day Feast is the occasion when the Spiritual Assembly makes its reports to the community and invites discussion of plans and suggestions for new and better methods of service. The consultative or administrative period of the Feast not only provides the opportunity for individuals to gain experience in the practice of the necessary spiritual qualities, the intellectual and administrative skills associated with consultation, but it also constitutes "a vital medium for maintaining close and continued contact between the believers themselves, and also between them and the body of their elected representatives in the local community."[39]

Beyond the acquisition of personal skills, the Nineteen Day Feast provides a dynamic setting in which its participants learn "the essentials of responsible citizenship." Thus the Feast has been described as "an arena of democracy at the very root of society, where the Local Spiritual Assembly and the members of the community meet on common ground, where individuals are free to offer their gifts of thought, whether as new ideas or constructive criticism, to the building processes of an advancing civilization."[40]

THE NURTURING ROLE OF THE
NATIONAL SPIRITUAL ASSEMBLY

To assist the Local Spiritual Assemblies to understand the need to establish the Nineteen Day Feast in their local area, and to ensure that the Bahá'ís understood their responsibility in relation to learning the art of consultation, the National Spiritual Assembly of the United States and Canada took a number of important initiatives. In assessing the state of the American Bahá'í community in 1934, the National Assembly identified the need to develop the Nineteen Day Feast as one of the areas of community functioning requiring special attention. The extent of the reorientation of individual understanding and of the change in behavior required is illustrated in the following excerpt from the Assembly's report:

> The basis and foundation of collective Bahá'í progress and achievement is right use of the universal principle of consultation. Let us banish all personal limitations in our Bahá'í consultation, all griefs, suspicions and fears, all dependence upon personal influence, and frankly and whole-heartedly participate in those general discussions devoted to purely Bahá'í ends. It is a pity that here and there the Nineteen Day Feast is not yet appreciated, but some of the friends appear still to feel that conversation in a little, intimate group is more interesting and important than those general meetings held for the entire community.[41]

To give an extra impetus to the process of change and to encourage attendance at the Feast, the National Spiritual Assembly decided to send its individual members to meet with the Local Spiritual Assemblies. In preparation for these gatherings, the National Assembly adopted a list of topics to be discussed in the meetings with the local Assemblies. One of the subject for discussion was "How are the Nineteen Day Feasts carried on and are they attended by all members of the community?" In addition, the National Spiritual Assembly appointed a special committee to prepare "a form of Bahá'í parliamentary procedure for use by local Assemblies in conducting their own meetings and also the Nineteen Day Feast . . ."[42] This document was later adopted by the National Spiritual Assembly of the United States and Canada and is published in *The Bahá'í World*, vol. VI. It describes, among other things, the approach to Bahá'í consultation, sets out the functions of the Local Spiritual Assembly, and the procedures for the conduct of Assembly meetings and for the Assembly's consultation with the community. In relation to the latter the document states:

> The institution of the Nineteen Day Feast provides the recognized and regular occasion for general consultation on the part of the community, and for consultation between the Spiritual Assembly and the members of the community. The conduct of the period of consultation at the Nineteen Day Feast is a vital function of each Spiritual Assembly.[43]

To ensure the smooth and efficient functioning of the administrative period of the Feast, the document sets out the order of business—the reports made by the Assembly and its committees to the community concerning matters that concern the Faith, a general consultation on these reports, and the offering of recommendations and suggestions by individual members to the Assembly. Summarizing the importance and tone of this period of consultation, and its inherently spiritual nature, the document states: "Upon each member of the community lies the obligation to make his or her utmost contribution to the consultation, the ideal being a gathering of Bahá'ís inspired with one spirit and concentrating upon the one aim to further the interests of the Faith."[44]

Through the example of 'Abdu'l-Bahá, the patient guidance of Shoghi Effendi, and the careful monitoring by the National Spiritual Assembly of the United States and Canada, the institution of the Nineteen Day Feast was gradually embedded in the heart of each local area. With greater understanding of the significance of this institution, the American Bahá'ís made a concerted and more conscious effort to acquire the spiritual qualities and administrative skills necessary to promote social cohesion and fellowship. They also gained a deeper sense of belonging to the Bahá'í community and a keener sense of personal responsibility for working to ensure the progress of the Bahá'í Faith. The systematic development of the Nineteen Day Feast, not only illustrated the application of society-building processes aimed at the development of the spiritual, administrative, and social aspects of life within the Bahá'í community, but it might also be said that these same processes are essential to laying the foundations of a future world civilization.

THE INSTITUTION OF THE BAHÁ'Í SUMMER SCHOOL

The future world commonwealth, which represents the fruition of the evolving Bahá'í Administrative Order, is destined to witness the coming of age of, and the unification of, the whole of humankind, and to provide an unprecedented stimulus to "the intellectual, the moral and spiritual life of the entire human race."[45] Shoghi Effendi links the establishment of the Bahá'í summer school to this evolutionary process. He describes the wide-ranging educational purpose of this institution and highlights the unique contribution of the American Bahá'í community to its unfoldment. He writes:

> Equally important as a factor in the evolution of the Administrative Order has been the remarkable progress achieved, particularly in the United States of America, by the institution of the summer schools designed to foster the spirit of fellowship in a distinctly Bahá'í atmosphere, to afford the necessary training for Bahá'í teachers, and to provide facilities for the study of the history and teachings of the Faith, and for a better understanding of its relation to other religions and to human society in general.[46]

GREEN ACRE BAHÁ'Í SCHOOL

One of the first Bahá'í summer schools in the Western Hemisphere was established at Green Acre, in the eastern United States in Maine. Initially established as a forum for free thinkers, Green Acre served as a center for the open discussion of and experimentation with new ideas in the realms of science, religion, and the arts. Its founder was Miss Sarah Jane Farmer, who in later years became a member of the Bahá'í Faith, and thereafter progressively attempted to imbue the program with more of a focus on the teachings and history of the religion.[47]

'Abdu'l-Bahá visited and spoke at Green Acre during his travels in the West in 1912. He spent time with the aged and fragile Miss Farmer. He counseled and encouraged her, and inspired her with his vision for the future of Green Acre. An account of this historic visit and details of the events that transpired have been recorded elsewhere.[48] His talks were delivered to large audiences, which included people from a wide range of backgrounds and areas of interest. His presentations provided innovative contexts within which to consider themes of interest to his listeners, and served as bridges to introduce the audience to Bahá'í conceptions of education and human development and the study of reality. In relation to the search for truth, for example, 'Abdu'l-Bahá in one of his talks offered the following advice:

> Every subject presented to a thoughtful audience must be supported by rational proofs and logical arguments. Proofs are of four kinds: first, through sense perception; second, through the reasoning faculty; third, from tradition or scriptural authority; fourth, through the medium of inspiration. That is to say, there are four criteria or standards of judgment by which the human mind reaches its conclusions.[49]

He then proceeded to demonstrate the potential limitations inherent in each of these criteria, and systematically illustrated his thesis by applying the criteria to a discussion of love.

Beyond providing standards for intellectual activity, 'Abdu'l-Bahá also called attention to the importance of the atmosphere in which such activity was carried out. For example, commenting on the physical beauty of Green Acre and the comparative lack of attention to the spiritual, he conveyed his desire that "a spiritual charm may surround and halo it; then its beauty will be perfect." In yet another talk, anticipating the great future in store for Green Acre, he expressed the hope that this institution would provide a living example of the beneficial interaction among the spiritual, intellectual, and social aspects of life. Thus: "Are you all well and happy? This is a delightful spot; the scenery is beautiful, and the atmosphere of spirituality haloes everything. In the future, God willing, Green Acre shall become a great center, the cause of the unity of the world of humanity, the cause of uniting hearts and binding together the East and the West. This is my hope."[50] 'Abdu'l-Bahá's address then sets out in detail the Bahá'í perspective on one of the pressing issues of contemporary society, the oneness of humankind. He states:

> I wish to speak upon the oneness of the world of humanity. This is one of the important subjects of the present period. If the oneness of the human world were established, all the differences which separate mankind would be eradicated. Strife and warfare would cease, and the world of humanity would find repose. Universal peace would be promoted, and the East and West would be conjoined in a strong bond. All men would be sheltered beneath one tabernacle. Native lands would become one; races and religions would be unified. The people of the

world would live together in harmony, and their well-being would be assured.[51]

'Abdu'l-Bahá's historic visit to Green Acre focused special attention on the intellectual development of Bahá'í community life and underlined the creative interaction between intellectual and spiritual development and their potential implications for the processes of social and community development. This triple emphasis on spiritual, intellectual, and social development is reflected and consciously amplified in the operation of the institution of the Bahá'í summer school.

THE ROLE OF SUMMER SCHOOLS

As the American Bahá'í community continued to attract new members, the Spiritual Assemblies were confronted with an urgent need to find ways to increase the new believers' understanding of and sense of commitment to the religion they had embraced. Highlighting the importance of education, Shoghi Effendi indicated that "Bahá'u'lláh considered education as one of the most fundamental factors of a true civilization." Elaborating on this theme, the Guardian cautions that "in order to be adequate and fruitful," education "should be comprehensive in nature and should take into consideration not only the physical and the intellectual side of man but also his spiritual and ethical aspects."[52]

As part of their religious duty, Bahá'ís are called upon to take individual responsibility to study the Bahá'í teachings and to become familiar with the writings of the Faith. To assist the members of the local Bahá'í community, Spiritual Assemblies frequently arrange study classes and other programs, which are conducted by knowledgeable Bahá'ís. However, the Bahá'í community has no category of professional ministers or fulltime paid teachers. Therefore, to hasten the process of deepening, Shoghi Effendi called attention to the important role Bahá'í summer schools might play in educating the Bahá'í community, indicating that they can be "of the greatest help to the friends, new and old Bahá'ís alike, for in them they can study, and enjoy the feeling of Bahá'í companionship."[53] Beyond the potential benefit to the individual, Shoghi Effendi regarded attendance at these schools as a means of ensuring the steady development of the American Bahá'í community, of raising its level of understanding of the message of Bahá'u'lláh, and increasing both its human and administrative resources and its social cohesion. He therefore encouraged the Bahá'ís, acting under the leadership of their National Spiritual Assembly and its committees, to give attention to the establishment of Bahá'í summer schools.

To generate interest in these gatherings, Shoghi Effendi explained their overall purposes and the advantages that accrued from participating in these activities. He made specific suggestions about the content of the programs, suggestions that took into consideration the changing needs of the evolving Bahá'í community. He suggested different approaches to study, and continually called for the upgrading of the courses. He described the potential spiritual and social benefits that Bahá'ís and individuals who are investigating the Bahá'í Faith might derive from being immersed in a distinctive Bahá'í atmosphere. A letter written on behalf of Shoghi Effendi by his secretary to a member of a committee charged with the organization of a summer school, spells out the capacity of the summer school to demonstrate the Faith in action. We read:

> He hopes your Committee will continue to endeavour in raising the standard, both intellectual and spiritual, of the school, and make it an attractive centre not only to the believers but especially to non-Bahá'ís. It is, indeed, the teaching value of the

school which you should particularly emphasize. The courses, lectures and general activities conducted by the friends should be arranged in such a way as to attract the attention of the outside public to the Cause. The Summer School is a high occasion for teaching the Message.

Through daily association with the believers, non-Bahá'ís will come to see the Cause functioning as an active and living community entirely dedicated to the service of what is best and highest in the world. The lectures will familiarize them with the principles underlying the New World Order, while their participation in the social life of the believers will enable them to see the way in which these very same principles are put into operation.[54]

Although Bahá'ís had participated in the programs at Green Acre from the early days of the Bahá'í Faith in North America, it was not until 1929 that Green Acre was formally recognized as a Bahá'í educational institution. In addition, two other schools were established at Geyserville, in California in 1927, and at the Louhelen Ranch, near Davison, in Michigan in 1931. Commenting on the significance of the wide-ranging program initiatives taken by "these three embryonic Bahá'í educational institutions," Shoghi Effendi affirmed that they "set an example worthy of emulation by other Bahá'í communities in both the East and the West."[55] Elaborating on this theme, he writes:

Through the intensive study of Bahá'í Scriptures and of the early history of the Faith; through the organization of courses on the teachings and history of Islam; through conferences for the promotion of inter-racial amity; through laboratory courses designed to familiarize the participants with the processes of the Bahá'í Administrative Order; through special sessions devoted to Youth and child training; through classes in public speaking; through lectures on Comparative Religion; through group discussion on the manifold aspects of the Faith; through the establishment of libraries; through teaching classes; through courses on Bahá'í ethics and on Latin America; through the introduction of winter school sessions; through forums and devotional gatherings; through plays and pageants; through picnics and other recreational activities, these schools, open to Bahá'ís and non-Bahá'ís alike, have set so noble an example as to inspire other Bahá'í communities in Persia, in the British Isles, in Germany, in Australia, in New Zealand, in India, in Iraq and in Egypt to undertake the initial measures designed to enable them to build along the same lines institutions that bid fair to evolve into the Bahá'í universities of the future.[56]

It is evident that the breadth of these programs, which were open to all without discrimination, and directed at the spiritual, intellectual, artistic, and social aspects of life, differs dramatically from the formal academic courses traditionally offered in schools of theology and religious studies. In addition to providing a setting in which participants gain intellectual and spiritual knowledge, the Bahá'í summer school serves as a "laboratory" in which to practice and experience a new way of life!

The establishment of Bahá'í summer schools has been a gradual process, reflecting the needs of a steadily growing and diversifying membership. Likewise the programs offered evolve and are designed to meet the particular stage of development of the community. Hence when the committees appointed by the National Spiritual Assembly to organize the programs for the Bahá'í summer schools sought the guidance of Shoghi Effendi, the advice he offered set the priorities for immediate action. For example, at the earliest stage, when the greatest need was for the members of the community to gain a more systematic understanding of the Faith, its history, and its administrative structure as a means of raising the vision of the community, he advised concentration "on *The Dawn-Breakers* as well as on the needs, the principles and the purpose of Bahá'í Administration." His advice was based on the assessment of the priority needs of the American Bahá'í community: "The Cause in your land is still in its formative period. It needs men and women of vision, of capacity and understanding."[57] Writing on his behalf in 1934, Shoghi Effendi's secretary conveyed his advice concerning the importance of understanding the connection between the Administrative Order and the expansion of the Faith:

> He feels that in your next summer meetings continued emphasis should be laid upon the teaching of the administration, especially in its relation to the outside world, so as to impress the non-Bahá'í attendants at the School with the nature, character and world significance of the World Order of Bahá'u'lláh. The teaching of the Administration should, indeed, be considered as forming a permanent and vital feature of every Bahá'í summer school. For upon its thorough and intelligent understanding by the entire community of the believers must inevitably depend the effectiveness and continued expansion of Bahá'í activities throughout the world.[58]

At a later period, when the North American Bahá'í community was embarking on the First Seven Year Plan, designed to expand the Bahá'í Faith in Central and South America and to lay the foundations of its administrative structure throughout the Americas, Shoghi Effendi addressed a weighty letter to the American Bahá'ís.[59] The letter called for the acquisition of certain qualities and virtues that were needed to enable them to fulfill their spiritual destiny—a destiny that was not only linked to the systematic spread of the Faith, but also to the emergence of a community capable of laying the foundations of a future civilization. The members of the American Bahá'í community were challenged to make a concerted effort to rise above the prevailing prejudices, the corruption, and the decadence of the society in which they lived, and to demonstrate a high standard of ethical and moral behavior. Shoghi Effendi specified that the cultivation of these spiritual qualities was essential to the successful completion of the Plan, as well as to the regeneration of the Bahá'í community and the redemption of the society at large. Highlighting the importance of the "preeminent and vital" qualities to which the Bahá'í community must aspire, the Guardian writes:

Of these spiritual prerequisites of success, which constitute the bedrock on which the security of all teaching plans, Temple projects, and financial schemes, must ultimately rest, the following stand out as preeminent and vital, which the members of the American Bahá'í community will do well to ponder. Upon the extent to which these basic requirements are met, and the manner in which the American believers fulfill them in their individual lives, administrative activities, and social relationships, must depend the measure of the manifold blessings which the All-Bountiful Possessor can vouchsafe to them all. These requirements are none other than a high sense of moral rectitude in their social and administrative activities, absolute chastity in their individual lives, and complete freedom from prejudice in their dealings with peoples of a different race, class, creed, or color.[60]

While all Bahá'ís are called upon to uphold these high moral standards, Shoghi Effendi indicates that "a high sense of moral rectitude" has specific, but not exclusive relevance to the conduct of the elected members of the Bahá'í administrative bodies. Likewise, a chaste and holy life is "mainly and directly concerned with the Bahá'í youth." However, the exhortation to free oneself from forms of prejudice, applies equally to all members of the Faith. Shoghi Effendi states, that freedom from prejudice

> . . . should be the immediate, the universal, and the chief concern of all and sundry members of the Bahá'í community, of whatever age, rank, experience, class, or color, as all, with no exception, must face its challenging implications, and none can claim, however much he may have progressed along this line, to have completely discharged the stern responsibilities which it inculcates.[61]

Stressing the pernicious and destructive influence of racial prejudice on society, and especially on American society, Shoghi Effendi directed that "Freedom from racial prejudice, in any of its forms, should . . . be adopted as the watchword of the entire body of the American believers." To make concrete the extent of the effort required by the believers in confronting the need to overcome prejudice in their personal lives, he calls for the deliberate cultivation of this important Bahá'í principle, specifying that freedom from race prejudice "should be consistently demonstrated in every phase of their activity and life, whether in the Bahá'í community or outside it, in public or in private, formally as well as informally, individually as well as in their official capacity as organized groups, committees and Assemblies."[62]

Given the importance of the "spiritual prerequisites of success," and their indispensability to the attainment of the goals of the First Seven Year Plan (and indeed, all subsequent Plans), Shoghi Effendi called for the inclusion of these subjects in the programs of the Bahá'í summer schools. He also emphasized the need for the participants at the schools to exemplify in their personal lives these spiritual qualities, qualities which have such profound social implications. A letter written in May 1939 on behalf of Shoghi Effendi provided the following guidance concerning the program for the three Bahá'í summer schools in North America:

> The course on character building, . . . the Guardian feels, is particularly important and should be given due emphasis and studied carefully and thoroughly, especially by the young believers in attendance at the school. These standards of Bahá'í conduct, which he himself has set forth in his last general epistle, *The Advent of Divine Justice,* and which it should be the paramount duty of every loyal and conscientious believer to endeavour to uphold and promote, deserve serious study and meditation, and should constitute the main central theme of this year's programme at all the three Bahá'í Summer Schools in the States.
>
> Since the purpose of the Summer School is not only to impart knowledge of the Teachings, but to infuse in the hearts of all those present such spirit as will enable them to translate the ideals of the Cause into daily deeds of constructive spiritual living, it is more than fitting therefore that this year's meetings should be principally devoted to the study of Bahá'í morals, not only in their theoretical aspect, but first and foremost in their relation to the present-day needs and requirements of Bahá'í community life.
>
> The principles and methods laid down by the Guardian in his *Advent of Divine Justice* on the vital subject of Bahá'í ethics should indeed prove of valuable inspiration and guidance to all the students and friends attending the Summer School classes,

and thus prepare them to better appreciate the privileges, and more adequately discharge the responsibilities, of their citizenship in the World Order of Bahá'u'lláh.[63]

Furthermore given the increasing racial and cultural diversity of the participants at the Bahá'í summer schools, Shoghi Effendi reminded the believers that these gatherings presented an opportunity for the type of close and informal associations that can naturally and gradually begin to erode ingrained prejudice. He thus advised that freedom from racial prejudice "should be deliberately cultivated through the various and everyday opportunities, no matter how insignificant, that present themselves, whether in their homes, their business offices, their schools and colleges, their social parties and recreation grounds, their Bahá'í meetings, conferences, conventions, summer schools and Assemblies."[64]

PROGRAMS FOR RACE UNITY
AT BAHÁ'Í SUMMER SCHOOLS

The elimination of all forms of prejudice is one of the fundamental principles of the Bahá'í Faith and a critical element in a future civilization giving expression to the oneness of the human family. This spiritual and moral principle is clearly set out in the writings of Bahá'u'lláh and 'Abdu'l-Bahá. No doubt, the early American Bahá'ís were familiar with this aspect of the Bahá'í teachings. They are also likely to have gained a much deeper understanding of the significance of its application in everyday life from the example of the conduct of 'Abdu'l-Bahá while he was in their midst. During his sojourn in North America, he not only associated with people of all classes and diverse colors but also spoke in a forthright manner about the issues of race and prejudice in his public addresses. Moreover, he demonstrated the absolute Bahá'í commitment to racial equality and amity by "the exemplary act He performed by uniting in wedlock two of His followers of different nationalities, one of the white, the other of the Negro race," an action, which in the estimation of Shoghi Effendi ranks "among the outstanding functions associated with His visit to the community of the American believers." The individuals in question were Mr. Louis Gregory, an African American lawyer and Miss Louisa Mathew, a university educated English woman. Both were middle-aged. They met while on pilgrimage, and with encouragement from 'Abdu'l-Bahá, who perceived the potential of their friendship, they were married on 27 September 1912 in New York City. The marriage took place at a time when American society was wracked by intense racial prejudice, and interracial marriage was, in much of the United States, illegal. For some time the Gregorys made their home in Washington, D.C., where their marriage was legal; however, as the social pressures, both within and outside the Bahá'í community, were intense, the couple decided to engage in independent Bahá'í activities, at least for part of each year, with Mrs. Gregory spending time promoting the Bahá'í Faith in Europe and Mr. Gregory concentrating his efforts in the United States. The couple acquired a small cottage near the Green Acre Bahá'í school and happily spent the summer months together. Morrison has, in her biography of Louis Gregory, recounted the events that led up to this extraordinary and historic marriage. She describes the distinguished contribution of these two believers to the development of the Bahá'í community, in particular, Mr. Gregory's outstanding services to the cause of race unity. In addition, Morrison sets out, in a forthright manner, the difficulties experienced by the American Bahá'ís as they struggled to confront the issue of prejudice in their personal lives and within the Bahá'í community, and she describes their efforts to rise above the destructive habits and social customs of the society in which they were immersed.[65]

From the days of 'Abdu'l-Bahá, Bahá'ís have made systematic attempts to promulgate the principle of the oneness of humankind and to combat racial prejudice both within the Bahá'í community and in society at large.[66] Early in his ministry, Shoghi Effendi stressed the importance of this issue for "the future growth and prestige of the Cause." He challenged "every conscientious upholder of the universal principles of Bahá'u'lláh" to "cleanse their souls form every lingering trace of racial animosity so subversive of the Faith they profess." Elaborating on this theme Shoghi Effendi offers the following pointed guidance:

> In their relations amongst themselves as fellow-believers, let them not be content with the mere exchange of cold and empty formalities often connected with the organizing of banquets, receptions, consultative assemblies, and lecture-halls. Let them rather, as equal co-sharers in the spiritual benefits conferred upon them by Bahá'u'lláh, arise and, with the aid and counsel of their local and national representatives, supplement these official functions with those opportunities which only a close and intimate social intercourse can adequately provide. In their homes, in their hours of relaxation and leisure, in the daily contact of business transactions, in the association of their children, whether in their study-classes, their playgrounds, and club-rooms, in short under all possible circumstances, however insignificant they appear, the community of the followers of Bahá'u'lláh should satisfy themselves that in the eyes of the world at large and in the sight of their vigilant Master they are the living witnesses of those truths which He fondly cherished and tirelessly championed to the very end of His days. If we relax in our purpose, if we falter in our faith, if we neglect the varied

opportunities given us from time to time by an all-wise and gracious Master, we are not merely failing in what is our most vital and conspicuous obligation, but are thereby insensibly retarding the flow of those quickening energies which can alone insure the vigorous and speedy development of God's struggling Faith.[67]

To encourage the Bahá'ís to take constructive action, Shoghi Effendi pointed to the important role to be played by Bahá'í schools, including Green Acre, describing them as "a testing ground for the application of those ideals and standards that are the distinguishing features of the Revelation of Bahá'u'lláh." And, he expresses the hope that the friends assembled at such gatherings might "so exemplify that spirit of universal love and fellowship as to evoke in the minds of their associates the vision of that future City of God which the almighty arm of Bahá'u'lláh can alone establish."[68]

Race Unity Conferences had been held at regular intervals at the Green Acre summer school from the 1920s. These events involved Bahá'í speakers as well as prominent experts in the fields of race relations and human rights, drawn from the African American and other racial and ethnic communities. The aim of such gatherings was to foster greater awareness of the issue of race, to promote understanding of the Bahá'í perspective on this subject, and to cultivate a sense of fellowship among the participants.[69]

To give impetus to the process of change and to assist the American Bahá'ís to understand the long-term personal commitment that was required to confront and progressively overcome racial prejudice, Shoghi Effendi set out the particular responsibilities facing all sections of the Bahá'í community, both white and black alike, in overcoming this long-standing, socially destructive force. Furthermore, he highlighted the kind of behavior the members of the community should manifest in order to demonstrate freedom from prejudice, by calling attention to the inspiring example of 'Abdu'l-Bahá. He counsels the American Bahá'ís as follows:

As to racial prejudice, the corrosion of which, for well-nigh a century, has bitten into the fiber, and attacked the whole social structure of American society, it should be regarded as constituting the most vital and challenging issue confronting the Bahá'í community at the present stage of its evolution. The ceaseless exertions which this issue of paramount importance calls for, the sacrifices it must impose, the care and vigilance it demands, the moral courage and fortitude it requires, the tact and sympathy it necessitates, invest this problem, which the American believers are still far from having satisfactorily resolved, with an urgency and importance that cannot be overestimated. White and Negro, high and low, young and old, whether newly converted to the Faith or not, all who stand identified with it must participate in, and lend their assistance, each according to his or her capacity, experience, and opportunities, to the common task of fulfilling the instructions, realizing the hopes, and following the example, of 'Abdu'l-Bahá. Whether colored or non-colored, neither race has the right, or can conscientiously claim, to be regarded as absolved from such an obligation, as having realized such hopes, or having faithfully followed such an example. A long and thorny road, beset with pitfalls, still remains untraveled, both by the White and the Negro exponents of the redeeming Faith of Bahá'u'lláh. On the distance they cover, and the manner in which they travel that road, must depend, to an extent which few among them can imagine, the operation of those intangible influences which are indispensable to the spiritual triumph of the American believers and the material success of their newly launched enterprise.

Let them call to mind, fearlessly and determinedly, the example and conduct of 'Abdu'l-Bahá while in their midst. Let them remember His courage, His genuine love, His informal and indiscriminating fellowship, His contempt for and impatience of criticism, tempered by His tact and wisdom. Let them revive and perpetuate the memory of those unforgettable and historic episodes and occasions on which He so strikingly demonstrated His keen sense of justice, His spontaneous sympathy for the downtrodden, His ever-abiding sense of the oneness of the human race, His overflowing love for its members, and His displeasure with those who dared to flout His wishes, to deride His methods, to challenge His principles, or to nullify His acts.[70]

With the publication of *The Advent of Divine Justice* early in 1939, renewed emphasis was placed on the vitally important theme of race unity at all of the Bahá'í summer schools. Courses on race, taught by racially diverse instructors, were included in the curriculum with the aim of educating the Bahá'ís themselves and of instilling more positive attitudes about various ethnic groups and a greater appreciation of racial diversity.

EXTENSION OF RACE UNITY ACTIVITIES

By 1940, as the community became more aware of the guidance contained in Bahá'í writings, it embarked on a concerted and systematic campaign to introduce the Bahá'í Faith to the ethnic minorities in North America. The National and Local Spiritual Assemblies working in collaboration with a number of national Bahá'í committees spearheaded the work. The scope of these activities was broad, as suggested by the following excerpt from a 1940 report of the Race Unity Committee:

Some of the Assemblies have undertaken unique work of their own along these lines. Chicago held her third annual unity banquet, conducted an exhibition at the National Negro Exposition, followed this with public and fireside meetings in several parts of the city, entertained at an International Night, and recently has sponsored a tour which visited the Chicago [Bahá'í] Center in celebration of Oriental Day. Milwaukee reports unusual success with Indian councils and visits to the Oneida tribes, and within the year two full-blooded Oneida Indians have become members of the Milwaukee Community. A Milwaukee Youth series has included a Jewish night, German, Mexican, Eskimo, and Hungarian nights. Milwaukee has participated in the Race Unity work of the Council of Churches, the Jewish Center, and the Urban League. Other cities have reported success in radio, dinner meetings, and fraternization on public occasions. Fourteen new local Race Unity Committees have appeared this year and growing cooperation and enthusiasm is widespread.[71]

Particular emphasis was also given to a special program in which Bahá'í speakers were offered to colleges and universities initially in the southern states. The lecture program, initiated by the Bahá'í Race Unity Committee, set out to present Bahá'í perspectives on the creation of a unified world society with the issue of the oneness of humanity being included as an integral, though not central component. Two of the individuals who participated as speakers in this project were Mr. Louis Gregory and Mrs. Dorothy Baker, both of whom were serving as members of the National Spiritual Assembly of the United

States and Canada and also of the Race Unity Committee appointed by that institution. Morrison captures the extent of their heroic travels, reporting that in November 1940, Mr. Gregory spoke in Georgia and the Carolinas, while Mrs. Baker visited a total of 30 colleges in Tennessee, Alabama, and Florida. Likewise, in 1941–42, Mrs. Baker lectured in nearly fifty colleges—white, black, and Indian—while in the months of March and April alone, Mr. Gregory's circuit took him to the African American state universities in West Virginia, Virginia, and the Carolinas, and he also visited Ohio, Michigan, Minnesota, and Washington, D.C.[72]

The work of the southern college project expanded to the point where it required the attention of a separate organizing body. In January 1943, the National Spiritual Assembly appointed the Bahá'í College Speakers Bureau for the purpose of carrying on a widespread campaign of teaching among university student bodies. The aim of the Bureau, acting in collaboration with the Race Unity Committee and the Spiritual Assemblies and with the assistance of a number of prepared teachers, was initially to bring the Bahá'í Faith to college chapels, clubs, and classrooms, then to provide speakers at these institutions on an annual basis, and finally to establish groups or clubs on each campus for the study of the Bahá'í Faith. In the first years of this initiative, Mrs. Baker devoted her energies to the Southwest, visiting six states and speaking in twenty-seven colleges. Mr. Gregory traveled through Ohio, Michigan, Tennessee, Kansas, Oklahoma, Texas, Mississippi, Alabama, Louisiana, West Virginia, Virginia, and North Carolina. In his lectures in black colleges, he spoke directly on the Faith, and in white schools he presented the Bahá'í teachings on race relations. A report in *Bahá'í News* provides a fascinating glimpse of the impact of Mr. Gregory's presentations: "In the heart of Mississippi, where race feeling runs so high as to make such a subject well-nigh impossible, the students waited in long rows in the hall, to shake his hand and wish him well. It was their first adventure in receiving a colored speaker, and only their second experience with the Faith of Bahá'u'lláh."[73]

In addition to the ongoing activities in the area of race unity in the Bahá'í summer schools and the efforts to introduce the Bahá'í Faith to the Southern states, in 1943, the National Spiritual Assembly initiated a nationwide proclamation program on the theme of race unity. This program, which coincided with a period of heightened racial tensions within North America, resulted in an upsurge of activity within the Bahá'í community and several notable conferences in San Francisco, New York, and Flint, Michigan.[74]

The contribution of Louis Gregory and Dorothy Baker to furthering race unity was clearly outstanding and, indeed, heroic. But, it would not be correct to assume that they were alone and unaided in their labors. Their efforts have, over the years, been supported by the unnamed rank and file members of the Bahá'í community, acting with the encouragement and direction of the Spiritual Assemblies and their committees. Nevertheless, the task of effecting a fundamental transformation in attitudes and values is an evolutionary process, and obviously far from being complete. Though, over the decades, a great deal of progress has been made within the Bahá'í community to overcome the prevailing prejudices that blight American society, the Bahá'ís are conscious of the need to continue to make concerted efforts to progressively transform their personal conduct and to demonstrate a way of life that is not only free of prejudice but also gives confident hope for the emergence of new forms of social interaction, and a new civilization.

THE FUTURE OF BAHÁ'Í SUMMER SCHOOLS

As with all Bahá'í institutions, Bahá'ís confidently anticipate that summer schools will evolve in their functions in a manner and at a rate that is commensurate with the development of the Bahá'í community. The earliest indication of the future shape of the Bahá'í summer schools came during 'Abdu'l-Bahá's sojourn in North America. It was during his historic visit to Green Acre that he shared with Sarah Farmer and others, his vision for the future of Green Acre. One day when visiting Monsalvat, an elevated area within the precincts of the Green Acre property, 'Abdu'l-Bahá indicated the spot where the second Mashriqu'l-Adhkár in America would be built, and beside it the great institution of learning. Regrettably, the actual words spoken by 'Abdu'l-Bahá on that occasion have not been recorded. Nevertheless, a number of individuals who witnessed the scene have written their accounts of what transpired. For example, one observer reports that, pointing to an area that encompassed the top of the hill and the surrounding land, 'Abdu'l-Bahá stated that this is where the first Bahá'í university will be built. And, motioning to a spot in the center of this area, he indicated that it is where a second Bahá'í House of Worship in North America will be erected. The same observer refers to 'Abdu'l-Bahá's prediction concerning the high rank of this university and the quality of its international student body, and to the beneficial influence of the university being in close proximity to the Bahá'í House of Worship—with students streaming up and down the hill to some department in the university and to the House of Worship for prayer.[75]

While the Master envisioned that the first Bahá'í university is to be established at Green Acre, the vision for the future development of Bahá'í universities is not confined to Green Acre. Shoghi Effendi generalized this notion, applying it more broadly to Bahá'í summer schools. For example, writing to Bahá'í youth groups in the United States, his secretary states: "The obligation to teach is essentially the responsibility of young believers. Their whole training should therefore be directed in such a way as to make them competent teachers. It is for this very purpose that Bahá'í summer schools, which constitute the very basis upon which the Bahá'í universities of the future will be established, should be widely attended by young believers."[76]

Recognizing the long-term effort required to bring about the transformation of the institution of the Bahá'í school into the future "ideal Bahá'í University," Shoghi Effendi's secretary, writing on his behalf to the attendants at the Louhelen Bahá'í summer school, stressed the important contribution of youth to this organic process and defined the actions that were required in order to move the process forward toward the long-term objective. The letter states:

> Remembering the strong emphasis repeatedly laid by the Guardian on the importance of the institutions of the summer school, both as a center for the preparation and training of prospective teachers and pioneers, and for the commingling and fellowship of various elements in the Bahá'í community, the Bahá'í Youth, on whom Louhelen Ranch has exercised a particular and indeed irresistible appeal, and whose sessions they have so frequently and in such large numbers attended, have a peculiar responsibility to shoulder in connection with its development into that ideal Bahá'í University of the future, which should be the aim of every existing Bahá'í Summer School to establish in the fullness of time.
>
> Through their regular attendance at each and every session of the school, and their participation in all phases of its activities, intellectual, spiritual, social and recreational, and above all by their faithful and close adherence to those high standards of Bahá'í life and conduct, they can best and most effectively contribute towards the growth of that institution and attract to it the attention and interest of the non-Bahá'í world outside.[77]

While the way forward will, no doubt, be long and slow, Shoghi Effendi expressed his satisfaction with the efforts being exerted by the American Bahá'ís, inquiring: "What other community has shown the foresight, the organizing ability, the enthusiastic eagerness, that have been responsible for the establishment and multiplication, throughout its territory, of those initial schools which, as time goes by, will, on the one hand, evolve into powerful centers of Bahá'í learning, and, on the other, provide a fertile recruiting ground for the enrichment and consolidation of its teaching force?"[78]

CIVILIZATION BUILDING

The evolutionary development of the Bahá'í community is driven by the dynamic interaction between the spiritual and practical aspects of life. It derives its inspiration from the concept of the Mashriqu'l-Adhkár, the spiritual center of every Bahá'í community around which, in the fullness of time, dependencies dedicated to the social, humanitarian, educational, and scientific advancement of humankind, will progressively be established and flourish. The concept of social and economic development is, therefore, embedded in the teachings of the Bahá'í Faith, and its application underlies the reconstruction of society.

Central to the capacity of a Bahá'í community to give leadership to a process of social transformation is the ability of its members and the Bahá'í institutions to apply the teachings of Bahá'u'lláh to various aspects of life, thereby establishing consistent patterns of change and upraising the quality of life. To effect such change, the Universal House of Justice attests,

The steps to be taken must necessarily begin in the Bahá'í Community itself, with the friends endeavoring, through their application of spiritual principles, their rectitude of conduct and the practice of the art of consultation, to uplift themselves and thus become self-sufficient and self-reliant. Moreover, these exertions will conduce to the preservation of human honor, so desired by Baha'u'llah. In the process and as a consequence, the friends will undoubtedly extend the benefits of their efforts to society as a whole, until all mankind achieves the progress intended by the Lord of the Age.[79]

During the ministry of Shoghi Effendi, the membership of the North American Bahá'í community was still rather small and its human and financial resources were relatively limited. Lacking the capacity to take on large-scale projects in the realms of social and economic development, the community gave priority to creating a sense of Bahá'í identity; fostering an educated, enlightened, and diverse membership; laying the foundations of Bahá'í community life; and strengthening its evolving institutions; thereby setting in motion processes that had implications for social change beyond the confines of the Bahá'í community. The examples provided in this chapter—the systematic institution of the Nineteen Day Feast, the establishment of Bahá'í summer schools, and the conscious emphasis given to the elimination of racial prejudice—illustrate the realistic, evolutionary, and multifaceted approach to social transformation and some of the processes involved in laying the foundations of a future civilization, a civilization that fosters creativity and allows the spiritual, intellectual, and social dimensions of life to flourish.

Without doubt, the North American Bahá'ís have made a unique contribution to the potential upliftment of human society. Acknowledging their role in this process and their willingness to engage in the challenging task, Shoghi Effendi states:

The Community of the Most Great Name, the leaven that must leaven the lump, the chosen remnant that must survive the rolling up of the old, discredited, tottering order, and assist in the unfoldment of a new one in its stead, is standing ready, alert, clear-visioned, and resolute. The American believers, standard-bearers of this world-wide community and torch-bearers of an as yet unborn civilization, have girt up their loins, unfurled their banners and stepped into the arena of service. Their Plan has been formulated. Their forces are mobilized. They are steadfastly marching toward their goal.[80]

As the Bahá'í community continues to evolve and the dependencies of the Mashriqu'l-Adhkár are established and begin to demonstrate the Bahá'í ideal of worship and service, the capacity of the Bahá'ís to serve humankind and to influence the forces of change will be greatly enhanced.

9

STANDARD-BEARERS OF THE EMANCIPATION AND TRIUMPH OF THE BAHÁ'Í FAITH

The machinery of the Administrative Order, established with such enthusiasm and sacrificial devotion, was used with great effect by the American Bahá'ís as a tool for pursuing the emancipation and recognition of the Bahá'í Faith throughout the world. This chapter explores the meaning and significance of the emancipation of the Bahá'í religion and examines the role of the American Bahá'í community as "the standard-bearers of the emancipation and triumph of the Bahá'í Faith,"[1] with particular emphasis on their unique contribution to the alleviation of the sufferings of their coreligionists in Iran.

The challenging reality confronting each new religious dispensation is to make known its aims and teachings, to demonstrate the religion's relevance to the present needs of an evolving humanity, and to achieve recognition of its independent status among the existing world religions. This challenge is compounded by the invariably hostile reaction of people in authority who, typically, are motivated by the belief that they are in danger of losing their power and authority if the new religion gains widespread recognition. Bahá'u'lláh attests that "In the beginning of every Revelation adversities have prevailed, which later on have turned into great prosperity."[2] He illustrates the operation of this pattern of challenge and rejection and its impact on the founders of the religion and their followers, in the following tablet:

Consider the former generations. Witness how every time the Daystar of Divine bounty hath shed the light of His Revelation upon the world, the people of His Day have arisen against Him, and repudiated His truth. They who were regarded as the leaders of men have invariably striven to hinder their followers from turning unto Him Who is the Ocean of God's limitless bounty.

Behold how the people, as a result of the verdict pronounced by the divines of His age, have cast Abraham, the Friend of God, into fire; how Moses, He Who held converse with the Almighty, was denounced as liar and slanderer. Reflect how Jesus, the Spirit of God, was, notwithstanding His extreme meekness and perfect tender-heartedness, treated by His enemies. So fierce was the opposition which He, the Essence of Being and Lord of the visible and invisible, had to face, that He had nowhere to lay His head. He wandered continually from place to place, deprived of a permanent abode. Ponder that which befell Muḥammad, the Seal of the Prophets, may the life of all else be a sacrifice unto Him. How severe the afflictions which the leaders of the Jewish people and of the idol-worshipers caused to rain upon Him, Who is the sovereign Lord of all, in consequence of His proclamation of the unity of God and of the truth of His Message! . . .

Thou hast known how grievously the Prophets of God, His Messengers and Chosen Ones, have been afflicted. Meditate a while on the motive and reason which have been responsible for such a persecution. At no time, in no Dispensation, have the Prophets of God escaped the blasphemy of their enemies, the cruelty of their oppressors, the denunciation of the learned of their age, who appeared in the guise of uprightness and piety. Day and night they passed through such agonies as none can ever measure, except the knowledge of the one true God, exalted be His glory.[3]

Shoghi Effendi's secretary, writing on his behalf, explains the purpose and significance of this historical process, and its eventual outcome, observing that "every Divine Cause, cannot be effectively established unless it encounters and valiantly triumphs over the forces of opposition with which it is assailed." He indicates that: "Trials and persecutions have always been, and will continue to be, the lot of the chosen ones of God. But these they should consider as blessings in disguise, as through them their faith will be quickened, purified and strengthened. Bahá'u'lláh compares such afflictive trials to the oil which feeds the lamp of the Cause of God." In this same letter the religion's adherents are encouraged to mobilize and take constructive action in the face of persecutions and the letter provides assurance of the ultimate triumph of a "Faith born of God." The letter states,

> The friends should, therefore, not assume an attitude of mere resignation in the face of persecutions. They should rather welcome them, and utilize them as [a] means for their own spiritual uplift and also for the promotion of the Cause. . . . A Faith born of God and guided by His Divine and all-pervasive spirit cannot but finally triumph and firmly establish itself, no matter how persistent and insidious the forces with which it has to contend. The friends should be confident, and act with the utmost wisdom and moderation, and should particularly abstain from any provocative act. The future is surely theirs.[4]

The history of the Bahá'í Faith, especially in the land of its birth, clearly illustrates the processes described above. Commenting on the underlying dynamic of the "resistless march of the Faith of Bahá'u'lláh," Shoghi Effendi indicates that it "resolves itself into a series of rhythmic pulsations, precipitated, on the one hand, through the explosive outbursts of its foes, and the vibrations of Divine Power, on the other, which speed it, with ever-increasing momentum, along that predestined course traced for it by the Hand of the Almighty."[5]

From its inception, the Bahá'í community in Iran has suffered intermittent and often violent persecutions at the hands of the civil and ecclesiastical authorities who, feeling threatened by the spread of its modern teachings, sought to halt the growth of its influence through the exile and imprisonment of its Founders, through malicious attempts to spread false information about the teachings and history of the religion, and through the martyrdom of thousands of the followers of the Báb and Bahá'u'lláh. These violent and concerted attacks, however, failed to annihilate the new religion; rather they strengthened the resolve of its members. Undefeated by the calamity and atrocities confronting them, confident of the eventual outcome, and drawing on the spiritual powers inherent in the religion, the Persian Bahá'ís took decisive action. As described in earlier chapters, they made heroic attempts to clarify the true nature of the Faith's history, aims, and teachings. They also directed reasoned and passionate appeals for justice toward the country's government and religious leadership. Such appeals generally fell on deaf ears; and, in some instances raised up fresh adversaries, which, in turn, served to rally the Bahá'ís and communicate a fresh impulse to the onward march of the Faith. Inevitably, the emancipation of the Bahá'í Faith, in Iran and elsewhere, will be a long and arduous process, extending far into the future. Nevertheless, Bahá'u'lláh confidently testifies to the power of His Cause and its ability to overcome the machinations of its adversaries, asserting:

By the righteousness of God! Should they cast Him [the Manifestation of God] into a fire kindled on the continent, He will assuredly rear His head in the midmost heart of the ocean and proclaim: "He is the Lord of all that are in heaven and all that are on earth!" And if they cast Him into a darksome pit, they will find Him seated on earth's loftiest heights calling aloud to all mankind: "Lo, the Desire of the World is come in His majesty, His sovereignty, His transcendent dominion!" And if He be buried beneath the depths of the earth, His Spirit soaring to the apex of heaven shall peal the summons: "Behold ye the coming of the Glory; witness ye the Kingdom of God, the Most Holy, the Gracious, the All-Powerful!" And if they shed His blood, every drop thereof shall cry out and invoke God in this Name through which the fragrance of His raiment hath been diffused in all directions.[6]

EMANCIPATION OF THE BAHÁ'Í FAITH

The emancipation of the Bahá'í Faith is destined to be an evolutionary process, extending over a long period of time. This process is driven by the dynamic of crisis and victory and will pass through a number of stages. It will ultimately result in the recognition of the Faith as "an independent religion established on a basis of absolute equality with its sister religions, enjoying the unqualified protection of the civil authorities for its followers and its institutions, and fully empowered, in all matters related to personal status, to apply without any reservations the laws and ordinances ordained in the Most Holy Book."[7]

The movement toward the emancipation of the Faith received an initial impetus in 1848 when eighty-one disciples of the Báb gathered at the conference of Badasht for the purpose of not only proclaiming the independence of the new religion but also initiating the practice of its laws and teachings. The aim of the gathering was to demonstrate the Báb's spiritual authority "by a sudden, a complete and dramatic break with the past—with its order, its ecclesiasticism, its traditions, and ceremonials." It was Ṭáhirih, the lone woman participant at the conference, who stepped forward and challenged her fellow believers to act on their new religious beliefs. As a result of her initiative "the most challenging implications of a revolutionary and as yet dimly grasped Dispensation were laid bare before her fellow disciples and the new Order permanently divorced from the laws and institutions of Islám." By courageously raising the clarion call she announced the "formal extinction of the old, and the inauguration of the new Dispensation." Ṭáhirih's actions had profound and far-reaching consequences. "The call she sounded," was, in the words of Shoghi Effendi, "the death-knell of the twelve hundred year old law of Islám."[8]

The revelation by Bahá'u'lláh in 1873 of the Kitáb-i-Aqdas, His Most Holy Book, announcing the formulation of the laws of His Dispensation, was a further significant step in the process of asserting the independence of the Bahá'í Faith and releasing forces that would lead, with the passage of time, to the emancipation of the new Faith not only from Islam, but from all the earlier religious Dispensations, and to its eventually being afforded recognition and protection by civil, legal, and governmental authorities.

The continued progress toward the emancipation of the Faith will inevitably challenge and test the resolve and resourcefulness of the Bahá'í community and its institutions and will raise up a formidable range of religious and civil adversaries. In a letter written in 1927, Shoghi Effendi predicts that, as the Faith grows "from strength to strength, the fanatical defendants of the strongholds of Orthodoxy, whatever their denomination, realizing the penetrating influence of this growing Faith, will arise and strain every nerve to extinguish its light and discredit its name."[9] Writing in 1930, the Guardian identifies more precisely the types of adversaries and foreshadows the nature of their anticipated attacks:

> Peoples, nations, adherents of diverse faiths, will jointly and successively arise to shatter its unity, to sap its force, and to degrade its holy name. They will assail not only the spirit which it inculcates, but the administration which is the channel, the instrument, the embodiment of that spirit. For as the authority with which Bahá'u'lláh has invested the future Bahá'í Commonwealth becomes more and more apparent, the fiercer shall be the challenge which from every quarter will be thrown at the verities it enshrines.[10]

Shoghi Effendi envisions that the Faith's movement toward emancipation will be "painful, yet persistent," and will be achieved in stages. Elaborating on this theme, he outlines in broad and visionary terms the sequence in which these stages are likely to unfold. Thus he states, that "a sore tried Faith" must

> . . . pass through the successive stages of unmitigated obscurity, of active repression, and of complete emancipation, leading in turn to its being acknowledged as an independent Faith, enjoying the status of full equality with its sister religions, to be followed by its establishment and recognition as a State religion, which in turn must give way to its assumption of the rights and prerogatives associated with the Bahá'í state, functioning in the plenitude of its powers, a stage which must ultimately culminate in the emergence of the worldwide Bahá'í Commonwealth, animated wholly by the spirit, and operating solely in direct conformity with the laws and principles of Bahá'u'lláh.[11]

THE PATH TO EMANCIPATION

The progressive emancipation of the Bahá'í Faith involves both the individual members of the community and its administrative institutions in actions designed to promote among its followers a deeper understanding of the religion and adherence to its laws and teachings, to increase public recognition of the Faith's independent status, and to defend the Faith from intermittent attacks and persecution.

On the level of the individual, each person who chooses to become a member of the Bahá'í community after investigating its teachings, is challenged to develop a Bahá'í identity by endeavoring to conform his or her conduct to the standards set by the Faith. The dramatic challenge facing the disciples of the Báb at the conference at Bada<u>sh</u>t—to make a break with the practices of the past—might well be considered as the archetypal challenge of this nature. By their personal commitment to demonstrating a Bahá'í way of life and to promoting its teachings, individual Bahá'ís in contemporary times are directly contributing to the recognition of the independent status of the Faith and its eventual emancipation.

Likewise, as described in earlier chapters, Bahá'í administrative institutions are engaged in a range of activities intended to enhance the spiritual, intellectual, and social aspects of Bahá'í community life, through the provision of educational programs and through the guidance offered to individual members by the Spiritual Assemblies. In addition, these Spiritual Assemblies play a vital role in the systematic expansion of the Bahá'í Faith. They actively and widely promote understanding of its aims, its teachings, and the nature of its Administrative Order, through the organization of meetings, publications, and other events, designed to reach all sections of society, including those in authority and leaders of thought.

Recognition of the independent status of the Bahá'í Faith involves more than simply an intellectual understanding by the general population that the Faith claims to be a new world religion. Rather, it needs to involve recognition by the civil authorities and to be reinforced by legal recognition, such that the rights of the community are protected by the provisions of the legal system. The groundbreaking efforts by the American Bahá'ís to legally register and incorporate their Spiritual Assemblies and the subsequent recognition of these institutions as legal entities empowered to hold property and to engage in various contractual arrangements represents a major contribution to the emancipation of the Faith in North America, and inspired other Bahá'í communities to follow its example.

The growing awareness of the independent status of the Bahá'í Faith and the legal recognition of its institutions have important practical implications in times when the Faith is subject to attack. In addition to having recourse to the protection of the law, it is also possible under such conditions for the institutions to appeal to governmental authorities, and to use the media to bring the assault to the attention of the public. Shoghi Effendi stressed the importance of setting in place such defensive measures. He envisaged that, with the passage of time, the American Bahá'í community would be subject to opposition. He alerts them to the possibility that

> ... storms of abuse and ridicule, and campaigns of condemnation and misrepresentation, may be unloosed against them. Their Faith, they may soon find, has been assaulted, their motives misconstrued, their aims defamed, their aspirations derided, their institutions scorned, their influence belittled, their authority undermined ...

He cautions the community not to be "afraid of any criticism that might be directed against it," and issues the following guidance to assist the community:

Let it not be deterred by any condemnation with which the tongue of the slanderer may seek to debase its motives. Let it not recoil before the threatening advance of the forces of fanaticism, of orthodoxy, of corruption, and of prejudice that may be leagued against it. The voice of criticism is a voice that indirectly reinforces the proclamation of its Cause. Unpopularity but serves to throw into greater relief the contrast between it and its adversaries, while ostracism is itself the magnetic power that must eventually win over to its camp the most vociferous and inveterate amongst its foes.[12]

And, in another letter addressed to the American Bahá'í community Shoghi Effendi assured them that, irrespective of the practical obstacles, complications, and unforeseen difficulties that are likely to arise, Bahá'ís can confidently anticipate a positive outcome in the long-term, since their religion "unlike any other human organization . . . inspires a spirit of Faith and Devotion" in its members, and motivates them "to make sincere and renewed efforts to face these difficulties and smooth any differences that may and must arise."[13]

DEFENSE OF THE BAHÁ'Í COMMUNITY IN IRAN

The American Bahá'ís, the spiritual descendants of the dawn-breakers in the West are called upon to make a major contribution to the emancipation of the Bahá'í Faith, not only in North America, but throughout the world. Addressing the members of the American Bahá'í community as "the outstanding protagonists of the Cause of God; the stout-hearted defenders of its integrity, its claims and its rights," Shoghi Effendi acknowledges the role they have played and will continue to play as "the chief succorers of the down-trodden, the needy and the fettered among its followers." Indeed, he clearly foresees a vital role for the American Bahá'ís in "the deliverance of Bahá'í communities from the fetters of religious orthodoxy in such Islamic countries as Persia, Iraq, and Egypt," and in devising "precautionary and defensive measures" to counteract "the full force of the inescapable attacks which the organized efforts of ecclesiastical organizations of various denominations will progressively launch and relentlessly pursue." Underlining the outstanding contribution of the American Bahá'í community to the protection of the Bahá'í Faith, Shoghi Effendi poses the following question: "what other community has had the privilege, and been granted the means, to succor the needy, to plead the cause of the downtrodden, and to intervene so energetically for the safeguarding of Bahá'í edifices and institutions in countries such as Persia, Egypt, 'Iráq, Russia, and Germany, where, at various times, its fellow-believers have had to suffer the rigors of both religious and racial persecution?"[14]

The remaining sections of this chapter examine the role of the American Bahá'í community in its capacity as "the standard-bearers of the emancipation and triumph of the Bahá'í Faith,"[15] by analyzing a number of critical interventions this community and its administrative institutions have made in defense of their coreligionists in Iran.

The reputation of America in upholding justice and defending the weak and downtrodden is well established in the historical record. What may be less well known is that America is also singled out in the writings of the Founder of the Bahá'í Faith. Bahá'u'lláh, in His book of laws, the Kitáb-i-Aqdas, revealed around 1873, addressed "the Rulers of America and the Presidents of the Republics therein" calling upon them to "adorn . . . the temple of dominion with the ornament of justice and of the fear of God," and He counseled them to "bind . . . with the hands of justice the broken" and "crush" the "oppressor" with "the rod of the commandments of their Lord, the Ordainer, the All-Wise."[16]

From the earliest days of the Bahá'í Faith, the Persian Bahá'ís sought the protection and intervention of the American government. Prior to the revelation of the Kitáb-i-Aqdas and almost a quarter of a century before the introduction of the Bahá'í Faith to North America, on 16 March 1867, a group of fifty-three Bahá'ís in the small city of Shushtar affixed their personal seals on a petition addressed to the United States Congress, and requested its assistance in alleviating the imprisonment and exile of Bahá'u'lláh. In the latter part of the twentieth century, the historic document was located in the United States government archives. The petition, which was written in Arabic, was apparently entrusted to a German traveler in Baghdad. The traveler sent the document to Beirut where it found its way into the hands of the American Consul, who forwarded it along with an English translation to the Secretary of State in Washington, D.C. in July 1867. The petition informs the representatives of the government about the advent of "a perfect man and a learned sage," summarizes His teachings, describes the opposition to which His Faith has been subjected, mentions His exiles, and invites the Congress to send "a judicious representative" to inquire into the case with a view to finding a way "to bring that oppressed person relief from tyranny and oppression."[17] While there does not appear to be any clear evidence that the United States government took steps to respond to the petition, the fact that the appeal was made illustrates the remarkable confidence placed in the American nation by the less fortunate and needy peoples of the world. It also foreshadows the actions undertaken in later years by the American Bahá'ís in their attempts to defend their harassed coreligionists in Iran and to alleviate the persecutions that continue, intermittently, to be inflicted on them.

RESPONSE OF THE AMERICAN BAHÁ'Í COMMUNITY

The express aim of the persecution of the Bahá'ís in Iran, from the time of the turbulent and violent attacks on the hapless followers of the Báb in the middle of the nineteenth century, which are described in an earlier chapter, has been to eliminate the new religion—a religion that claims to represent a more recent expression of divine guidance, particularly in the social life of humankind, and is therefore perceived, especially by the clergy, as a rival to the Shí'ih sect of Islam, the dominant faith of Iran. While the methods adopted by the persecutors have taken different forms, they all seek to pressure the Iranian Bahá'ís to recant their beliefs, as a way of eradicating the new religion and of demonstrating the superiority of Islam.

During the thirty-six years of Shoghi Effendi's ministry, and continuing in contemporary times, there have been repeated and violent outbreaks, on both a local and national scale, of brutal and repressive opposition to the followers of the Bahá'í Faith in Iran. Three episodes, spanning the lifetime of Shoghi Effendi, are described below. They illustrate the nature of the opposition and the defensive measures taken by the American Bahá'ís and their institutions to alleviate the sufferings and protect the human rights of the Persian Bahá'ís.

THE EARLY YEARS—1920s

The Qájár regime whose rulers, acting in collusion with the ecclesiastical authorities, had mercilessly and willingly harassed the Báb's followers, the dawn-breakers of the Heroic Age, was overthrown in 1925 and replaced by the Pahlavi regime, headed by Rezá Sháh. The new regime, which initially enjoyed the support of the clergy, ushered in a period of change in Iran. However, the alliance with the clergy proved to be short-lived as Rezá Sháh embarked on a program of modernization that soon threatened the traditional privileges, the areas of responsibility, and sources of financial gain of the clergy. The sháh and his government introduced a number of revolutionary reforms in "matters of education, trade and finance, means of transportation and travel, and the development of the country's internal resources," and they also strictly limited "the number, the rights and the prerogatives of high ecclesiastical officials." These reforms were designed, slowly but surely, to transform "the very basis and structure of Persia's primitive society," and to fuel a process of gradual secularization in the society, a process that the Guardian believed was, at a future time, likely to give rise to "the formal and complete separation of Church and State," thereby smoothing the way for the emancipation of the Faith.[18]

For a short while the changes in society permitted the Persian Bahá'ís greater freedom to practice their religion. Under the direction of their Spiritual Assemblies, the Bahá'ís in Iran seized the opportunity to establish a number of Bahá'í schools. In addition, they built hostels, libraries, and public baths, held public gatherings, constructed official headquarters for their administrative work, and took steps, when not in conflict with the law of the land, to apply the laws and ordinances of the Kitáb-i-Aqdas to their personal lives. This respite was destined to be brief.

In 1926, a fresh outbreak of persecutions rocked the Bahá'í community. These attacks were instigated in part by "religious hostility," and partly for "political purposes and selfish motives."[19] In Jahrum, in southern Iran, twelve Bahá'ís, including a number of women and a child, were brutally martyred. Others were severely beaten and injured; their homes were pillaged and their property confiscated. In other parts of Iran the Bahá'ís were denied "the civic rights and privileges extended to every citizen of the land." Explaining the plight of these believers, Shoghi Effendi reports that:

They have been refused the use of the public bath, and been denied access to such shops as provide the necessities of life. They have been declared deprived of the benefit and protection of the law, and all association and dealing with them denounced as a direct violation of the precepts and principles of Islám. It has even been authoritatively stated that the decencies of public interment have been refused to their dead, and that in a particular case every effort to induce the Muslim undertaker to provide the wood for the construction of the coffin, failed to secure the official support of the authorities concerned.[20]

Shoghi Effendi's response to these events was immediate. Through the National Spiritual Assembly of Persia, he addressed, on behalf of the Bahá'ís of the world, a cable to the Head of State. He also requested all Local Spiritual Assemblies in Iran to send a similar message to the authorities appealing for full protection and justice. At the same time, Shoghi Effendi used this event to initiate a process of training of the Western Bahá'ís and their embryonic administrative institutions to prepare them to take appropriate and effective defensive measures on behalf of their afflicted brethren in the East. To this end, he called upon "every conscientious promoter of the Cause to bestir himself and undertake in consultation with the friends in his locality such measures of publicity as will lead to the gradual awakening of the conscience of the civilized world to what is admittedly an ignominious manifestation of a decadent age." Likewise, all National Assemblies were instructed "to devise ways and means that will secure the fullest publicity for our grievances," and to endeavor "to secure the sympathy and hospitality of the leading journals and periodicals in the Western world."[21]

Addressing the National Spiritual Assembly of the United States and Canada, Shoghi Effendi not only emphasized the importance of publicity, he also stressed the need "to devise every possible means that will alleviate the fears and sorrows of the silent sufferers" in Iran. In a later letter he reminded the Americans that because they enjoyed the benefits of the freedom and religious toleration in their homeland, they were in the enviable position of being able to play a unique role in defending the Faith. He instructed the Assemblies to engage in prayerful, intelligent, and persistent efforts to use every means at their disposal "to arouse . . . the conscience of unheeding humanity, and to direct the attention of men of vision and authority to these incredibly odious acts which in their ferocity and frequency cannot but constitute in the eyes of every fair-minded observer the gravest challenge to all that is sacred and precious in our present-day civilization."[22]

The National Assembly responded to this weighty assignment with alacrity. It mobilized the Bahá'í community, calling attention to the need for publicity to make known the situation of the Bahá'ís in Iran, as well as to inform the general public more about the aims, history, and teachings of the Bahá'í Faith. A Publicity Committee was also constituted to coordinate these activities. In the first phase of the response to the Guardian's call for assistance, the National Spiritual Assembly itself sent publicity direct to some four hundred newspapers throughout North America.[23]

A groundbreaking initiative undertaken by the National Spiritual Assembly was the preparation of a long, dignified, yet forthright petition, which was addressed directly to the Persian monarch, Rezá Sháh Pahlavi. On 16 July 1926 this petition was transmitted to the sháh on behalf of all the Local Spiritual Assemblies and Bahá'í groups in the United States and Canada. The American National Assembly's appeal to Rezá Sháh set out in detail the nature of the recent persecutions afflicting the Bahá'ís in Iran. It named the martyrs, countered misunderstandings and corrected misinformation being circulated about the Faith, called attention to the condition of "moral and civic anarchy" existing in that country, and called for religious freedom for the beleaguered Persian Bahá'í community. The document formally appealed to the sháh to investigate the situation and to "initiate whatever measures are necessary to terminate this long and frightful chapter of unmerited woe."[24] The National Spiritual Assembly's petition concludes with the following words:

> We await your Majesty's assurance that our respectful appeal has achieved its aim. Our love for these oppressed Bahá'í brothers and sisters makes it imperative that we continue our efforts to rescue them from their sea of calamity, until assured that henceforth they shall be protected by the full power of the Imperial Government, and just restitution made them for losses already sustained.[25]

The National Spiritual Assembly's appeal to the sháh was given the widest possible circulation. The Assembly sent copies of the petition to every member of the United States Government in Washington, D.C.; to the British Foreign Office; the League of Nations; all the members of the Persian Cabinet; and about one thousand leading individuals, organizations, and libraries in North America. In addition, through the efforts of the local Spiritual Assemblies and Bahá'í groups, the story about the persecutions of the Bahá'ís in Iran and the petition to the sháh was published in many of the major newspapers in the United States.[26]

A number of individual Bahá'ís also seized the opportunity to bring the teachings of the Faith and the plight of the Persian Bahá'ís to the attention of prominent people. Miss Martha Root, for example, achieved the unique distinction of introducing the Faith to Queen Marie of Romania and of obtaining from her, written and public tributes to the power of Bahá'u'lláh's teachings and their transformative effect on humankind. Further, the artist, Miss Juliet Thompson painted a portrait of the wife of Calvin Coolidge, the President of the United States, and was able to give her information about the Faith. Commenting on the contributions of such individuals, the National Spiritual Assembly noted:

> While these examples by no means exhaust the achievements rendered by individual believers this year, they may be taken as indications of how individual initiative, when allied with understanding of and loyalty to the Cause, is confirmed, and such instances should inspire us all to nobler intention and more ardent effort.[27]

Shoghi Effendi expressed his deep appreciation for "the prompt and wise measures" taken by the American Bahá'í community. Writing to the National Assembly, the Guardian underlines the significance of these measures and their impact on the Persian Bahá'ís, indicating that the "noble appeal" addressed to his highness the sháh, and "the wide range of publicity" that was undertaken by the community were "truly providential in character, and will undoubtedly prove an inspiration and solace to those who still continue to be trampled under the heel of an odious and inveterate enemy." Shoghi Effendi informs the National Assembly of actions he had taken in relation to the appeal, and he allies the promising steps taken by the American Bahá'ís with the unique contribution they are destined to make in the emancipation of the Faith of Bahá'u'lláh in Iran. He writes: "I have had your appeal translated into Persian and sent to all Centers throughout the Orient that the suffering in Persia may learn of your bold and courageous intervention, and witness the signs of their promised redemption which, as foretold by 'Abdu'l-Bahá, must first be made manifest through the efforts of their brethren in that great freedom-loving Republic of the West."[28]

The National Spiritual Assembly of the United States and Canada followed up its appeal to the sháh with a statement on the Faith addressed to the heads of the Muslim religion in Ṭihrán. The Bahá'í community of Ṭihrán translated the document into Persian, and printed copies of the statement were sent to many hundreds of influential people in Iran. The purpose of this communication was "to plead for peace in the realm of religion, that there may be peace among the nations of East and West." The letter made clear the high regard the Bahá'í Faith has for Muḥammad and His religion and describes the talks of 'Abdu'l-Bahá in the West, in which He "publicly proclaimed to large and distinguished audiences . . . the verity of the Prophethood of Muḥammad." The National Assembly's letter laments the persistent persecutions that were being inflicted on the Persian Bahá'ís because of the apparent misunderstanding among the Muslims in that land about "the motives and teachings of Bahá'u'lláh," and calling upon the Muslim leaders to take firm action against those who commit atrocities against the Bahá'ís in the name of religion, the letter concludes: "Thus it would be a true service to Islám, as well as to humanity, if the chiefs of the religion of Muḥammad should now counsel mercy and give forth teachings of peace."[29]

Despite the heroic efforts exerted on behalf of the Bahá'ís in Iran, the National Spiritual Assembly's appeals brought no noticeable response, and the opposition to the Faith in the land of its birth continued unchecked. Nevertheless, in the course of their activities, the Bahá'í community and its institutions had succeeded not only in bringing the Bahá'í Faith to the attention of an increasingly large audience, but they also were gaining invaluable skills and experience in defending the Faith. They were embarked on the long-term process of gradually and systematically achieving the eventual emancipation of their religion.

THE UNIQUE CONTRIBUTION OF
MRS. KEITH RANSOM-KEHLER

In January 1932 the American National Spiritual Assembly again addressed petitions to the sháh and his prime minister, this time calling for the ban on the entry and circulation of Bahá'í literature in Iran to be lifted. When these formal petitions failed, Shoghi Effendi decided that the matter was too important to be dropped, even though he knew it would be very difficult to achieve the desired goal.[30] He chose Mrs. Keith Ransom-Kehler, a courageous American Bahá'í to undertake the important and delicate assignment of interceding, in person, with the Persian government. In a land where women were still largely secluded in the home, Mrs. Ransom-Kehler was required to relate, at the highest level, to government ministers and members of parliament in her efforts to have the Bahá'í petition brought to the attention of the sháh.

As the designated representative of the National Spiritual Assembly of the United States and Canada, Mrs. Ransom-Kehler traveled to Iran in June 1932. Her task was to present in person the National Spiritual Assembly's petition to the sháh.

In August, following a meeting with the court minister in Ṭihrán, she was able to inform the National Assembly that the Persian government had agreed to lift the ban on the importation and circulation of Bahá'í literature in Iran. The National Spiritual Assembly immediately cabled the court minister expressing its appreciation to the sháh and his government. The Assembly also brought the matter to the attention of the Persian minister in Washington, D.C., and it issued a statement to the American press "reporting that Mrs. Ransom-Kehler had received assurance from the Court Minister that the postal regulations under which Bahá'í literature had been confiscated would be immediately annulled."[31]

As the months passed, it became evident that the anticipated change in government policy did not take place. It emerged that, in the volatile political climate of the times, the court minister with whom Mrs. Ransom-Kelher had consulted had been dismissed, and the ban on the entry of Bahá'í literature continued. So, Mrs. Ransom-Kelher renewed her efforts to find ways to present the petition on behalf of the National Spiritual Assembly of the United States and Canada. In the first instance, she turned to the secretary charged with American affairs at the Foreign Office in Ṭihrán. He gave her three reasons why Bahá'í literature could not circulate in Persia:

> First, that it is contrary to the constitution of Persia to recognize any religion founded after Islam, and since the Bahá'í religion cannot legally receive recognition it follows that our literature must remain unrecognized. Second, that it is contrary to the constitution of Persia to permit the circulation of any literature opposed to Islam. Third, that the circulation of Bahá'í literature at this time might cause grave internal disorders that would bring much suffering to the Bahá'ís themselves.[32]

To verify the information conveyed by the representative of the Foreign Ministry, Mrs. Ransom-Kehler made an exhaustive study of the Persian constitution in order to see what provisions it might contain concerning the status of religions founded after Islam. Finding no reference to this subject in the constitution, in February 1933, she addressed another letter to the sẖáh, reporting on the meeting with the official and seeking clarification of the information provided by his Foreign Office. Her appeal to the sẖáh received no response.

Meanwhile, the National Spiritual Assembly, realizing that its report to the press concerning the lifting of the ban was incorrect, dispatched to its representative in Iran another letter to be presented to the sháh. The letter informed the sháh that, in order for the National Assembly to maintain its reputation with American newspaper editors for accurate and reliable reporting, it was necessary for the Assembly to notify the press that the information, with which the media had, in good faith, been earlier provided, must now be withdrawn. Mrs. Ransom-Kehler presented the National Spiritual Assembly's letter to the sháh in April 1933, and in yet another letter to him she called attention to her obligation to report the results of her mission to the National Assembly.

In June 1933, when no response was forthcoming and new reports of fresh attacks on the Persian Bahá'ís were received from Iran, Shoghi Effendi turned to the delegates assembled at the American National Bahá'í Convention for additional assistance. He instructed them to give special attention to this grave issue. As a result, the National Spiritual Assembly opened "a new phase in the progress of the matter" by sending two representatives with a communication to meet the Persian minister in Washington, D.C.[33] Concerned that their petitions were not reaching the person of the sháh, despite the best efforts of Mrs. Ransom-Kehler, the National Spiritual Assembly's representatives provided the Persian minister with a summary of the content of the earlier appeals. Forthright in its expression, the document presented to the Persian minister states

The Bahá'ís of America assert very frankly to your Excellency their unhappiness because of the fact that unfounded prejudice against the Bahá'ís of Persia, whether emanating from atheistic or from ecclesiastical sources, can in this day and age find sanction from authorities of the State. Without this sanction, active or passive, it would be impossible to forbid the entry and circulation of a sacred literature which one day will be recognized as the glory of Persia, while at the same time permitting the entry and circulation of other religious literature the essential purpose of which is to defame the founder of Islam and overthrow the very foundation of Persian culture and ideals.[34]

The document concludes with the hope that the National Spiritual Assembly's appeal on behalf of the Persian Bahá'ís would be successful.

In Iran, Mrs. Ransom-Kehler, who was now physically ill, increased her efforts to achieve the desired results. During the months of June and July 1933, she addressed yet another letter to the Persian sháh in order to leave no stone unturned in her efforts to change the official attitude and to bring relief to her coreligionists. She also forwarded to every cabinet minister and to the president of the Persian parliament, a statement containing a summary of the steps she had, so far, taken to alleviate the situation of the Persian Bahá'ís. Her statement concluded with the following impassioned plea: "I now with the most intense fervor supplicate and implore your Majesty to put a final stop to these fanatical persecutions that disgrace in the eyes of men the annals of Persia's former rulers, by removing this ban against Bahá'í literature, that bids fair if it continues to involve the world in contempt for this sacred land."[35] The minister of education was the only one to respond. He informed her that the circulation of publications that were considered contrary to the official religion or the political interests of the country was prohibited.

Finally, to assess the outcome of the resolutions at the National Convention concerning the protection of the Persian Bahá'ís, and in a further attempt to call the Persian government to account, the National Spiritual Assembly forwarded to their intrepid representative a summary of the actions taken by American Bahá'ís in relation to the conditions affecting the Bahá'ís in Iran, with the request that she communicate the facts and the attitude of the American believers to the officials of the Persian government. The National Assembly requested that Mrs. Ransom-Kehler report the government officials' response so that it could convey the information to the members of the American Bahá'í community. The outcome of this request came in a cable from Mrs. Ransom-Kehler on 10 September 1933: "Petition unanswered."[36]

For over a year Mrs. Ransom-Kehler encountered formidable obstacles, broken promises, and conflicting advice from the Persian government. In the end, the petition was never answered. Yet despite such difficulties she persisted, undeflected in bringing to bear her keen intelligence, great eloquence, wise and strategic judgment, and sensitivity to her assigned task. Disappointed at the failure of her mission and exhausted from her constant efforts to visit and address Bahá'í gatherings throughout Iran, Mrs. Ransom-Kehler fell victim to smallpox and passed away in Iṣfahán on 23 October 1933.

When informed of Mrs. Ransom-Kehler's sudden death, Shoghi Effendi lamented the loss of such an outstanding and capable believer. In recognition of her unique services, the Guardian designated her as the "first and distinguished martyr" drawn from the American Bahá'í community. He also characterized her as the "valiant emancipator" of the Persian Bahá'í community, and bestowed upon her the high rank of Hand of the Cause of God.[37]

Given her close association with Persia and with the agreement of her family, Shoghi Effendi arranged for Mrs. Ransom-Kehler to be buried in Iṣfahán. He specified that her grave was to be in the vicinity of the final resting place of the King of Martyrs, one of the outstanding figures of the Heroic Age of the Bahá'í Faith. Commenting on the befitting nature of the proximity of these graves, the Guardian observed that it "will pass down through the ages as the symbol of the unity of the East and West."[38]

While Mrs. Keith Ransom-Kehler's untimely death was a significant blow to the campaign, Shoghi Effendi, nevertheless, called on the National Spiritual Assembly of the United States and Canada to take immediate steps to renew their representations to the Persian minister in Washington, D.C. and to persevere in their efforts on behalf of the Persian Bahá'ís. Writing on his behalf, the Guardian's secretary provided the following guidance to the National Assembly:

> To cease pressing our case at this critical time will give the authorities the impression that our representations were mere formalities and without any solid foundation. To create such a highly unfavorable impression about the Cause is, indeed, an irreparable mistake which may greatly retard the administrative development of the Cause not only in Persia but also in the West.[39]

Shoghi Effendi highlights the importance of giving sustained and systematic attention to the defense of the Bahá'í Faith in Iran in another letter written at this time to a member of the National Spiritual Assembly. He writes:

> With the passing of Keith, that indefatigable, brilliant and wholly consecrated international champion of the Cause, the Persian believers may be entering upon a period of systematic persecution reminiscent of a by-gone day. I urge your Assembly to obtain the fullest and up-to-date information from the Ṭihrán Assembly and to exert the utmost pressure on the Persian Minister in Washington.[40]

In this encounter with the adversaries of the Bahá'í Faith in Iran, the American Bahá'í community offered up its first martyr. The National Spiritual Assembly began to take a more active role in the international affairs of the Faith, especially in relation to its protection from attack. The actions of the delegates at the 1933 National Bahá'í Convention, and the subsequent delegations sent to meet with the Persian minister in Washington, D.C. gave additional impetus to the process of emancipation. Further, by sending its representative to Ṭihrán, the National Assembly was not only able to play a more direct role in interceding with the Persian government on behalf of the suffering Persian Bahá'í community, but her presence in that country served as an encouragement to the Bahá'ís there and facilitated a greater level of mutual understanding and collaboration between the two Bahá'í communities.

THE ATTACKS OF 1955–57

A fresh attack on the Bahá'ís in Iran was launched with "dramatic suddenness" in 1955, during the month of Ramaḍán—the Muslim month of fasting. Being "of exceptional severity," and "unpredictable in its immediate consequences," this new wave of persecution was seen as exceptionally dangerous since it threatened to engulf "the overwhelming majority" of the followers of Bahá'u'lláh in the land of His birth. Indeed, when turning to the American Bahá'ís and their institutions for assistance, Shoghi Effendi foreshadowed that this situation was, to date, the most "grievous" of "the intermittent crises which have more or less acutely afflicted the Faith since the inception . . . of the Formative Age of the Bahá'í Dispensation." So severe was this crisis that he regarded it as being "tragically reminiscent of the tribulations experienced by the dawn-breakers of the Heroic Age of the Faith at the hour of its birth in that sorely tried, long-agitated land."[41]

Despite the sudden outbreak, this "premeditated campaign" of attack had, in actuality, been "slowly and secretly developing." The precipitating factor appears to be linked to the significant, systematic progress of the Faith throughout the world, including the Muslim world, as a consequence of the launching of the Ten Year Spiritual Crusade. Commenting on the timing of the outbreak of hostilities, Shoghi Effendi attests that it "came to a head, as the result of the ceaseless intrigue of the fanatical and determined ecclesiastical opponents of the Faith, ever ready to seize their chance, in times of confusion, and to strike mercilessly, at an opportune hour, at the very root of that Faith and of its swiftly developing, steadily consolidating administrative institutions."[42]

During the month of Ramaḍán, the Muslims traditionally gather at midday in the mosque to pray and to listen to the sermons delivered by their religious leaders. In one of the mosques in Ṭihrán the speaker, Shaykh Muḥammad Taqí, known as Falsafí, used his pulpit to call upon his hearers to rise up against "false" religions, unjustly accusing the Bahá'í Faith of being an enemy of Islam. His repeated public denunciations of the Faith were broadcast throughout the country by government radio, and covered in the press. Each day, his words became more defamatory and increased in vehemence. His violent and passionate sermons succeeded in stirring up widespread suspicion and antipathy against the Bahá'ís. This campaign of vilification received formal endorsement in May 1955, when the Majlis, the Persian Parliament, officially outlawed the Faith and banned its activities in Iran.

The immediate aftermath of the government's action was the demolition of the dome of the Bahá'í Central Administrative Headquarters in Ṭihrán, which was soon followed by the seizure and occupation of all Bahá'í administrative headquarters throughout the provinces. However, beyond the loss of property, the action of the government proved to be immeasurably more dangerous. It served as "the signal for the loosing of a flood of abuse, accompanied by a series of atrocities simultaneously and shamelessly perpetrated in most of the provinces, bringing in its wake desolation to Bahá'í homes, economic ruin to Bahá'í families, and staining still further the records of Shí'ah Islám in that troubled land."[43] The scope and nature of the attacks that were precipitated by the government's suppression of the Faith are vividly captured in the following report:

> This was followed by an orgy of senseless murder, rape, pillage and destruction the like of which has not been recorded in modern times. The dome of the Ḥaḍíratu'l-Quds in Ṭihrán was demolished; the House of the Báb was twice desecrated and severely damaged; Bahá'u'lláh's ancestral home at Tákur was occupied; the house of the Báb's uncle was razed to the ground; shops and farms were plundered; crops burned; livestock destroyed; bodies of Bahá'ís disinterred in the cemeteries and mutilated; private homes broken into, damaged and looted; adults execrated and beaten; young women abducted and forced to marry Muslims; children mocked, reviled, beaten and expelled from schools; boycott by butchers and bakers was imposed on hapless villagers; young girls were raped; families murdered; Government employees dismissed and all manner of pressure brought upon the believers to recant their Faith.[44]

Shoghi Effendi swiftly rallied the Bahá'ís throughout the world to spring to the assistance of the beleaguered Bahá'ís in Iran. Countermeasures were immediately taken. Turning, once more, to the members of the American Bahá'í community, "the outstanding defenders of the Faith," he called upon them to utilize the machinery of its elected administrative institutions to publicize the situation of their coreligionists and to find ways of alleviating the suffering of the Persian believers. Being "blessed with a freedom so cruelly denied the vast majority of their brethren, and equipped with the means and instruments needed to make that publicity effective," Shoghi Effendi placed great confidence in the ability of the American Bahá'í community to play a major role in this critical task.[45]

The American Bahá'í community's defensive campaign was launched in mid-August 1955, following a particularly brutal criminal attack in which "a mob of many hundreds marched upon the hamlet of Hurmuzak, to the beating of drums and the sounding of trumpets, and armed with spades and axes, fell upon a family of seven, the oldest eighty, the youngest nineteen, and, in an orgy of unrestrained fanaticism, literally hacked them to pieces." At the behest of Shoghi Effendi, who fearing the likelihood of a more widespread massacre in the immediate future, all the Bahá'í groups and Spiritual Assemblies in the United States sent a cable to President Eisenhower, in which they appealed to the president to intervene to protect the Persian Bahá'ís from further massacres, and to safeguard their human rights. In addition to the cable, the National Spiritual Assembly also addressed a letter to the president, which included a detailed list of the atrocities that had taken place. A short time later, it was learned from a press report that President Eisenhower, who "was the first to make mention of the attacks launched against the Faith," referred to the plight of the Bahá'ís in Iran during a press conference in Washington, D.C.[46]

The American Bahá'ís, together with the Bahá'ís and their institutions from all continents of the globe, joined in a united wave of protest by sending cables to the sháh, the prime minister and the members of the Persian Parliament, in the hope of stemming the tide of persecutions that was threatening to engulf the entire Persian Bahá'í community. More than a thousand such appeals were addressed to these prominent figures in Iran, impressing on them, perhaps for the first time, that the Bahá'í Faith was not simply an insignificant local phenomenon but a worldwide, tightly-knit, independent religious community.

Furthermore, a widespread campaign of publicity was initiated in the expectation that the arousal of world public opinion might serve as a restraining influence on those who were either condoning or perpetrating the atrocities. The American Bahá'ís were assigned the task of intensifying and giving effective leadership to the publicity campaign. This "sacred task" was supplementary to the already onerous responsibilities involving the expansion of the Bahá'í Faith and the establishment of its administrative institutions that were associated with the prosecution of the Ten Year Crusade. To reinforce the effectiveness of their publicity efforts, and at a time when there were many other competing calls on its limited financial resources, the National Spiritual Assembly allocated a sizeable sum of money for the purpose of securing the assistance of an expert publicity agent.[47] Acknowledging the determination of the American Bahá'ís to give priority to this activity, Shoghi Effendi spelled out its significance, relating it to the eventual emancipation of the Faith:

> Let them remember, as they pursue diligently this sacred task, that such a publicity, following closely upon such dire tribulations, afflicting so large a number of their brethren, in so sacred a land, cannot but prove to be a prelude, however slow the process involved, to the emancipation of these same valiant sufferers from the galling fetters of an antiquated religious orthodoxy, which, great as has been its decline in the course of over a century, still wields considerable power and exercises a widespread influence in high circles as well as among the masses. Such an emancipation, which cannot be confined to Bahá'u'lláh's native land, will, in varying measure, have its repercussions in Islamic

countries, or may be even preceded by a similar phenomenon in neighboring territories, hastening and adding fresh impetus to the bursting of the bonds that fetter the freedom of the followers of God's infant Faith.[48]

The widespread campaign of publicity prepared the way for an appeal to the United Nations by the Bahá'í International Community. Before lodging the appeal to the United Nations, the National Spiritual Assembly of the United States wrote once more to the sháh of Iran and his prime minister, explaining that, since it had received no response to its earlier letters, the National Assembly had no option but to document the persecutions of the Persian Bahá'ís and to present the case to the United Nations. The National Spiritual Assembly's letters also called attention to the fact that as a signatory to the United Nations Charter and Bill of Rights, Iran had assumed a responsibility in the eyes of the world to uphold the basic human rights of all their citizens.[49]

By way of background, it is interesting to note that Shoghi Effendi had encouraged the establishment of formal association with the United Nations Organization. He saw it as providing the means of giving the Bahá'í Faith suitable publicity as an agency working for the recognition of the oneness of humankind and for world peace. In 1947 the National Spiritual Assembly of the United States and Canada was accredited as a national nongovernmental organization qualified to be represented at United Nations conferences through an observer. In the following year the eight National Spiritual Assemblies that existed at the time were collectively recognized as an international nongovernmental organization under the title of "Bahá'í International Community."[50] Shoghi Effendi was extremely pleased with this development. He related it to the recognition of the independent status of the Faith and foreshadowed its relevance to the protection of the Bahá'í community. In a letter addressed to the American National Assembly he stated:

> The recognition given your Assembly (as representative of the other National Spiritual Assemblies) by UNO as a non-governmental body entitled to send representatives to various UNO conferences marks an important step forward in the struggle of our beloved Faith to receive in the eyes of the world its just due, and be recognized as an independent World Religion. Indeed, this step should have a favorable reaction on the progress of the Cause everywhere, especially in those parts of the world where it is still persecuted, belittled, or scorned, particularly in the East."[51]

In July 1955, concerned about the possibility of a widespread massacre of the Persian Bahá'ís, Shoghi Effendi cabled the Bahá'í International Community, calling upon it to lodge an appeal for immediate assistance for the protection of the Bahá'ís in Iran with the United Nations, through its Economic and Social Council. By a fortunate coincidence, the Economic and Social Council of the United Nations was meeting in Geneva, Switzerland. A Committee of Bahá'ís from five different countries, including the American representative, Mrs. Mildred Mottahedeh, was immediately dispatched to Geneva.

Conscious of the urgency of the situation and aware of the challenge of securing the intervention of the United Nations in time to save their coreligionists in Iran, the committee worked tirelessly. It endeavored to get one of the members of the Economic and Social Council to present the Bahá'í case from the floor of the Council. To this end, the committee interviewed the Council members, informing them about the situation of the Persian Bahá'ís, and it pressed for an interview with the secretary-general of the United Nations, Mr. Dag

Hammarskjöld. When it became evident that no delegate or organization was willing to speak up for the Bahá'ís, the committee sought the assistance of a competent lawyer to frame a formal appeal. This appeal, together with the evidence of the persecutions, was widely distributed. It was presented to the secretary-general, to all members of the Economic and Social Council who had been interviewed by the committee, to the Human Rights Commission, and to a variety of United Nations agencies and international nongovernmental organizations. Unable to take further action in Geneva, and fearing that their efforts had failed, the committee held a press conference to circulate the news of the appeal, prior to returning to their home countries to launch a publicity campaign aimed at arousing the public conscience.

Just days before the anticipated widespread attack on the Persian Bahá'ís in 1955, the committee of the Bahá'í International Community received the unexpected news that the secretary-general of the Untied Nations, yielding to the pleas of the American delegates to the Economic and Social Council and of the High Commissioner for Refugees, decided to send the latter to Bonn, Germany, to meet with the chief Iranian delegate to the United Nations and the Minister of Foreign Affairs. The Bahá'í International Community reported that the Iranian government

> . . . had been certain that the United Nations would not intervene to save the Bahá'ís since the provisions of the Charter for upholding human rights and fundamental freedoms were morally, but not legally, binding. The intervention of the Secretary-General astounded the Iranian government. This intervention, the efforts of prominent Bahá'ís in Iran, the appeals of the National Spiritual Assembly of the United States to the American State Department, and the publicity campaign brought an

immediate end to the physical persecution and lifted the danger of massacre.[52]

The Persian government took some initial steps to redress the situation. However, the clergy, who were responsible for fomenting the attacks, continued to protest, the population remained hostile, and the provincial authorities were slow to act to protect the Bahá'ís. Nevertheless, the immediate threat of massacre had been averted. But the situation was far from being resolved.[53] Economic reprisals against the Bahá'ís continued, and those who had been dismissed from employment were not reinstated. The Bahá'ís in Iran continued to be denied the fundamental religious right of assembly for worship, and their meeting places were still being held by the governmental authorities.

The American Bahá'ís intensified their publicity campaign. The National Spiritual Assembly took the case to the media and sought the support of academics, leaders of thought, and people of prominence who were willing to raise their voice in protest against the persecution of the Persian Bahá'ís. Meanwhile, the Bahá'í International Community prepared and circulated a comprehensive statement concerning the banning of the Bahá'í Faith in Iran. The statement, entitled *Bahá'í Appeal for Religious Freedom in Iran*, summarized the attempts that had been made to have the ban lifted; catalogued the persecutions perpetrated against the believers; and listed and publicly refuted the false and misleading accusations that were being leveled against the Bahá'ís by the Iranian Parliament, and spread throughout the country by the radio and the press. The statement ends with an appeal for freedom of religion, and the defense of the rights of the people of all faiths.

Despite the massive media campaign, persistent attempts by individual Bahá'ís in Ṭihrán, and many appeals the American National

Spiritual Assembly addressed to the State Department of the American government, it became evident that the assurances, given previously by the Iranian foreign minister to the secretary-general of the United Nations, were not being carried out. In June 1956, the Bahá'í International Community launched a second appeal to the United Nations. As in the first instance, the committee was unable to find any of the delegates to the Social and Economic Council willing to present the Bahá'í case. However, as before, at the eleventh hour, someone stepped forward. This time, it was the delegate from Ecuador, who was also chairman of the Social Commission. In opening the session of that commission, he referred to the plight of the Bahá'ís in Iran, affirming: "I believe this matter should receive the close attention of the Subcommittee on Prevention of Discrimination and Protection of Minorities and should receive equal attention with other instances of religious discrimination. This new religion should be respected like all other religions in the world."[54] The delegate from Ecuador not only spoke in defense of the Bahá'ís, but he also acknowledged the independent status of the Bahá'í Faith in this important international setting.

Although the Bahá'ís in Iran continued to labor under some restrictions, it was clear that this phase of the battle had been won. By 1957, all but a few of the local administrative headquarters had been returned, the government had issued an order for the return of the National Bahá'í administrative building, and the house of the Báb in Shíráz was restored to the Bahá'í community.[55]

Summarizing the outstanding contributions of the American Bahá'í community to the defense of their oppressed brethren in Iran during this challenging two year period, Shoghi Effendi begins by expressing his admiration and gratitude for the community's "swift" and "energetic" response. He then calls attention to:

The spontaneity with which the rank and file of this community as well as the body of its elected representatives, have contributed to the "Save the Persecuted Fund" established for the succor of the victims of these savage and periodically recurring barbarities; the measure of publicity accorded them in the American press, as well as over the radio; the timely and efficacious intervention of men of prominence, in various walks of life, on behalf of the oppressed and the down-trodden; the repeated and direct appeals addressed by them to the highest authorities in Persia, as well as to their representative in the United States; the immense number of written and cabled appeals, made by the local as well as the national elected representatives of the community, to the chief magistrate of Persia, his ministers and parliament; the numerous messages addressed by the same representatives to the chief executive of the United States, urging his personal intervention, the pleading of the cause of an harassed, sorely-tried community in the course of repeated representations made to the State Department in Washington; the part played in the presentation of the Bahá'í case to the United Nations officials in both Geneva and New York; the allocation of a sizeable sum for the purpose of securing the assistance of an expert publicity agent, in order to reinforce the publicity already being received in the public press.

The Guardian concludes by underlining the significance of all the measures taken by the American Bahá'ís. He testifies that they, "proclaim, in no uncertain terms, the dynamic and decisive nature of the aid accorded, in a hour of trial and emergency, by the champions of the Faith of Bahá'u'lláh, raised up in the great republic of the West, at such a crucial hour in the evolution of His Plan, for both His Faith and the world at large, to the vast body of the descendants of the dawn-breakers of the Apostolic Age of that same Faith in the land of its birth."[56]

THE EMERGENCE OF
THE FUTURE WORLD ORDER

The three examples described above provide brief snapshots of the contribution made by the American Bahá'í community and its administrative institutions to the defense of the Bahá'í community in Iran and, more generally, to the emancipation of the Faith. Although the process has been engaged and some modest victories achieved, the complete story of the emergence of the Bahá'í Faith from obscurity in the land of its birth and of its recognition as an independent religion remains to be written.

The path to emancipation stretches far into the future. It is destined to involve periodic challenges and setbacks. Since its inception in Iran, the Bahá'í Faith has been, and, even to the present day, continues to be, subjected to intermittent outbreaks of opposition from those who, threatened by its growing strength, attempt to stem its society-building influence. Driven by the dynamic interaction of the forces of crisis and victory, these attacks may temporarily retard the Faith's development. Paradoxically, they also serve to mobilize the Bahá'ís and strengthen their sense of identity. Opposition also catalyzes the actions of their coreligionists throughout the world, who, stirred by a burning sense of justice, arise to campaign for the human rights and freedom of religion on behalf of the Persian believers.

As the "standard-bearers of the emancipation and triumph"[57] of the Faith, the American Bahá'ís have a significant continuing role to play in this evolutionary process. The three examples, drawn from the ministry of Shoghi Effendi, demonstrate the response of the Americans, the ways in which they arose to meet the challenge, the kinds of skills they acquired in the course of their exertions, and the increasing range of actions they were able to take as their administrative institutions matured in their functioning.

In the case of the first incident, which took place during the 1920s, perhaps the principal and immediate outcome of the American Bahá'í community's interventions was that it led to an increased understanding about the aims, teachings, and history of the religion among the general public, in both Iran and North America. In the second situation in the 1930s, the American Bahá'ís assumed greater responsibility and took a more direct international role. The dispatch of their representative, Mrs. Keith Ransom-Kehler, to Iran to intercede in person with the Persian government made it more difficult for the authorities to ignore the appeal. Her very physical presence demanded a response! She was an intelligent and formidable defender of the Faith. Her presence in the Persian capital demonstrated the scope and caliber of the international membership of the religion, contributing thereby to its recognition and prestige even though in the short term the government refused to respond to her appeals for the religious freedom of the Persian Bahá'ís.

The final example illustrates the growing capacity of a maturing administrative machinery to take on major new responsibilities for protecting the Bahá'ís in Iran, while at the same time pursuing the demanding goals of the Ten Year Spiritual Crusade. In this instance, the National Spiritual Assembly working in collaboration with the recently constituted Bahá'í International Community, an agency created to promote the emancipation of the Bahá'í Faith and to serve as a vehicle for its protection, successfully mobilized world public opinion through an extensive publicity campaign, and, through the actions of the United Nations Organization, secured the intervention of the nations of the world in defense of the Persian Bahá'í community. This same forum accorded a degree of international recognition of the independence of the Faith by publicly acknowledging that the Bahá'í Faith, as well as other religions, had the right to be respected.

In the course of these, and other similar interventions, the American Bahá'ís and their institutions set in motion processes that will, over time, not only facilitate the emancipation of the Bahá'í community in Iran, and indeed throughout the world, but will also lead to the universal recognition of the Bahá'í Faith as an independent religion enjoying equal status with the world's major religions. Such recognition is an important step in the eventual emergence of the World Order envisioned in the writings of Bahá'u'lláh. In anticipation of that future day, when the Faith will have achieved universal recognition, Shoghi Effendi writes:

> Such a consummation will, in its turn, pave the way for the recognition of that Faith as an independent religion established on a basis of absolute equality with its sister religions, enjoying the unqualified protection of the civil authorities for its followers and its institutions, and fully empowered, in all matters related to personal status, to apply without any reservations the laws and ordinances ordained in the Most Holy Book.[58]

Addressing the American Bahá'í community, whose members are destined to make a critical and continuing contribution to this evolutionary process, Shoghi Effendi not only expresses appreciation for their willingness to take on the "supplementary task" of defending the Persian Bahá'ís, but he also recounts the exemplary functions they are performing in relation to the expansion of the Cause and the establishment of its administrative institutions. He writes:

> That the members of the American Bahá'í Community—the outstanding protagonists of the Cause of God; the stout-hearted

defenders of its integrity, its claims and its rights, the champion-builders of its Administrative Order; the standard-bearers of its crusading hosts; the torchbearers of its embryonic civilization; the chief succorers of the down-trodden, the needy and the fettered among its followers—that the members of such a community, may, whilst discharging, fully and unflinchingly, their specific tasks in accordance with the provisions of the Ten-Year Plan, seize the present God-sent opportunity, and hasten, through a proper discharge of this supplementary task, the consummation of such ardent hopes for so signal a victory, is a prayer constantly in my heart, and a wish which I treasure above all others.[59]

10

THE DESTINY
OF AMERICA

The earlier chapters of this book described the dramatic and tumultuous events associated with the inception of the Bahá'í Faith in Iran,
distinguished by the heroic exploits of its valiant followers in the land
of its birth, and examined the significance of the members of the
American Bahá'í community's designation as the spiritual descendants of the dawn-breakers of the Faith's Heroic Age. In the course
of our analysis, we have not attempted to write a comprehensive history of the Bahá'í Faith and its development in the West. Rather, the
aim has been to illustrate the high degree of personal commitment
required, and the multiplicity of interconnected challenges involved
in establishing a new religion, particularly one that does not have a
clergy. Attention was, therefore, focused on an exploration of some
of the evolutionary processes set in motion by the North American
Bahá'í community in its endeavor to expand the religion throughout
the world, establish its administrative institutions, and to use these
institutions as vehicles for achieving the further consolidation and
emancipation of the Faith. These same processes continue now to
drive the work of the Bahá'í community, though the ways in which
they are actualized tend to reflect the particular evolutionary stage of
the community.

Having examined the unique contribution of the North American Bahá'ís to the development of this new religious dispensation, principally during the lifetime of Shoghi Effendi, it is appropriate to reflect on the reasons this continent has been singled out in the literature of the Bahá'í Faith for such a high destiny, to understand the role it is anticipated to play in the future unfoldment of the World Order envisioned in the writings of Bahá'u'lláh, and to examine the relationship between the destiny of the American Bahá'í community and that of the American nation.

HISTORICAL PATTERNS

A supreme and distinguishing feature of the revelation of Bahá'u'lláh and the Báb is "the calling into being of a new race of men."[1] There are historical parallels between the reasons the Persian dawn-breakers of the Heroic Age and their spiritual descendants in North America were singled out from among the other peoples and nations of the world. Both were selected to illustrate the transformative influence of the visionary teachings of the new revelation, and to serve as a creative minority inspiring change. As a background against which to consider this theme, it is useful to reflect on the more general issue of why a particular nation is selected to serve as the cradle of a new revelation

The primary reason a nation is chosen to receive the unique honor of being the land in which the call of the new revelation is raised, is paradoxically not because of its inherent superiority, but rather because of the decadent social conditions prevailing in that land at the time of the advent of the Messenger of God. Referring to a recurring general pattern in religious history, Shoghi Effendi observes that invariably, "the Prophets of God" have "chosen to appear, and deliver their Message in countries and amidst peoples and races, at a time when they were either fast declining, or had already touched the lowest depths of moral and spiritual degradation." He characterizes the appalling social conditions that existed at the time of the appearance of Moses, Jesus, and Muḥammad, and comments on "the indescribable state of decadence, with its attendant corruption, confusion, intolerance, and oppression, in both the civil and religious life of Persia," which pertained "at the hour of the Revelation of Bahá'u'lláh."[2]

Underlining the "inescapable" lesson to be drawn from this general principle, Shoghi Effendi issues the following caution:

> To contend that the innate worthiness, the high moral standard, the political aptitude, and social attainments of any race or nation is the reason for the appearance in its midst of any of these Divine Luminaries would be an absolute perversion of historical facts, and would amount to a complete repudiation of the undoubted interpretation placed upon them, so clearly and emphatically, by both Bahá'u'lláh and 'Abdu'l-Bahá.[3]

It is critical therefore for those who belong to "such races and nations," and who have responded to "the call which these Prophets have raised," to appreciate the uniqueness of the situation. They must have a clear understanding of both the motive underlying the action of the Manifestation of God, and of the creative potential for social transformation inherent in the new revelation. In the words of Shoghi Effendi, the challenge is to

> . . . unreservedly recognize and courageously testify to this indubitable truth, that not by reason of any racial superiority, political capacity, or spiritual virtue which a race or nation might possess, but rather as a direct consequence of its crying needs, its lamentable degeneracy, and irremediable perversity,

has the Prophet of God chosen to appear in its midst, and with it as a lever has lifted the entire human race to a higher and nobler plane of life and conduct. For it is precisely under such circumstances, and by such means that the Prophets have, from time immemorial, chosen and were able to demonstrate their redemptive power to raise from the depths of abasement and of misery, the people of their own race and nation, empowering them to transmit in turn to other races and nations the saving grace and the energizing influence of their Revelation.[4]

PERSIA—CRADLE OF THE NEW REVELATION

The "fundamental principle" outlined above explains "the primary reason why the Báb and Bahá'u'lláh chose to appear in Persia." At that time, in the middle of the nineteenth century, Persia, "of all the peoples and nations of the civilized world, . . . had . . . sunk to such ignominious depths, and manifested so great a perversity, as to find no parallel among its contemporaries." Commenting on the significance of this choice, Shoghi Effendi writes:

For no more convincing proof could be adduced demonstrating the regenerating spirit animating the Revelations proclaimed by the Báb and Bahá'u'lláh than their power to transform what can be truly regarded as one of the most backward, the most cowardly, and perverse of peoples into a race of heroes, fit to effect in turn a similar revolution in the life of mankind. To have appeared among a race or nation which by its intrinsic worth and high attainments seemed to warrant the inestimable privilege of being made the receptacle of such a Revelation would in the eyes of an unbelieving world greatly reduce the efficacy of that Message, and detract from the self-sufficiency of its omnipotent power.[5]

The Guardian underscores the transformative power of the new revelation by contrasting the actions and demeanor of the Persian Bahá'ís in the Heroic Age of the Faith with the behavior of their fellow citizens. Noting the striking distinction between "the heroism that immortalized the life and deeds of the Dawn-Breakers and the degeneracy and cowardice of their defamers and persecutors," Shoghi Effendi attests that it serves as "a most impressive testimony to the truth of the Message of Him Who had instilled such a spirit into the breasts of His disciples." As described in earlier chapters, the exploits of "the trail-breakers of the New Day," their "standard of faith and . . . code of conduct" not only "challenged and revolutionized the lives of their countrymen," but their "unparalleled deeds" were "responsible for the birth of the Faith itself." Referring to this historical record, the Guardian concludes that "in the face of the overwhelming evidence," it is not possible for "any believer of that race to maintain that the excellence of his country and the innate nobility of its people were the fundamental reasons for its being singled out as the primary receptacle of the Revelations of the Báb and Bahá'u'lláh."[6]

AMERICA—CRADLE OF THE WORLD ORDER OF BAHÁ'U'LLÁH

The Bahá'í writings designate the American Bahá'í community as "the cradle of the World Order of Bahá'u'lláh,"[7] and envisage that it will play a predominating role in the birth of the future world civilization, to which their religion will give rise in the fullness of time. What, we might ask, is the basis for the selection of this nation? Why is it singled out for such an important and noble function?

In clarifying this issue, Shoghi Effendi draws a parallel between the principle that applied in the case of Persia at the time of the advent of Bahá'u'lláh, and the application of this same principle, though to "a lesser degree," to the situation in North America. Addressing the

American Bahá'ís, the Guardian instructs them not to "imagine for a moment that for some mysterious purpose or by any reason of inherent excellence or special merit Bahá'u'lláh has chosen to confer upon their country and people so great and lasting a distinction." The fundamental reason for this special station, he explains, is "precisely" due to the pernicious influence of "an excessive and binding materialism," which gives rise to a number of "patent evils" in American society. In providing the rationale for the seemingly paradoxical operation of the divine will, Shoghi Effendi also describes some of the most pressing social issues confronting the nation, and he calls attention to the responsibility of the Bahá'ís to demonstrate the power of the revelation to transform human behavior and bring about significant social change.[8] He writes,

> It is by such means as this that Bahá'u'lláh can best demonstrate to a heedless generation His almighty power to raise up from the very midst of a people, immersed in a sea of materialism, a prey to one of the most virulent and long-standing forms of racial prejudice, and notorious for its political corruption, lawlessness and laxity in moral standards, men and women who, as time goes by, will increasingly exemplify those essential virtues of self-renunciation, of moral rectitude, of chastity, of indiscriminating fellowship, of holy discipline, and of spiritual insight that will fit them for the preponderating share they will have in calling into being that World Order and that World Civilization of which their country, no less than the entire human race, stands in desperate need. Theirs will be the duty and privilege, in their capacity first as the establishers of one of the most powerful pillars sustaining the edifice of the Universal House of Justice, and then as the champion-builders of that New World Order

of which that House is to be the nucleus and forerunner, to inculcate, demonstrate, and apply those twin and sorely needed principles of Divine justice and order—principles to which the political corruption and the moral license, increasingly staining the society to which they belong, offer so sad and striking a contrast.[9]

In underlining the role of the American Bahá'í community, Shoghi Effendi stresses the importance of having a clear and balanced understanding of the complexity of the nature of American society and the qualities of its peoples. He cautions against focusing exclusively on the negative aspects of society, since this would, necessarily, "blind us to those virtues and qualities of high intelligence, of youthfulness, of unbounded initiative, and enterprise which the nation as a whole so conspicuously displays, and which are being increasingly reflected by the community of believers within it." Rather, he indicates that the American Bahá'í community's ability "to lay a firm foundation for the country's future role in ushering in the Golden Age of the Cause of Bahá'u'lláh," must, ultimately, depend "Upon these virtues and qualities, no less than upon the elimination of the evils referred to."[10]

THE AMERICAN NATION AND THE BAHÁ'Í COMMUNITY

The Bahá'í writings foreshadow the potential contribution that both the American Bahá'í community and the American nation are destined to make to the world at large, and they also provide insight into the nature of the complex and dynamic interactions between the two. To explore this relationship, it is first necessary to reflect on the central theme of Bahá'u'lláh's revelation and to examine the Bahá'í vision of social evolution and the emergence of world order.

RELIGION AND SOCIAL EVOLUTION

According to the Bahá'í teachings there is a close connection between religion and social evolution. Both unfold at a measured pace. Shoghi Effendi characterizes this relationship, as follows:

Just as the organic evolution of mankind has been slow and gradual, and involved successively the unification of the family, the tribe, the city-state, and the nation, so has the light vouchsafed by the Revelation of God, at various stages in the evolution of religion, and reflected in the successive Dispensations of the past, been slow and progressive. Indeed the measure of Divine Revelation, in every age, has been adapted to, and commensurate with, the degree of social progress achieved in that age by a constantly evolving humanity.[11]

Each of the world's great religions has "one central theme"—a theme that judges and encapsulates the needs of society at the time of the coming of the Manifestation of God, and establishes the pattern for the subsequent evolution of the spiritual and social order. For example, the message associated with the Faith of Jesus Christ, which was revealed at a time when the whole surface of the globe was largely unexplored and the peoples of the world had not been organized into nations, "stressed, as its central theme, the necessity of inculcating a high standard of morality and discipline into man, as the fundamental unit in human society." Similarly, "Islám, the succeeding link in the chain of Divine Revelation, introduced . . . the conception of the nation as a unit and a vital stage in the organization of human society," a principle that was required to further the course of the evolution of human society at that time. Hence, the "conception of nationality" introduced by the Prophet Muḥammad, progressively led to "the attainment to the state of nationhood," a new social reality, "in the course of which the nations and races of the world, and particularly in Europe and America, were unified and achieved political independence."[12]

The advent of the Báb and Bahá'u'lláh in the middle of the nineteenth century coincides with a time of fundamental change in the economic and political life of society and an increasing trend toward the interdependence of the peoples and nations of the earth. The new and expanded possibilities for social evolution, resulting from the change in circumstances are described by 'Abdu'l-Bahá:

> In cycles gone by, though harmony was established, yet, owing to the absence of means, the unity of all mankind could not have been achieved. Continents remained widely divided, nay even among the peoples of one and the same continent association and interchange of thought were wellnigh impossible. Consequently intercourse, understanding and unity amongst all the peoples and kindreds of the earth were unattainable. In this day, however, means of communication have multiplied, and the five continents of the earth have virtually merged into one. And for everyone it is now easy to travel to any land, to associate and exchange views with its peoples, and to become familiar, through publications, with the conditions, the religious beliefs and the thoughts of all men. In like manner all the members of the human family, whether peoples or governments, cities or villages, have become increasingly interdependent. For none is self-sufficiency any longer possible, inasmuch as political ties unite all peoples and nations, and the bonds of trade and industry, of agriculture and education, are being strengthened every day. Hence the unity of all mankind can in this day be achieved.[13]

The world indeed, is, in the words of Shoghi Effendi, "contracting into a neighborhood, and the fortunes of its races, nations and peoples "are becoming "inextricably interwoven."[14]

THE ONENESS OF HUMANKIND— FOUNDATION OF WORLD ORDER

'Abdu'l-Bahá identifies the central theme of the Bahá'í era as "the consciousness of the Oneness of Mankind." He indicates that, in the Dispensation of Bahá'u'lláh, the oneness of humankind is "the foundation of the Faith of God and the distinguishing feature of His Law."[15]

The Bahá'í principle of the oneness of humankind, "the pivot around which all the teachings of Bahá'u'lláh revolve," has broad and far-reaching practical implications. Elaborating on the significance of this principle, its particular relevance to contemporary times and its potential impact on social organization, Shoghi Effendi writes:

Its implications are deeper, its claims greater than any which the Prophets of old were allowed to advance. Its message is applicable not only to the individual, but concerns itself primarily with the nature of those essential relationships that must bind all the states and nations as members of one human family. . . . It implies an organic change in the structure of present-day society, a change such as the world has not yet experienced. . . . It calls for no less than the reconstruction and the demilitarization of the whole civilized world—a world organically unified in all the essential aspects of its life, its political machinery, its spiritual aspiration, its trade and finance, its script and language, and yet infinite in the diversity of the national characteristics of its federated units.

It represents the consummation of human evolution—an evolution that has had its earliest beginnings in the birth of family life, its subsequent development in the achievement of tribal solidarity, leading in turn to the constitution of the city-state, and expanding later into the institution of independent and sovereign states.[16]

The unification of the human race is the goal of the new world order anticipated in the revelation of Bahá'u'lláh. Commenting on "the achievement of this organic and spiritual unity of the whole body of nations," Shoghi Effendi indicates that it should "be regarded as signalizing through its advent the *coming of age of the entire human race*," and "as marking the last and highest stage in the stupendous evolution of man's collective life on this planet." From the perspective of social organization, it is envisaged that the new order will, among other things, involve "the eventual application of the principle of federalism . . . to the relationships now existing between the nations and peoples of the world."[17]

The Guardian calls attention to some of the outcomes of and the future benefits that are likely to be derived from this new stage in the collective life of humankind. He foresees

The emergence of a world community, the consciousness of world citizenship, the founding of a world civilization and culture—all of which must synchronize with the initial stages in the unfoldment of the Golden Age of the Bahá'í Era—should, by their very nature, be regarded, as far as this planetary life is concerned, as the furthermost limits in the organization of human society, though man, as an individual, will, nay must indeed as a result of such a consummation, continue, indefinitely to progress and develop.[18]

Stressing the importance of the concept of humanity's coming of age and its application and timeliness, Shoghi Effendi observes that "the stage of maturity inevitable in the life of the individual and the development of the fruit . . . must have its counterpart in the evolution of the organization of human society," and he points to the enhanced, long-term benefits that accrue both to the individual and society from such an administrative structure. "A similar stage producing an even more striking phenomenon in world relations, and endowing the whole human race with such potentialities of well-being as shall provide, throughout the succeeding ages, the chief incentive required for the eventual fulfillment of its high destiny."[19]

The unification of the entire human race, the foundation and hallmark of the new world order foreshadowed in the writings of the Bahá'í Faith, is destined to pass through stages and to emerge in the fullness of time. The course of its evolution is likely to be influenced by social, economic, political, and technological movements that promote change and social cohesion. Its progress is also likely to be dislocated by the increasingly chaotic state of world events, and disrupted by the forces of conservatism, fanaticism, and repression. Its emergence will necessarily be gradual, leading at first to the establishment of the Lesser Peace by the nations of the world. This step will involve "the reconstruction of mankind, as a result of the universal recognition of its oneness and wholeness," which, in turn, "will bring in its wake the spiritualization of the masses, consequent to the recognition of the character, and the acknowledgement of the claims, of the Faith of Bahá'u'lláh—the essential condition to that ultimate fusion of all races, creeds, classes, and nations which must signalize the emergence of His New World Order," a stage to be followed by "the coming of age of the entire human race," the hoisting of "the banner of the Most Great Peace," and birth of a "world civilization.[20]

RELATIONSHIP BETWEEN BAHÁ'Í
ADMINISTRATIVE ORDER AND WORLD ORDER

The Bahá'í writings contain specific provisions for the establishment of an administrative system to conduct the affairs of the Bahá'í community, and also foreshadow changes in the political realm that give rise to the emergence of world order. There is also a dynamic relationship between the two, which is destined to unfold in an evolutionary manner.

The Bahá'í Administrative Order derives its inspiration and direction from the writings of Bahá'u'lláh and 'Abdu'l-Bahá. The sacrifice of the early Persian believers was the seminal act that initiated the process of its development. Shoghi Effendi states: "Its seed is the blood of no less that twenty thousand martyrs who have offered up their lives that it may be born and flourish."[21] Discussion in this book has focused primarily on the sustained heroic efforts made by the American Bahá'ís to water and nurture these precious seeds, thereby laying the foundations of the worldwide Bahá'í administrative system, in the form of the election of Spiritual Assemblies at the local, national, and international levels of society. As these institutions grow in maturity and the status of the Faith as an independent world religion is increasingly recognized, they will take on functions concomitant with the new evolutionary stage. Commenting on the future of the Administrative Order, Shoghi Effendi predicts,

> It will, as its component parts, its organic institutions, begin to function with efficiency and vigor, assert its claim and demonstrate its capacity to be regarded not only as the nucleus but the very pattern of the New World Order destined to embrace in the fullness of time the whole of mankind.[22]

He further attests that:

The central, the underlying aim which animates it is the establishment of the New World Order as adumbrated by Bahá'u'lláh. . . . Its watchword is the unification of the human race; its standard the "Most Great Peace"; its consummation the advent of that golden millennium—the Day when the kingdoms of this world shall have become the Kingdom of God Himself, the Kingdom of Bahá'u'lláh.[23]

While progress toward the establishment of both the Bahá'í Administrative Order and world order is destined to evolve and go through stages, there is no detailed timeline of how these two processes will unfold. The responsibility for the emergence of the Administrative Order rests with the Bahá'í community, while the nations of the world have primary responsibility for furthering the development of world order. In the following section the unique contribution of the American Bahá'í community and the American nation will be examined in relation to the establishment of the Administrative Order and the unfoldment of world order.

CONTRIBUTIONS OF THE AMERICAN BAHÁ'Í COMMUNITY AND THE AMERICAN NATION TO WORLD ORDER

The Bahá'í writings single out both the American Bahá'í community and the American nation and envisage that each will make unique contributions to the unfoldment of a world-embracing order, the creation of world civilization, and the emergence of peace. While each has a defined role to play, Shoghi Effendi attests that the "ultimate destiny" of the American Bahá'í community is linked to that of the nation of which it forms a part. For both, the path ahead is likely to be thorny. It will proceed "through experiment and trial, slowly, painfully, unwittingly and irresistibly advancing towards the goal destined for it both by Bahá'u'lláh and 'Abdu'l-Bahá." It will involve "the workings of two simultaneous processes, [that were] generated as far back as the concluding years of the Heroic Age of our Faith."[24] Commenting on the relationship between these processes Shoghi Effendi indicates that "each [is] clearly defined, each distinctly separate, yet closely related and destined to culminate, in the fullness of time, in a single glorious consummation." Elaborating on this theme, the Guardian describes the historic events that set the separate processes in motion, highlights their unique arena of operation, and foreshadows their ultimate convergence in the distant future. He writes:

> One of these processes is associated with the mission of the American Bahá'í Community, the other with the destiny of the American nation. The one serves directly the interests of the Administrative Order of the Faith of Bahá'u'lláh, the other promotes indirectly the institutions that are to be associated with the establishment of His World Order. The first process dates back to the revelation of those stupendous Tablets constituting the Charter of 'Abdu'l-Bahá's Divine Plan. . . . It will be consummated through the emergence of the Bahá'í World Commonwealth in the Golden Age of the Bahá'í Dispensation.

> The other process dates back to the outbreak of the first World War that threw the great republic of the West into the vortex of the first stage of a world upheaval. It received its initial impetus through the formulation of President Wilson's Fourteen Points, closely associating for the first time that republic with the fortunes of the Old World. . . . It must, however long and tortuous the way, lead, through a series of victories and reverses . . . to the emergence of a world government and the establishment of the

Lesser Peace, as foretold by Bahá'u'lláh and foreshadowed by the Prophet Isaiah. It must, in the end, culminate in the unfurling of the banner of the Most Great Peace, in the Golden Age of the Dispensation of Bahá'u'lláh.[25]

CONTRIBUTION OF THE
AMERICAN BAHÁ'Í COMMUNITY

The unique mission of the North American Bahá'í community has been described in detail in earlier chapters. Suffice it to say that, from its inception, this community was selected for special attention. It was nurtured and trained by 'Abdu'l-Bahá. Perceiving its potential and youthful vitality, he addressed to its members innumerable tablets aimed at educating and guiding the Bahá'ís and he dispatched a number of knowledgeable teachers to that land to deepen the community members' understanding of the religion they had embraced. During his visit to the United States and Canada he participated in activities that served to set in motion evolutionary processes that were, at a later stage, to give rise both to the inauguration of the Bahá'í administrative machinery and lay the foundation for Bahá'í community life. And, in the evening of his life, 'Abdu'l-Bahá revealed the Tablets of the Divine Plan, which set out the American Bahá'í community's spiritual world-embracing mission—its mandate to promote the interests of the religion in the five continents of the globe.

When Shoghi Effendi called for the establishment of the institutions of the Bahá'í Administrative Order, the American Bahá'í community, designated as "the cradle and stronghold of the Administrative Order of the Faith of Bahá'u'lláh," was "the first among all other Bahá'í communities to fix its pattern, to erect its fabric, to initiate its endowments, to establish and consolidate its subsidiary institutions, and to vindicate its aims and purposes." As these embryonic institutions gained in strength and experience, the community, under the leadership of the National Spiritual Assembly and its committees, embarked upon the implementation of 'Abdu'l-Bahá's Divine Plan, thereby expanding the interests of the Faith and laying the foundations of the structural basis of its administrative system, initially in all the republics of Central and South America, then in Europe and Africa, and subsequently in all areas of the world. In addition, this community had the unique distinction of erecting "in the heart of the North American continent, the first Mashriqu'l-Adhkár of the West," of championing "the cause of the down-trodden and persecuted among their brethren in Persia" and in other lands, and in stretching "a generous helping hand to the needy among them, to defend and safeguard the interests of their institutions, and to plead their cause before political and ecclesiastical adversaries." As the community continues to evolve and mature it assumes additional functions—functions that reflect the needs of its particular stage of development. This evolutionary process will, progressively, increase in momentum and give rise to the emergence of the Bahá'í World Commonwealth in the Golden Age of the Bahá'í Dispensation.[26]

CONTRIBUTION OF THE AMERICAN NATION

In the Kitáb-i-Aqdas Bahá'u'lláh issued a summons to the presidents of the republics of the American continent, calling on them "to seize their opportunity in the Day of God and to champion the cause of justice." He thus singled out the American nation and charged it with playing an important role in the future political and social reconstruction of humankind, and a key contribution to the establishment of world peace. The writings of 'Abdu'l-Bahá elucidate the nature of America's potential contribution. In a talk delivered on 6 May 1912 during his travels in North America, he affirmed that "This revered nation presents evidences of greatness and worth," and he expressed the hope that "this just government will stand for peace so that warfare may be abolished throughout the world and the standards of national unity and reconciliation be upraised." "This," he states, "is the greatest attainment of the world of humanity." He avers: "This American nation is equipped and empowered to accomplish that which will adorn the pages of history, to become the envy of the world and be blest in the East and the West for the triumph of its democracy. I pray that this may come to pass, and I ask the blessing of God in behalf of you all."[27]

Shoghi Effendi cites a number of visionary statements from the writings of 'Abdu'l-Bahá, which highlight the role of America, in the following passage. Referring to America, a "nation that has achieved undisputed ascendancy in the entire Western Hemisphere," Shoghi Effendi notes that it

. . . has been acclaimed by 'Abdu'l-Bahá as the "home of the righteous and the gathering-place of the free," where the "splendors of His light shall be revealed, where the mysteries of His Faith shall be unveiled" and belonging to a continent which, as recorded by that same pen, "giveth signs and evidences of very great advancement," whose "future is even more promising," whose "influence and illumination are far-reaching," and which "will lead all nations spiritually." Moreover, it is to this great republic of the West that the Center of the Covenant of Bahá'u'lláh [i.e. 'Abdu'l-Bahá] has referred as the nation that has "developed powers and capacities greater and more wonderful than other nations," and which "is equipped and empowered to accomplish that which will adorn the pages of history, to become the envy of the world, and be blest in both the East and the West for the triumph of its people." It is for this same American democracy that He expressed His fervent hope that it might be "the first nation to establish the foundation of international agreement," "to proclaim the unity of mankind," and "to unfurl the Standard of the Most Great Peace," that it might become "the distributing center of spiritual enlightenment, and all the world receive this heavenly blessing," and that its inhabitants might "rise from their present material attainments to such a height that heavenly illumination may stream from this center to all the peoples of the world." It is in connection with its people that He has affirmed that they are "indeed worthy of being the first to build the Tabernacle of the Great Peace and proclaim the oneness of mankind."[28]

What kind of contribution is this "signally blest"[29] nation making to the evolution of a system of global governance that recognizes the oneness of the human family and ensures its peaceful existence? Recurrent international crises in the twentieth and twenty-first centuries have tended to increase the American nation's participation in the affairs of the world, imbuing it with a sense of world solidarity and increasing awareness of the need for the creation of an international order capable of establishing and maintaining peace in the world. Its contributions are both direct and indirect.

As to its direct contribution, the United States is distinguished for its willingness to expend its human and material resources for "the relief of human suffering and the rehabilitation of the peoples and nations."[30] It has also taken visionary initiatives to establish lasting peace at the cessation of periods of warfare, and has actively participated in consultations aimed at creating institutions to preserve the peace, in the form of the League of Nations and, later, the United Nations.

'Abdu'l-Bahá pays tribute to President Woodrow Wilson for striving "day and night that the rights of all men may be preserved safe and secure, that even small nations, like greater ones, may dwell in peace and comfort, under the protection of Righteousness and Justice." While Wilson's efforts were thwarted and the League of Nations ultimately foundered and gave way to the United Nations, it nevertheless represented a critical first step toward recognition of the necessity of a system of collective security. Its importance lies in the fact that "For the first time in the history of humanity the system of collective security, foreshadowed by Bahá'u'lláh and explained by 'Abdu'l-Bahá, has been seriously envisaged, discussed and tested. . . . For the first time in human history tentative efforts have been exerted by the nations of the world to assume collective responsibility, and to supplement their verbal pledges by actual preparation for collective action."[31] Commenting on the immediate and long-term significance of President Wilson's actions, Shoghi Effendi writes:

> To her President, the immortal Woodrow Wilson, must be ascribed the unique honor, among the statesmen of any nation, whether of the East or of the West, of having voiced sentiments so akin to the principles animating the Cause of Bahá'u'lláh, and of having more than any other world leader, contributed to the creation of the League of Nations—achievements which the pen of the Center of God's Covenant acclaimed as signalizing the dawn of the Most Great Peace, whose sun, according to that same pen, must needs arise as the direct consequence of the enforcement of the laws of the Dispensation of Bahá'u'lláh.[32]

The process of furthering the cause of peace was given renewed impetus by the American government's initiatives in relation to the establishment of the United Nations, the successor of the League of Nations, and in the subsequent actions it has taken over the years to employ the machinery of this still imperfectly functioning world body to protect peace. While the American nation has demonstrated its readiness to become the standard-bearer of world peace, peace is destined to unfold in phases and will, to some extent, depend on the creation of an international body committed to implementing the principle of collective security. The creation of such a body is, in turn, dependent on the leaders of the nations of the world becoming "thoroughly imbued with a sense of world solidarity,"[33] and clearly understanding that the structure of political institutions must needs reflect the social reality of the oneness of the human family.

By providing a working model of an evolved system of governance, the United States is expected to make an indirect, albeit important contribution to the emergence of a future international governing body. In this regard, 'Abdu'l-Bahá affirmed that: "The United States may be held up as the example of future government—that is to say, each province will be independent in itself, but there will be federal union protecting the interests of the various independent states."[34]

Highlighting the pressing need for a new form of global governance, Shoghi Effendi compares the situation of humanity in contemporary times to the situation that existed at the time of the establishment of the American Republic. "Such a unique and momentous crisis in the life of organized mankind," he writes, "may be likened to the culminating stage in the political evolution of the great American Republic—the stage which marked the emergence of a unified community of federated states." Commenting on the implications of this enlarged political unity, he calls attention to

The stirring of a new national consciousness, and the birth of a new type of civilization, infinitely richer and nobler than any which its component parts could have severally hoped to achieve, may be said to have proclaimed the coming of age of the American people. Within the territorial limits of this nation, this consummation may be viewed as the culmination of the process of human government. The diversified and loosely related elements of a divided community were brought together, unified and incorporated into one coherent system.

Shoghi Effendi lays emphasis on the creative potential for future development within the unified nation, which is the outgrowth of this development in the political realm, asserting:

Though this entity may continue gaining in cohesive power, though the unity already achieved may be further consolidated, though the civilization to which that unity could alone have given birth may expand and flourish, yet the machinery essential to such an unfoldment may be said to have been, in its essential structure, erected, and the impulse required to guide and sustain it may be regarded as having been fundamentally imparted. No stage above and beyond this consummation of national unity can, within the geographical limits of that nation, be imagined, though the highest destiny of its people, as a constituent element in a still larger entity that will embrace the whole of mankind, may still remain unfulfilled. Considered as an isolated unit, however, this process of integration may be said to have reached its highest and final consummation.[35]

The achievement of a federation of states and the consolidation of the internal institutions within the United States marks its "coming of age as a political entity," and provides a viable working model for the coming of age of the world polity—the emergence of an international federal system of governance that will embrace all the nations of the world, take into consideration the needs of an evolving humanity, and be capable of establishing peace among the nations. The Bahá'í writings anticipate that this nation will play a preponderating role "in the hoisting of the standard of the Lesser Peace, in the unification of mankind, and in the establishment of a world federal government on this planet." While it is not possible to know in advance exactly how this process will unfold, how long it will take, and the exact nature of America's contribution, it is envisaged that the United States will play a significant role in fostering the eventual evolution of such a world body. Looking to the future, Shoghi Effendi attests that the American nation will "through the active and decisive part it will have played in the organization and peaceful settlement of the affairs of mankind, have attained the plenitude of its powers and functions as an outstanding member, and component part of a federated world."[36]

THE DESTINY OF AMERICA

The American Bahá'í community and the American nation are each pursuing different but related agendas. The one is involved in establishing the Bahá'í Faith in all continents of the globe and constructing a community based on the practice of the religion's spiritual and social teachings, and is engaged in building the framework of its administrative institutions which will ultimately prove to be the nucleus and pattern of the emerging world order. While the record of the American Bahá'í community has been outstanding and reminiscent "in some of its aspects, of the exploits with which the dawn-breakers of an heroic Age have proclaimed the birth of the Faith itself, the task associated with the name of this privileged community is, far from approaching its climax, only beginning to unfold."[37] Foreshadowing its future contribution and outlining some of its tasks, Shoghi Effendi writes:

> The community of the organized promoters of the Faith of Bahá'u'lláh in the American continent—the spiritual descendants of the dawn-breakers of an heroic Age, who by their death proclaimed the birth of that Faith—must, in turn, usher in, not by their death but through living sacrifice, that promised World

Order, the shell ordained to enshrine that priceless jewel, the world civilization, of which the Faith itself is the sole begetter . . . this community . . . deriving continual sustenance from the mandate with which the Tablets of the Divine Plan have invested it, is now busily engaged in laying the foundations and in fostering the growth of those institutions which are to herald the approach of the Age destined to witness the birth and rise of the World Order of Bahá'u'lláh.[38]

The American nation is pursuing separate and independent initiatives in the political arena—initiatives that indicate a gradually increasing awareness of the practical implications of the interdependence of the nations of the world and the associated need for changes in the world's political and organizational structures to reflect the new social and political reality. In an address delivered during his visit to the United States, 'Abdu'l-Bahá set out the mission of America. He states: "America has become renowned for her discoveries, inventions and artistic skill, famous for equity of government and stupendous undertakings; now may she also become noted and celebrated as the herald and messenger of universal peace. Let this be her mission and undertaking, and may its blessed impetus spread to all countries." Through its engagement in this pursuit, the American nation will, thereby, be "in a position to raise its voice in the councils of the nations, itself lay the cornerstone of a universal and enduring peace, proclaim the solidarity, the unity, and maturity of mankind, and assist in the establishment of the promised reign of righteousness on earth."[39]

The evolutionary processes to which the activities of the American Bahá'í community and the American nation give rise are long-term and are inevitably subject to challenge and periods of testing, which will, in turn, provide the discipline and the experience necessary to promote subsequent stages in the unfoldment of the fundamental transformation that must necessarily accompany the coming of age of the human race. The Bahá'í writings envisage, in the distant future, an eventual convergence between the mission and aspirations of the American nation and "the community of the American believers within its heart." This critical conjunction opens the way for the fulfillment of America's destiny. "Then, and only then," asserts Shoghi Effendi, "will the American nation accomplish 'that which will adorn the pages of history,' 'become the envy of the world and be blest in both the East and the West.'"[40]

NOTES

INTRODUCTION

1. Shoghi Effendi, *The Advent of Divine Justice,* ¶15.

2. Ibid., ¶15.

3. Shoghi Effendi, "The Faith of Bahá'u'lláh, A World Religion," *World Order,* volume XIII, no. 7, p. 2.

4. Ibid.

5. For additional information refer to a letter dated 5 July 1947 by Shoghi Effendi in *Citadel of Faith,* p. 7.

6. Ibid.

7. Shoghi Effendi, *God Passes By,* p. 3.

8. Ibid., p. 256.

9. Ibid., p. 256.

CHAPTER 1: DRAMA OF THE HEROIC AGE

1. Shoghi Effendi, *God Passes By,* p. 3.

2. George Townshend, in "Introduction," *The Dawn-Breakers,* p. xxiv.

3. Shoghi Effendi, *God Passes By,* p. 4.

4. Shoghi Effendi, *The Promised Day Is Come,* ¶188; Renan cited in ibid., ¶188.

5. Shoghi Effendi, *God Passes By,* p. 5.

6. Ibid., pp. 6–7.

7. Ibid., p. 7.

8. The Báb, in *The Dawn-Breakers*, pp. 92–94.

9. Shoghi Effendi, *God Passes By*, p. 11.

10. For a detailed account of these interviews refer to *The Dawn-Breakers: Nabíl's Narrative of the Early Days of the Bahá'í Revelation*, pp. 171–77.

11. Shoghi Effendi, *God Passes By*, pp. 16–20.

12. *Selections from the Writings of the Báb*, no. 1:4:12.

13. Shoghi Effendi, *God Passes By*, p. 20.

14. Ibid., p. 21.

15. The Báb, in *The Dawn-Breakers*, pp. 315–16.

16. Shoghi Effendi, *God Passes By*, pp. 25, 22–23; for additional details refer to Ibid., pp. 25–26.

17. Ibid., pp. 31, 32–33.

18. Ibid., pp. 35–36; p. 36; p. 37; pp. 37–38; p. 35.

19. Moojan Momen, *The Bábí and Bahá'í Religions 1844–1944, Some Contemporary Western Accounts*, p. 91.

20. Shoghi Effendi, *God Passes By*, p. 38.

21. Ibid.

22. Nabíl-i-A'ẓam, *The Dawn-Breakers*, pp. 430–31.

23. See Ibid., Chapter XXI; footnote pp. 458–59; p. 462.

24. Nabíl-i-A'ẓam, *The Dawn-Breakers*, Chapter XXII; Shoghi Effendi, *God Passes By*, p. 42; Nabíl-i-A'ẓam, *The Dawn-Breakers*, p. 486; Shoghi Effendi, *God Passes By*, p. 43.

25. Nabíl-i-A'ẓam, *The Dawn-Breakers*, p. 494.

26. Ibid., pp. 495–496.

27. Ibid., Chapter XXIV; p. 529.

28. Ibid., pp. 543–544.

29. Ibid., p. 546.

30. Shoghi Effendi, *God Passes By*, p. 45.

31. Ibid., pp. 44, 46.

32. Nabíl-i-A'ẓam, *The Dawn-Breakers*, Chapter XXIII.

33. Shoghi Effendi, *God Passes By*, pp. 62, 63–64, 65.
34. Ibid., pp. 74, 75.
35. Nabíl-i-A'ẓam, *The Dawn-Breakers*, p. 645.
36. Shoghi Effendi, *God Passes By*, p. 79.

CHAPTER 2: THE ROLE OF THE MARTYR

1. Cóilín Owens, "A Literary Preamble" in Rona M. Fields (ed.), *Martyrdom, The Psychology, Theology, and Politics of Self-Sacrifice*, p. 1; Rona M. Fields, "The Psychology and Sociology of Martyrdom" in ibid., p. 27; Cóilín Owens, cited in "A Conversation among the Collaborators," in ibid., p. 170; Abdu'l-Missagh Ghadirian, "Intergenerational Responses to the Persecution of Bahá'ís of Iran," in Yael Danieli (ed.) *International Handbook of Multigenerational Legacies of Trauma*, p. 518.

2. Rona M. Fields, "The Psychology and Sociology of Martyrdom" in *Martyrdom, The Psychology, Theology, and Politics of Self-Sacrifice*, p. 27.

3. Ibid., pp 39–40, 56.

4. Michael Berenbaum and Reuven Firestone, "The Theology of Martyrdom" in ibid., p. 117; Michael Berenbaum cited in "A Conversation among the Collaborators," in ibid., p. 152.

5. Valérie Rosoux, "The Politics of Martyrdom" in ibid., p. 84.

6. Ami Pedahzur, cited in Christian Caryl, "Why They Do It," in *The New York Times Review of Books* 52, no. 14 (September 22, 2005): p. 5.

7. A comprehensive list of references is found in John Jaeger, "Muslim Extremists and Violence, Bibliographic Essay," in *Choice*, December 2006, pp. 587–95.

8. Rona M. Fields, "The Psychology and Sociology of Martyrdom" in *Martyrdom, The Psychology, Theology, and Politics of Self-Sacrifice*, p. 35; Abdu'l-Missagh Ghadirian, "Intergenerational Responses to the

Persecution of Bahá'ís of Iran," in Yael Danieli (ed.) *International Handbook of Multigenerational Legacies of Trauma*, p. 518.

9. Extract from a letter dated 28 July 1950 written on behalf of Shoghi Effendi, published in *Unfolding Destiny*, p. 406.

10. See, for example, an extract from a letter dated 25 August 1939 written on behalf of Shoghi Effendi to an individual believer, published in *Lights of Guidance*, no. 1200; Extract from a letter dated 27 January 1933, written on behalf of Shoghi Effendi, published in ibid., no. 1928.

11. Bahá'u'lláh, in H. M. Balyuzi, *Eminent Bahá'ís in the Time of Bahá'u'lláh*, p.172; Bahá'u'lláh, *Epistle to the Son of the Wolf*, p. 25.

12. Abdu'l-Missagh Ghadirian, "Intergenerational Responses to the Persecution of Bahá'ís of Iran," in Yael Danieli (ed.) *International Handbook of Multigenerational Legacies of Trauma*, p. 517.

13. The Báb, *Selections from the Writings of the Báb*, no. 7:19:1–3.

14. Bahá'u'lláh, the Kitáb-i-Íqán, ¶249.

15. Ibid., ¶252, ¶261, ¶263.

16. Ibid., ¶264.

17. Shoghi Effendi, *God Passes By*, p. 5; Ibid., p. 4.

18. Ibid., p. 5.

19. Ibid., p. 81.

20. Nabíl-i-A'ẓam, *The Dawn-Breakers*, p. 179.

21. Ibid., pp. 330–331.

22. Ibid., p. 99.

23. Section XIV in the compilation "Fire and Light" in *The Bahá'í World*, volume XVIII, p. 27.

24. Shoghi Effendi, extract from a letter dated 21 March 1932, *The World Order of Bahá'u'lláh*, pp. 55–56.

CHAPTER 3: TRANSITION TO THE FORMATIVE AGE

1. Shoghi Effendi, *God Passes By,* p. xiv.

2. Ibid., p. xv.

3. Ibid., pp. 197, 198.

4. Ibid., p. 199.

5. Ibid., pp. 200, 201

6. Ibid., pp. 215, 218.

7. Ibid., pp. 239, 243.

8. For additional details refer to *God Passes By*, Chapter XV.

9. For additional details refer to *God Passes By*, Chapter XVIII.

10. Shoghi Effendi, *God Passes By*, pp. xv, 279, 280–81, 287–88, 295.

11. For a detailed treatment of the travels of 'Abdu'l-Bahá in the West, refer to *God Passes By*, Chapter XIX; Ibid., pp. 281–82.

12. Shoghi Effendi, extract from a letter dated 5 June 1947 to the American Bahá'ís, *Citadel of Faith,* p. 5.

13. Shoghi Effendi, *God Passes By*, pp. xv, 324, 325.

14. The Báb, cited in Ibid., pp. 324–325; Bahá'u'lláh, the Kitáb-i-Aqdas, ¶181.

15. Shoghi Effendi, *God Passes By*, p. 325.

16. Ibid., pp. 328, 325; For additional details see Ibid., Chapter XXII.

17. Ibid., p. 330.

18. Extract from a letter dated 3 August 1932 written on behalf of Shoghi Effendi, in *The Compilation of Compilations*, volume II, no. 1276.

CHAPTER 4: SEEDS OF WORLD ORDER

1. Shoghi Effendi, *God Passes By,* p. 79.

2. Ibid., p. 38.

3. Ibid., pp. 79–80.

4. Ibid., p. 36; For a comprehensive treatment of the episode at Shaykh Ṭabarsí, see *The Dawn-Breakers,* Chapters XIX and XX.

5. 'Abdu'l-Bahá, *A Traveller's Narrative,* p. 23.

6. Nabíl-i-A'ẓam, *The Dawn-Breakers,* p. 347.

7. Ibid., p. 349.

8. Ibid., p. 363.

9. Ibid., p. 365.

10. Ibid., p. 366.

11. Ibid., p. 383.

12. Ibid., p. 396.

13. 'Abdu'l-Bahá, *Memorials of the Faithful,* ¶2.6.

14. For details refer to *The Dawn-Breakers,* pp. 430–32; Ibid., p. 431.

15. Ibid., p. 413.

16. For details refer to *God Passes By,* pp. 38–42.

17. Extract from a letter dated 30 November 1930, written on behalf of Shoghi Effendi to an individual, *Unfolding Destiny,* p. 426.

18. Bernard Lewis, *The Crisis of Islam, Holy War and Unholy Terror,* p. 27; 'Abdu'l-Bahá, *A Traveller's Narrative,* pp. 33–34.

19. Bahá'u'lláh, *Epistle to the Son of the Wolf,* p. 25; Bahá'u'lláh, in "Introduction," *Dawn-Breakers,* p. xxxv.

20. Shoghi Effendi, *God Passes By,* p. 39; Nabíl-i-A'ẓam, in "Introduction," *The Dawn-Breakers,* p. xxxiv.

21. Shoghi Effendi, *God Passes By,* p. 39.

22. Nabíl-i-A'ẓam, *The Dawn-Breakers,* pp. 390–92.

23. Warren Bennis, "The Challenges of Leadership in the Modern World," *American Psychologist* 62, no. 1 (January 2007): pp. 2–5; Kathleen K. Reardon, "Courage as a Skill," *Harvard Business Review,* January 2007, pp. 58–64. See pp. 63–64.

24. Warren Bennis, "The Challenges of Leadership in the Modern World," *American Psychologist* 62, no. 1 (January 2007): pp. 2–5. See, p. 2; Ibid., p. 5.

25. Nabíl-i-A'zam, *The Dawn-Breakers*, p. 350.

26. Ibid., pp. 356–357; Ibid., p. 356.

27. Shoghi Effendi, *God Passes By*, p. 40.

28. Ibid. pp. 40–41.

29. H. M. Balyuzi, *Bahá'u'lláh, the King of Glory*, pp. 81–82.

30. Shoghi Effendi, *God Passes By*, pp. 38–39.

31. Nabíl-i-A'zam, *The Dawn-Breakers*, p. 388.

32. Ibid., p. 363.

33. Shoghi Effendi, *God Passes By*, p. 41.

34. Ibid., p. 38.

35. Ibid., p. 38.

36. Shoghi Effendi, extract from a letter dated 21 March 1932, *The World Order of Bahá'u'lláh*, p. 52.

37. Shoghi Effendi, extract from a letter dated 8 February 1934, ibid., p. 156; Ibid., p. 144; Shoghi Effendi, extract from a letter dated 11 March 1936, ibid., p. 168.

38. Shoghi Effendi, "The Faith of Bahá'u'lláh, A World Religion." A statement prepared for the United Nations Special Palestine Committee, July 1947, in *World Order Magazine* XIII, no. 7 (October 1947); Shoghi Effendi, extract from a letter dated 27 February 1929, *The World Order of Bahá'u'lláh*, p. 10.

39. Shoghi Effendi, extract from a letter dated 11 March 1936, *The World Order of Bahá'u'lláh*, p. 194; Shoghi Effendi, extract from a letter dated 21 March 1932, ibid., p. 67.

40. Extract from a letter dated 26 April 1932, written on behalf of Shoghi Effendi to the Bahá'ís of Montreal, in *Messages to Canada*, p. 37.

41. Shoghi Effendi, extract from a letter dated 5 June 1947, in *Citadel of Faith*, p. 5; Ibid., p. 22; Shoghi Effendi, extract from a letter dated 27 February 1929, *The World Order of Bahá'u'lláh*, p. 9.

42. Shoghi Effendi, "The Faith of Bahá'u'lláh, A World Religion." A statement prepared for the United Nations Special Palestine Committee, July 1947, in *World Order Magazine*, XIII, no. 7 (October 1947); Shoghi Effendi, extract from a letter dated 15 April 1940, *This Decisive Hour*, ¶70.2.

CHAPTER 5: THE DAWN-BREAKERS OF THE FORMATIVE AGE—THE ROLE OF THE WEST

1. For a detailed treatment of the rise and early establishment of the Bahá'í Faith in the West, see Shoghi Effendi, *God Passes By*, Chapter XVI.

2. Shoghi Effendi, extract from a letter dated 21 April 1933, *The World Order of Bahá'u'lláh*, pp. 85–86; Shoghi Effendi, extract from a letter dated 3 May 1953, *Messages to the Bahá'í World, 1950–1957*, p. 146.

3. The Báb, in *God Passes By*, p. 253; Bahá'u'lláh in ibid., p. 253.

4. 'Abdu'l-Bahá, in ibid., pp. 253–54.

5. Shoghi Effendi, extract from a letter dated 21 April 1933, *The World Order of Bahá'u'lláh*, pp. 73–74; Shoghi Effendi, extract from a letter dated 21 March 1932 to the Bahá'ís in the United States and Canada, ibid., p. 52.

6. Shoghi Effendi, *God Passes By*, pp. 396–97.

7. Shoghi Effendi, extract from a letter dated 21 April 1933, *The World Order of Bahá'u'lláh*, p. 87; Shoghi Effendi, *God Passes By*, p. 324.

8. Shoghi Effendi, *God Passes By*, p. 397.

9. Shoghi Effendi, extract from a letter dated 29 April 1953, *Citadel of Faith*, p. 109.

10. Shoghi Effendi, extract from a letter dated 25 December 1938, *The Advent of Divine Justice,* ¶12.

11. For a summary of Bahá'u'lláh's vision of the future World Order, see an extract from a letter dated 11 March 1936 written by Shoghi Effendi in *The World Order of Bahá'u'lláh,* pp. 203–4; William S. Hatcher & J. Douglas Martin, *The Bahá'í Faith, The Emerging Global Religion,* p. 135.

12. Shoghi Effendi, extract from a letter dated 8 February 1934, *The World Order of Bahá'u'lláh,* pp. 144, 145.

13. William S. Hatcher & J. Douglas Martin, *The Bahá'í Faith: The Emerging Global Religion,* p. 139.

14. For a discussion of this subject refer to Shoghi Effendi's analysis in *The Promised Day Is Come.*

15. William S. Hatcher & J. Douglas Martin, *The Bahá'í Faith: The Emerging Global Religion,* pp. 142–43.

16. Shoghi Effendi, extract from a letter dated 11 March 1936, *The World Order of Bahá'u'lláh,* pp. 203–4.

17. Shoghi Effendi, extract from a letter dated 5 June 1947, *Citadel of Faith,* p. 38; Shoghi Effendi, extract from a letter dated 11 March 1936, *The World Order of Bahá'u'lláh,* pp. 162–63.

18. Shoghi Effendi, extract from a letter dated 21 March 1930, *The World Order of Bahá'u'lláh,* p. 19.

19. Shoghi Effendi, *God Passes By,* p. 31.

20. Ibid., p. 31.

21. Nabíl-i-A'zam, *The Dawn-Breakers,* p. 293.

22. For details refer to Ibid., pp. 293–98.

23. Nabíl-i-A'zam, *The Dawn-Breakers,* pp. 294–95.

24. Ṭáhirih, in Shoghi Effendi, *God Passes By,* pp. 32–33.

25. Shoghi Effendi, *God Passes By,* p. 32; Ibid., p. 33.

26. 'Abdu'l-Bahá, *The Promulgation of Universal Peace,* p. 251.

27. Nabíl-i-A'ẓam, *The Dawn-Breakers,* pp. 297–98; Shoghi Effendi, *God Passes By,* p. 33.

28. Shoghi Effendi, *God Passes By,* pp. 33–34.

29. Shoghi Effendi, extract from a letter dated April 1957 to the National Convention of the Bahá'ís of the United States, in *Messages to the Bahá'í World, 1950–1957,* p. 120.

30. Bahá'u'lláh, the Kitáb-i-Aqdas, ¶1.

31. Shoghi Effendi, extract from a letter dated 25 December 1938, *The Advent of Divine Justice,* ¶61.

32. Shoghi Effendi, *God Passes By,* p. 33.

CHAPTER 6: THE CRADLE AND STRONGHOLD OF THE BAHÁ'Í ADMINISTRATIVE ORDER

1. Shoghi Effendi, *The Advent of Divine Justice,* ¶15.

2. Shoghi Effendi, extract from a letter dated 21 April 1933, *The World Order of Bahá'u'lláh,* pp. 85–86; Shoghi Effendi, extract from a letter dated 5 June 1947, *Citadel of Faith,* p. 34.

3. Shoghi Effendi, extract from a letter dated 8 February 1934, *The World Order of Bahá'u'lláh,* pp. 153–54.

4. For additional information refer to Janet A. Khan, "Rank and Station: Reflections on the Life of Bahíyyih Khánum," *Journal of Bahá'í Studies,* volume 17, no. 1/4, (March–December 2007), pp. 1–26.

5. Shoghi Effendi, extract from a letter dated 27 February 1929, *The World Order of Bahá'u'lláh,* p. 9.

6. Shoghi Effendi, extract from a letter dated 21 April 1933, *The World Order of Bahá'u'lláh,* p. 80.

7. Ibid., p. 82.

8. For detailed information about the groups addressed by 'Abdu'l-Bahá and the subjects of his talks, refer to *The Promulgation of Universal Peace: Talks Delivered by 'Abdu'l-Bahá during His Visit to the*

United States and Canada in 1912, rev. ed. (Wilmette: Bahá'í Publishing, 2007).

9. For details concerning the embryonic administrative institutions that existed in the last years of the Heroic Age, refer to Robert. H. Stockman, *The Bahá'í Faith in America: Origins 1892–1900,* vol. 1 (Wilmette: Bahá'í Publishing Trust, 1985) and Robert H. Stockman, Oxford: George Ronald, *The Bahá'í Faith in America, Early Expansion 1900-1912,* vol. 2 (Oxford: George Ronald, 1995).

10. Shoghi Effendi, extract from a letter dated 21 April 1933, *The World Order of Bahá'u'lláh,* p. 89.

11. Shoghi Effendi, extract from a letter dated 5 June 1947, *Citadel of Faith,* p. 34.

12. Ibid.

13. See, for example, Shoghi Effendi, *Bahá'í Administration: Selected Messages, 1922–1932* (Wilmette: Bahá'í Publishing Trust, 1974, 1998 printing); Shoghi Effendi, *The World Order of Bahá'u'lláh: Selected Letters.*

14. Horace Holley, "A Statement on Present-day Administration of the Bahá'í Cause," in *The Bahá'í World,* volume II, p. 69.

15. Horace Holley, in Introduction to *Bahá'í Administration: Selected Messages, 1922–1932,* pp. viii–ix.

16. Ibid., pp. ix–x.

17. Horace Holley, "A Statement on Present-day Administration of the Bahá'í Cause," in *The Bahá'í World,* volume II, p. 70.

18. Ibid., p. 70.

19. *The Bahá'í Year Book,* volume 1, pp. 101–103.

20. Shoghi Effendi, extract from a letter dated 5 March 1922, *Bahá'í Administration,* p. 20.

21. Ibid., p. 20.

22. 'Abdu'l-Bahá, in ibid., p. 21.

23. Shoghi Effendi, extract from a letter dated 5 March 1922, ibid., p. 24.

24. Shoghi Effendi, extract from a letter dated 3 June 1925, ibid., p. 88.

25. Shoghi Effendi, extract from a letter dated 23 February 1924, ibid., p. 64.

26. United States National Spiritual Assembly, United States *Bahá'í News*, no. 347 (January 1960): p. 2.

27. Shoghi Effendi, extract from a letter dated 10 April 1925, *Bahá'í Administration*, p. 82.

28 Shoghi Effendi, extract from a letter dated 12 May 1925, ibid., p. 85; Shoghi Effendi, extract from a letter dated 27 November 1924, ibid., p. 72.

29. Shoghi Effendi, extract from a letter dated 18 October 1927, ibid., p. 140.

30. Shoghi Effendi, extract from a letter dated 11 May 1926, ibid., p. 109; Ibid., p. 109.

31. Shoghi Effendi, extract from a letter dated 31 October 1926, ibid., p. 116.

32. Shoghi Effendi, extract from a letter dated 20 February 1927, ibid., p 128.

33. Shoghi Effendi, extract from a letter dated 12 April 1927, ibid., p. 129.

34. Ibid., p. 131.

35. Shoghi Effendi, extract from a letter dated 14 November 1926, ibid., p. 119.

36. Shoghi Effendi, extract from a letter dated 22 April 1926, ibid., p. 105.

37. Shoghi Effendi, extract from a letter dated 27 April 1927, ibid., p. 134.

38. William Sears, in "Memorial Gathering for Horace Holley Held at Request of the Hands of the Faith," in United States *Bahá'í News*, no. 355, September 1960, p. 4; Rúḥíyyih Khánum, "In Memoriam for Horace Hotchkiss Holley," *The Bahá'í World*, volume XIII, pp. 849–50.

39. Reported in article entitled, "Horace Holley Reviews Growth of Administrative Order at Farewell Meeting on Eve of Departure for Holy Land" in United States *Bahá'í News*, no. 348 (February 1960): p. 2.

40. Rúḥíyyih Khánum, "In Memoriam for Horace Hotchkiss Holley," *The Bahá'í World*, volume XIII, p. 854.

41. Ibid., p. 854.

42. Ibid., p. 855.

43. Ibid., p. 856.

44. Shoghi Effendi, *God Passes By*, pp. 334–35.

45. Shoghi Effendi, extract from a letter dated 28 July 1954, *Citadel of Faith*, p. 123; Shoghi Effendi, extract from a letter dated 21 March 1932, *The World Order of Bahá'u'lláh*, p. 53.

46. For details see the "Report of Legal Committee" in United States *Bahá'í News*, no. 17 (April 1927): pp. 11–12; Shoghi Effendi, *God Passes By*, p. 335.

47. Shoghi Effendi, *God Passes By*, p. 335.

48. Editorial entitled "The Spirit in the Body" in United States *Bahá'í News*, Special Number, May 1927, p. 1.

49. Ibid., pp. 1–2.

50. Shoghi Effendi, extract from a letter dated 27 May 1927, *Bahá'í Administration*, p. 135; Mention of the elaboration of the constitution refers to the establishment of the Universal House of Justice, which was elected for the first time in 1963. It issued its written Constitution in 1972; Shoghi Effendi, extract from a letter dated 18 October

1927, *Bahá'í Administration*, pp. 142–143; Shoghi Effendi, *God Passes By*, p. 335; Shoghi Effendi, *The Advent of Divine Justice*, ¶17.

51. Shoghi Effendi, *God Passes By*, p. 335.

52. Ibid., p. 336; Rúḥíyyih Rabbani, *The Priceless Pearl*, p. 303; Shoghi Effendi, *God Passes By*, p. 336.

53. Shoghi Effendi, *God Passes By*, p. 337.

54. Rúḥíyyih Rabbani, *The Priceless Pearl*, p. 303.

55. Shoghi Effendi, extract from a letter dated 21 March 1932, *The World Order of Bahá'u'lláh*, p. 64.

56. Shoghi Effendi, extract from a letter dated 11 February 1934 to an individual, in *Lights of Guidance*, no. 1454.

57. Ibid., no. 1455.

58. Shoghi Effendi, *God Passes By*, p. 372.

59. Shoghi Effendi, extract from a letter dated 21 March 1932, *The World Order of Bahá'u'lláh*, p. 64.

60. Ibid., 65.

61. Ibid., pp. 65–66.

62. Shoghi Effendi, extract from a letter dated 21 April 1933, ibid., p. 89.

63. Shoghi Effendi, *God Passes By*, p. 330.

64. Shoghi Effendi, extract from a letter dated October 1957, *Messages to the Bahá'í World, 1950–1957*, p. 127.

65. Shoghi Effendi, extract from a letter dated 20 August 1955, *Citadel of Faith*, p. 141; Shoghi Effendi, extract from a letter dated 18 July 1953, ibid., p. 110; Shoghi Effendi, extract from a letter dated 19 July 1956, ibid., p. 145.

66. Shoghi Effendi, *The Advent of Divine Justice*, ¶17.

67. Shoghi Effendi, extract from a letter dated 20 June 1954, *Citadel of Faith*, pp. 130–31.

CHAPTER 7: CHIEF EXECUTOR AND CUSTODIAN OF 'ABDU'L-BAHÁ'S DIVINE PLAN

1. Shoghi Effendi, *God Passes By*, p. 397; 'Abdu'l-Bahá, *Tablets of the Divine Plan*, p. 79.

2. 'Abdu'l-Bahá, *Tablets of the Divine Plan*, p. 40.

3. Extract from a letter dated 6 July 1942, written on behalf of Shoghi Effendi to an individual, in *Lights of Guidance*, no. 250.

4. Shoghi Effendi, extract from a letter dated 28 July 1954, *Citadel of Faith*, p. 123.

5. Shoghi Effendi, extract from a letter dated 26 May 1942, *This Decisive Hour*, ¶94.1; Shoghi Effendi, extract from a letter dated 21 April 1933, *The World Order of Bahá'u'lláh*, p. 87.

6. Abdu'l-Bahá, *Tablets of the Divine Plan*, pp. 40, 49–53.

7. Ibid., pp. 18. Amin Banani, Foreword to 1977 Edition, *Tablets of the Divine Plan*, p. xix.

9. Shoghi Effendi, extract from a letter dated 21 April 1933, *The World Order of Bahá'u'lláh*, p. 87; For details of Miss Root's life and exploits, see Mabel R. Garis, *Martha Root: Lioness at the Threshold* (Wilmette: Bahá'í Publishing Trust, 1983); The Universal House of Justice, extract from a letter dated January 1977 addressed to the International Teaching Conference, Bahia, Brazil, in *Messages from the Universal House of Justice, 1963–1986*, no. 185.3.

10. Shoghi Effendi, *God Passes By*, p. 308; Report in *The Bahá'í World*, volume 2 (New York City: Bahá'í Publishing Committee, 1928) p. 40.

11. Marzieh Gail, *Other People, Other Places*, pp, 188–90.

12. "In memoriam" for John Bosch, in *The Bahá'í World*, volume XI, pp. 488–494, quotation on p. 492. For additional details of the services of John and Louise Bosch refer to Louise Bosch, "A trip to Tahiti" in *The Bahá'í World*, volume III (New York City: Bahá'í Pub-

lishing Committee, 1930), pp. 368–371; "In memoriam" for Louise Bosch, in *The Bahá'í World,* volume XII, pp. 705–707.

13. Louise Bosch, "A trip to Tahiti" in *The Bahá'í World,* volume III, p. 371.

14. Shoghi Effendi, extract from a letter dated 21 April 1933, *The World Order of Bahá'u'lláh,* pp. 87–88.

15. Shoghi Effendi, extract from a letter dated 26 May 1942, *This Decisive Hour,* ¶94.1; See cable dated 29 April 1936 from Shoghi Effendi in *This Decisive Hour,* ¶20.1.

16. Shoghi Effendi, extract from a letter dated 14 November 1936, *This Decisive Hour,* ¶25.1.

17. Shoghi Effendi, extract from a letter dated 25 May 1941, ibid., ¶82.6.

18. Horace Holley, "Survey of Current Bahá'í Activities in the East and west" in *The Bahá'í World,* volume VII, p. 18.

19. Garreta Busey, "Uniting the Americas," in *The Bahá'í World,* volume IX, p. 188.

20. Shoghi Effendi, extract from a letter dated 4 June 1937, *This Decisive Hour,* ¶30.1.

21. See cable dated 24 January 1939 from Shoghi Effendi in ibid., ¶45.1. The nine states and provinces that needed to be opened to the Faith were Alaska, Delaware, Nevada, South Carolina, Utah, Vermont, West Virginia, Manitoba, and Nova Scotia.

22. Shoghi Effendi, in "In memoriam" for Honor Kempton, in *The Bahá'í World* volume 18, p. 748.

23. For details refer to the "In memoriam" for Honor Kempton, in ibid., pp. 748–751.

24. Shoghi Effendi, extract from a cable dated 26 April 1939, *This Decisive Hour,* ¶51.1; Shoghi Effendi, extract from a letter dated 25 December 1938, *The Advent of Divine Justice,* ¶102.

25. Shoghi Effendi, extract from a cable dated 26 May 1939, *This Decisive Hour,* ¶56.1.

26. For details of Mathew Kaszab's activities, see, "In memoriam" in *The Bahá'í World*, volume IX (Wilmette: Bahá'í Publishing Committee, 1945), pp. 614–16; For details concerning Panama refer to Daniel Nelson Wegener, *Divine Springtime, Louise Caswell Recalls the Early Years of the Bahá'í Faith in Central America and Panama* (Tegucigalpa, Honduras: Union Press, 1977).

27. Extract from a letter dated 5 July 1945, written on behalf of Shoghi Effendi, cited in ibid., p. 31.

28. Horace Holley, "Survey of current Bahá'í Activities in the East and West," *The Bahá'í World,* volume VIII, pp. 29–31.

29. See Shoghi Effendi, cable dated 23 October 1939, *This Decisive Hour,* ¶62.1; See Shoghi Effendi, cable dated 24 April 1939, ibid., ¶71.1.

30. Shoghi Effendi, extract from a cable dated 28 October 1940, ibid., ¶77.1.

31. Shoghi Effendi, extract from a letter dated 3 December 1940, ibid., ¶79.3.

32. Shoghi Effendi, extract from a cable dated 5 February 1942, ibid., ¶91.1; See also Shoghi Effendi, cable dated 25 April 1942, ibid., ¶93.1.

33. Shoghi Effendi, extract from a letter dated 15 August 1942, ibid., ¶98.1.

34. Ibid.

35. For additional information on these subjects see Shoghi Effendi, cable dated 13 January 1943, ibid., ¶104.1; Shoghi Effendi, letter dated 8 January 1943, ibid., ¶103.1; and communications dated 28 March 1943 and 14 April 1943 from Shoghi Effendi, ibid., ¶108.5,109.1.

36. See Shoghi Effendi, cables dated 25 May 1943 and 2 January 1944, ibid., ¶112.1, 121.1.

37. Shoghi Effendi, extract from a letter dated 16 November 1943, ibid., ¶119.1.

38. Garreta Busey, "Uniting the Americas," in *The Bahá'í World,* volume IX, pp. 196–97.

39. Leroy Ioas, "Teaching in North America, in *The Bahá'í World,* volume IX, p. 210, and pp. 213–14.

40. Shoghi Effendi, *A World Survey, the Bahá'í Faith 1844–1944,* pp. 8–9, 6.

41. Shoghi Effendi, extract from a letter dated 13 April 1944, *This Decisive Hour,* ¶125.1; For details concerning Latin America, see *The Bahá'í World,* volume IX, pp. 996–1002; for details concerning North America, see ibid., pp. 214–20.

42. Shoghi Effendi, extract from a letter dated 13 April 1944, *This Decisive Hour,* ¶125.3; Ibid., ¶125.5.

43. Ibid., ¶125.3.

44. Ibid., ¶125.4.

45. Ibid., ¶125.5.

46. Shoghi Effendi, extract from a letter dated 10 August 1945, ibid., ¶146.3–4.

47. Shoghi Effendi, extract from a cable dated 23 April 1946, ibid., ¶154.1; See Shoghi Effendi, cable dated 12 June 1946, ibid., ¶157.1.

48. Shoghi Effendi, extract from a letter dated 25 June 1946, ibid., ¶158.11; Shoghi Effendi, extract from a cable dated 2 December 1946, ibid., ¶165.1.

49. For details see Horace Holley, "International Survey of Current Bahá'í Activities in the East and West" in *The Bahá'í World,* volume XI (Wilmette, IL: Bahá'í Publishing Committee, 1952), pp. 44–45; Shoghi Effendi, *The Bahá'í Faith 1844–1952, Information Statistical and Comparative,* pp. 27–28, 32–33.

50. "International Survey of Current Bahá'í Activities" in *The Bahá'í World,* volume XII, pp. 57–60. For detailed information concerning the construction and dedication of the Bahá'í House of Worship in Wilmette refer to Bruce Whitmore, *The Dawning place: the building of*

a temple, the forging of the North American Bahá'í community (Wilmette, IL: Bahá'í Publishing Trust, 1984).

51. For details see Horace Holley, "International Survey of Current Bahá'í Activities in the East and West" in *The Bahá'í World*, volume XI, pp. 20–23; "International Survey of Current Bahá'í Activities" in *The Bahá'í World*, volume XII, pp. 66–67.

52. "International Survey of Current Bahá'í Activities" in *The Bahá'í World*, volume XII, p. 60.

53. Ibid., pp. 60–61.

54. Shoghi Effendi, extract from a letter dated 5 June 1945, *Citadel of Faith*, p. 20.

55. Ibid., pp. 20–21.

56. See Shoghi Effendi, cable dated 5 June 1946, *This Decisive Hour*, ¶156.1.

57. See detailed report entitled "Reestablishment of National Spiritual Assembly for Germany and Austria" in *The Bahá'í World*, volume X, pp. 18–30.

58. "International Survey of Current Bahá'í Activities," in *The Bahá'í World*, volume XI, pp. 23, 30–31.

59. The Universal House of Justice, in "In memoriam," Edna M. True, in *The Bahá'í World*, volume XX, p. 925; for additional details see ibid, pp. 925–927.

60. "International Survey of Current Bahá'í Activities," in *The Bahá'í World*, volume XI, p. 50.

61. Ibid., pp. 50–51.

62. Cited in ibid., p. 52.

63. "International Survey of Current Bahá'í Activities" in *The Bahá'í World*, volume XII, p. 64.

64. Shoghi Effendi, extract from a letter dated 23 November 1951, *Citadel of Faith*, p. 102; Shoghi Effendi, *The Bahá'í Faith 1844–1952, Information Statistical and Comparative*, pp. 36–37; Shoghi Effendi,

extract from a letter dated 30 June 1952, *Messages to the Bahá'í World, 1950–1957*, p. 31; "International Survey of Current Bahá'í Activities" in *The Bahá'í World*, volume XII, pp. 61–62.

65. Shoghi Effendi, extract from a letter dated 30 June 1952, *Messages to the Bahá'í World, 1950–1957*, pp. 33–35; Shoghi Effendi, extract from a cable dated 8 August 1952, ibid., p. 41

66. Shoghi Effendi, extract from a cable dated 8 August 1952, *Messages to the Bahá'í World, 1950–1957*, pp. 41–42. For a detailed summary of the goals and objectives of the Ten Year Spiritual Crusade see *The Bahá'í World*, volume XII, pp. 256–274; Shoghi Effendi, extract from a cable dated 8 August 1952, *Messages to the Bahá'í World, 1950–1957*, p. 43.

67. Shoghi Effendi, extract from a letter dated 4 May 1953, *Messages to the Bahá'í World, 1950–1957*, pp. 152–53.

68. See Shoghi Effendi, letter dated 29 April 1953, *Citadel of Faith*, pp. 106-109; Shoghi Effendi, extract from a cable dated 28 May 1953, *Messages to the Bahá'í World, 1950–1957*, p. 49.

69. For a detailed summary of the goals and objectives of the Ten Year Spiritual Crusade see *The Bahá'í World*, volume XII, pp. 256–274.

70. Shoghi Effendi, extract from a letter dated 29 April 1953, *Citadel of Faith*, pp. 106–109. This letter sets out the twenty-four goals assigned to the American Bahá'í community under the Ten Year Plan, 1953–1963.

71. Ibid., p. 109.

72. Shoghi Effendi, extract from a cable dated 28 May 1953, *Messages to the Bahá'í World, 1950–1957*, p. 49.

73. "International Survey of Current Bahá'í Activities" in *The Bahá'í World*, volume XIII, p. 270.

74. Shoghi Effendi, extract from a letter dated April 1957, *Messages to the Bahá'í World, 1950–1957*, p. 105.

75. See Shoghi Effendi, cable dated 21 March 1954, ibid., p. 57; Richard Thomas, "Spreading the Divine Fragrances: African-American Bahá'ís in the Global Expansion of the Bahá'í Faith, 1937–1963," in *Lights of the Spirit,* pp. 108–9.

76. See Shoghi Effendi, cable dated 21 March 1954, *Messages to the Bahá'í World, 1950–1957,* p. 57.

77. "In Memorial" for Alvin J. Blum, in *The Bahá'í World,* volume XV, pp. 439–41. The quotation appears on p. 441.

78. The Universal House of Justice, unpublished cable dated 7 June 1993 to the National Spiritual Assembly of the Solomon Islands.

79. "In memoriam" for Maude Elizabeth Todd Fisher in *The Bahá'í World,* volume XIII, pp. 902–5. The quotation appears on p. 905.

80. Shoghi Effendi, extract from a letter dated April 1957, *Messages to the Bahá'í World, 1950–1957,* p. 113. A list of the names of the Bahá'ís who were designated as Knights of Bahá'u'lláh during the course of the Ten Year Plan is found in *The Bahá'í World,* volume XIII, pp. 449–57.

81. Shoghi Effendi, extract from a letter dated April 1956, *Messages to the Bahá'í World, 1950–1957,* p. 100.

82. Shoghi Effendi, extract from a letter dated October 1957, ibid., pp. 124–25. Note unforeseen circumstances made it necessary to move the location of the conference, scheduled to take place in Djakarta, to Singapore. See report in *The Bahá'í World,* volume XIII, pp. 331–32; Shoghi Effendi, extract from a letter dated October 1957, *Messages to the Bahá'í World, 1950–1957,* p. 125; Ibid., p. 130.

83. Ibid., pp. 127–28.

84. For a report of the five conferences, refer to *The Bahá'í World,* volume XIII, pp. 317–32.

85. Shoghi Effendi, extract from a letter dated October 1957, *Messages to the Bahá'í World, 1950–1957,* p. 125.

86. For a summary of the achievements of the Ten Year Plan, see *The Bahá'í World,* volume XIII, pp. 459–478; Ibid., pp. 467, 468–69; *The Bahá'í World,* volume XIII, p. 270.

87. Shoghi Effendi, extract from a letter dated 21 September, *Citadel of Faith,* p. 153.

88. Ibid., pp. 151.

89. Ibid., p. 158; Shoghi Effendi, extract from a letter dated 16 March 1949, ibid., p. 66.

90. Shoghi Effendi passed away and was buried in London. See article entitled "The passing of Shoghi Effendi" in *The Bahá'í World,* volume XIII, pp. 207–25. The article is written by Rúḥíyyih <u>Kh</u>ánum, Shoghi Effendi's widow.

91. The Universal House of Justice, extract from a letter dated 7 May 1963 to the National Conventions of the Bahá'í World, in *Messages from the Universal House of Justice, 1963–1986,* ¶2.3.

92. Shoghi Effendi, extract from a letter dated 25 December 1938, *The Advent of Divine Justice,* ¶15.

93. Shoghi Effendi, extract from a letter dated 28 July 1954, *Citadel of Faith,* p. 127.

94. Shoghi Effendi, extract from a letter dated 21 December 1938, *The Advent of Divine Justice,* ¶33.

CHAPTER 8: LAYING THE FOUNDATIONS OF WORLD CIVILIZATION

1. Shoghi Effendi, from a letter dated 29 March 1951, *Citadel of Faith,* p. 97.

2. Shoghi Effendi, from a letter dated 29 April 1953, ibid., p. 109; Shoghi Effendi, extract from a letter dated 28 March 1943, *This Decisive Hour,* ¶108.2.

3. 'Abdu'l-Bahá, *Selections from the Writings of 'Abdu'l-Bahá,* no. 64.1.

4. Shoghi Effendi, *God Passes By*, p. 350; See, Bruce Whitmore, *The Dawning Place* (Wilmette: Bahá'í Publishing Trust, 1984), Nathan Rutstein, *Corinne True, Faithful Handmaiden of 'Abdu'l-Bahá* (Oxford: George Ronald, 1987); 'Abdu'l-Bahá, *Tablets of the Divine Plan*, p. 78.

5. Shoghi Effendi, extract from a letter dated 21 March 1932, *The World Order of Bahá'u'lláh*, p. 67.

6. Shoghi Effendi, extract from a letter dated 11 April 1949, *Citadel of Faith*, pp. 68–69.

7. Bahá'u'lláh, the Kitáb-i-Aqdas, ¶31, ¶115.

8. 'Abdu'l-Bahá, *Selections from the Writings of 'Abdu'l-Bahá*, no. 60.1.

9. Ibid., ¶64.1; Shoghi Effendi, extract from a letter dated 25 October 1929, *Bahá'í Administration*, p. 184.

10. Shoghi Effendi, extract from a letter dated 8 February 1934, *The World Order of Bahá'u'lláh*, pp. 156–57.

11. Shoghi Effendi, extract from a letter dated 25 October 1929, *Bahá'í Administration*, p. 185.

12. Ibid., p. 186.

13. Ibid., p. 186.

14. Ibid. p. 186.

15. Ibid., p. 184; Shoghi Effendi, *God Passes By*, pp. 339–40; Shoghi Effendi, extract from a letter of 4 July 1939, *This Decisive Hour*, ¶57.1.

16. Shoghi Effendi, extract from a letter dated 4 July 1939, *This Decisive Hour*, ¶57.1; Shoghi Effendi, extract from a letter dated 25 December 1938, *The Advent of Divine Justice*, ¶65.

17. Shoghi Effendi, *God Passes By*, p. 288.

18. The Universal House of Justice, extract from a letter dated 20 October 1983, *Messages from the Universal House of Justice, 1963–1986*, no. 379.2.

19. The Universal House of Justice, extract from a letter dated Naw-Rúz 1974, *Messages from the Universal House of Justice, 1963–1986*, no. 141.12–13.

20. Shoghi Effendi, extract from an unpublished letter dated 7 December 1923 to the Local Spiritual Assembly of New York.

21. Shoghi Effendi, extract from a letter dated 12 April 1927, *Bahá'í Administration*, p. 131.

22. Ibid., pp. 131–32.

23. Extract from a letter dated 2 November 1933, written on behalf of Shoghi Effendi in *Compilation of Compilations*, vol. II, no. 2259.

24. Shoghi Effendi, extract from a letter dated 12 March 1923, *Bahá'í Administration*, p. 39.

25. Ibid., p. 38.

26. Ibid., p. 39.

27. For a detailed discussion of the Bahá'í calendar refer to *The Bahá'í World* volumes.

28. The Universal House of Justice, extract from a letter dated 27 August 1989, in *Compilation of Compilations*, vol. I, p. 420.

29. Shoghi Effendi, *God Passes By*, p. 288.

30. Mirzá Maḥmúd, *Maḥmúd's Diary*, p. 150.

31. 'Abdu'l-Bahá, *The Promulgation of Universal Peace*, p. 214.

32. Ibid., p. 215.

33. Mirzá Maḥmúd, *Maḥmúd's Diary*, p. 150; 'Abdu'l-Bahá, *The Promulgation of Universal Peace*, p. 214.

34. Mirzá Maḥmúd, *Maḥmúd's Diary*, p. 151.

35. 'Abdu'l-Bahá, in ibid., p.151.

36. From a Statement of the National Spiritual Assembly of the United States and Canada, published in *Bahá'í News*, no. 75 (July 1933): p. 8 and cited in *Compilation of Compilations*, vol. I., pp. 432–33, 6n.

37. The Universal House of Justice, extract from a letter dated 27 August 1989, in *Compilation of Compilations*, vol. I, p. 422.

38. Ibid., p. 419.

39. From a letter dated 22 December 1934, written on behalf of Shoghi Effendi to an individual believer, in ibid., no. 957.

40. The Universal House of Justice, extract from a letter dated 27 August1989, in ibid., p. 421.

41. From the report, "Current Bahá'í Activities" in *The Bahá'í World*, vol. V, p. 76.

42. Ibid., p. 70; From a report, "Current Bahá'í Activities" in *The Bahá'í World*, vol. VI, p. 89.

43. From "A Procedure for the Conduct of the Local Spiritual Assembly," in *The Bahá'í World*, vol. VI, p. 192.

44. Ibid., p. 193.

45. Shoghi Effendi, extract from a letter dated 11 March 1936, *The World Order of Bahá'u'lláh*, p. 204.

46. Shoghi Effendi, *God Passes By*, p. 340.

47. For a detailed treatment of the history of Green Acre refer to Anne Gordon Atkinson, *Green Acre on the Piscataqua: A Centennial Celebration* (Eliot, Maine: Green Acre Bahá'í School Council, 1991).

48. See, for example, ibid., part 2; See *The Promulgation of Universal Peace*, pp. 253–75.

49. Ibid., pp. 253

50. Ibid., pp. 261, 264.

51. Ibid., pp. 264–65.

52. From a letter dated 9 July 1931, written on behalf of Shoghi Effendi in *Compilation of Compilations*, vol. II, no. 2246.

53. From a letter dated 18 July 1957, written on behalf of Shoghi Effendi in *Compilation of Compilations*, vol. I., no. 79.

54. From a letter dated 14 October 1936, written on behalf of Shoghi Effendi to an individual, in *Compilation of Compilations*, vol. I., no. 98.

55. Shoghi Effendi, *God Passes By*, p. 341.

56. Ibid., p. 341.

57. Postscript in the handwriting of Shoghi Effendi appended to a letter of 25 September 1933, written on his behalf, in *Compilation of Compilations*, vol. I, no. 87.

58. From a letter dated 6 November 1934, written on behalf of Shoghi Effendi in, ibid., no. 88.

59. The letter dated 25 December 1938 was published as *The Advent of Divine Justice*.

60. Shoghi Effendi, extract from a letter dated 25 December 1938, *The Advent of Divine Justice*, ¶36.

61. Ibid., ¶37, 36.

62. Ibid., ¶54.

63. From a letter dated 20 May 1939, written on behalf of Shoghi Effendi in *Compilation of Compilations*, vol. I., no. 91.

64. Shoghi Effendi, extract from a letter dated 25 December 1938, *The Advent of Divine Justice*, ¶54.

65. For a chronicle of 'Abdu'l-Bahá's journey in North America, see, for example, *Maḥmúd's Diary*. His speeches are published in *The Promulgation of Universal Peace: Talks Delivered by 'Abdu'l-Bahá during His Visit to the United States and Canada in 1912*; Shoghi Effendi, *God Passes By*, p. 288; Concerning Louis Gregory refer to Gayle Morrison, *To Move the World*.

66. See, for example, Richard Hollinger, ed. *'Abdu'l-Bahá in America: Agnes Parsons' Diary* (Los Angeles: Kalimát, 1996); Gayle Morrison, *To Move the World*; Gwendolyn Etter-Lewis and Richard Thomas, eds., *Lights of the Spirit: Historical Portraits of Black Bahá'ís in North America: 1898–2000* (Wilmette: Bahá'í Publishing, 2006).

67. Shoghi Effendi, extract from a letter dated 12 April 1927, Bahá'í Administration, pp. 129–31.

68. Ibid., p. 131.

69. For a description of some of these gatherings refer to Louis

G. Gregory, "Accelerated Progress in Race Relations" in *The Bahá'í World*, vol. IX, pp. 876–80.

70. Shoghi Effendi, *The Advent of Divine Justice*, ¶51–52.

71. Reported in *The Bahá'í World*, vol. IX, p. 71.

72. Gayle Morrison, *To Move the World*, p. 277.

73. Reported in *The Bahá'í World*, vol. IX, p. 73. Details of the activities undertaken by the expanded group of teachers are provided on pp. 73–76; Gayle Morrison, *To Move the World*, pp. 277–78.

74. Ibid., pp. 284–85.

75. For details refer to Anne Gordon Atkinson, *Green Acre on the Piscataqua: A Centennial Celebration*, pp. 53–57.

76. From a letter dated 15 May 1936, written on behalf of Shoghi Effendi to Bahá'í Youth Groups in North America, in *Compilation of Compilations*, vol. II., no. 2264.

77. From a letter dated 29 July 1939, written on behalf of Shoghi Effendi to the participants at Louhelen Bahá'í school, in *Lights of Guidance*, no. 1907.

78. Shoghi Effendi, *The Advent of Divine Justice*, ¶17.

79. The Universal House of Justice, extract from a letter dated 20 October 1983, *Messages from the Universal House of Justice, 1963–1986*, ¶379.3.

80. Shoghi Effendi, extract from a letter dated 5 July 1938, *This Decisive Hour*, ¶41.1.

CHAPTER 9: STANDARD-BEARERS OF THE EMANCIPATION AND TRIUMPH OF THE BAHÁ'Í FAITH

1. Shoghi Effendi, extract from a letter dated 22 April 1926, *Bahá'í Administration*, p. 105.

2. Bahá'u'lláh, in Shoghi Effendi, *The Advent of Divine Justice*, ¶112.

3. Bahá'u'lláh, *Gleanings from the Writings of Bahá'u'lláh*, no. 23.1–3.

4. From a letter dated 24 June 1936, written on behalf of Shoghi Effendi to an individual, in *The Compilation of Compilations*, vol. I, no. 287.

5. Shoghi Effendi, extract from a letter dated 12 August 1941, *This Decisive Hour*, ¶85.11.

6. Bahá'u'lláh, *Summons of the Lord of Hosts*, ¶1.116.

7. Shoghi Effendi, extract from a letter dated 20 August 1955, *Citadel of Faith*, p. 141.

8. Shoghi Effendi, *God Passes By*, p. 31; Ibid., p. 74; Ibid., pp. 33–34.

9. Shoghi Effendi, extract from a letter dated 12 February 1927, *Bahá'í Administration*, p. 123.

10. Shoghi Effendi, extract from a letter dated 21 March 1930, *The World Order of Bahá'u'lláh*, p. 18.

11. Shoghi Effendi, *God Passes By*, p. xvii; Shoghi Effendi, extract from a letter dated 25 December 1938, *The Advent of Divine Justice*, ¶25.

12. Shoghi Effendi, extract from a letter dated 25 December 1938, *The Advent of Divine Justice*, ¶60–61.

13. Shoghi Effendi, extract from a letter dated 23 December 1922, *Bahá'í Administration*, p. 28.

14. Shoghi Effendi, extract from a letter dated 20 August 1955, *Citadel of Faith*, pp. 141–42; Shoghi Effendi, extract from a letter dated 25 December 1938, *The Advent of Divine Justice*, ¶25; Ibid., ¶17.

15. Shoghi Effendi, extract from a letter dated 22 April 1926, *Bahá'í Administration*, p. 105.

16. Bahá'u'lláh, the Kitáb-i-Aqdas, ¶88.

17. For a description of the document and the available historical information pertaining to it refer to an article entitled "Persecution and Protection: Documents about Bahá'ís, 1867, 1897, and 1902" in *World Order,* 2006, volume 37, no. 3, pp. 31–38. Quotations appear on pp. 32–33.

18. Douglas Martin, "The Persecution of the Bahá'ís in Iran 1844–1984," *Bahá'í Studies,* volume 12/13, 1984, pp. 15–16; Shoghi Effendi, extract from a letter dated 6 December 1928, *Bahá'í Administration,* pp. 148, 149.

19. Shoghi Effendi, extract from a letter dated 22 April 1926, *Bahá'í Administration,* p. 104; Shoghi Effendi, extract from a letter dated 11 May 1926, ibid., p. 107.

20. Ibid.

21. Shoghi Effendi, extract from a letter dated 22 April 1926, ibid., p. 105.

22. Shoghi Effendi, extract from a letter dated 11 May 1926, ibid., p. 108; Shoghi Effendi, extract from a letter of 27 April 1927, ibid., p. 134.

23. See report in United States *Bahá'í News,* no. 15, January 1927, p. 4.

24. National Spiritual Assembly of the United States and Canada, extract from a letter dated 16 July 1926 to His Imperial Majesty Reza Shah Pahlavi, in *The Bahá'í World,* vol. II, p. 292; Ibid., p. 287.

25. Ibid., p. 294.

26. See report in United States *Bahá'í News,* no. 15, January 1927, pp. 4– 5.

27. See report in United States *Bahá'í News,* no. 17, April 1927, p.p. 7– 8.

28. Shoghi Effendi, extract from a letter dated 31 October 1926, *Bahá'í Administration,* p. 117.

29. See "The Unity of East and West," United States *Bahá'í News*, no. 80, January 1934, p. 10; "International Survey of Activities," in *The Bahá'í World*, vol. II., pp. 38–40.

30. From a letter dated 8 June 1932 written on behalf of Shoghi Effendi, in United States *Bahá'í News*, no. 67, October 1932, p. 4.

31. "The Unity of East and West," United States *Bahá'í News*, no. 80, January 1934, p. 11.

32. From a report of Mrs. Ransom-Kehler cited in ibid., p. 11.

33. "The Unity of East and West," United States *Bahá'í News*, no. 80, January 1934, p. 12.

34. From a document dated 10 July 1933, presented to the Persian Minister, cited in ibid., p. 14.

35. From a statement dated 3 July 1933 by Mrs. Ransom-Kehler, cited in ibid., p. 13.

36. Cable from Mrs. Ransom-Kehler cited in ibid., p. 14.

37. Shoghi Effendi, extract from a cable dated 28 October 1933, *This Decisive Hour*, no. 10.1.

38. From a letter dated 3 November 1933 written on behalf of Shoghi Effendi to the National Spiritual Assembly of the United States and Canada, in *Bahá'í News*, no. 80, January 1934, p. 4.

39. From a letter dated 9 November 1933 written on behalf of Shoghi Effendi to the National Spiritual Assembly of the United States and Canada, in ibid., p. 4.

40. Shoghi Effendi, extract from a letter dated 8 November 1933 to Mr. Allen B. McDaniel, in ibid., p. 4.

41. Shoghi Effendi, extract from a letter dated 20 August 1955, *Citadel of Faith*, p. 134; Ibid., pp. 133–34.

42. Shoghi Effendi, extract from a letter dated 20 August 1955, *Citadel of Faith*, p. 134.

43. Ibid., pp. 134–35.

44. "Survey of Current International Activities" in *The Bahá'í World*, vol. XIII, p. 292.

45. Shoghi Effendi, extract from a letter dated 20 August 1955, *Citadel of Faith*, p. 140.

46. Ibid., p. 135; For details see a letter dated 15 August 1955 from Shoghi Effendi in ibid., pp. 132–33; Shoghi Effendi, extract from a letter dated 20 August 1955, ibid., p. 136; Shoghi Effendi, extract from a cable dated 23 August, 1955, *Messages to the Bahá'í World, 1950–1957*, p. 89.

47. Shoghi Effendi, extract from a letter dated 20 August 1955, *Citadel of Faith,* p. 141; Shoghi Effendi, extract from a letter dated 19 July 1956, ibid., p. 144.

48. Shoghi Effendi, extract from a letter dated 20 August 1955, ibid., p. 141.

49. For details refer to Bahá'í International Community, *Bahá'í Appeal for Religious Freedom in Iran* (National Spiritual Assembly of the United Stated, 1956), pp. 8–9.

50. "The Bahá'í Faith and the United Nations, The Beginnings of Bahá'í Relationship with the United Nations," in *The Bahá'í World*, vol. XIII, p. 785.

51. Shoghi Effendi, extract from a letter dated 18 May 1948, in ibid., p. 786.

52. "The Bahá'í Faith and the United Nations, The Beginnings of Bahá'í Relationship with the United Nations," in *The Bahá'í World*, vol. XIII, p. 790.

53. "Survey of Current International Activities" in *The Bahá'í World*, vol. XIII, p. 294.

54. Cited in "The Bahá'í Faith and the United Nations, The Beginnings of Bahá'í Relationship with the United Nations," in *The Bahá'í World*, vol. XIII, p. 791.

55. "Survey of Current International Activities" in *The Bahá'í World*, vol. XIII, p. 296.

56. Shoghi Effendi, extract from a letter dated 19 July 1956, *Citadel of Faith*, pp. 143–44.

57. Shoghi Effendi, extract from a letter dated 22 April 1926, *Bahá'í Administration*, p. 105.

58. Shoghi Effendi, extract from a letter dated 20 August 1955, *Citadel of Faith*, p. 141.

59. Ibid., pp. 141–42.

CHAPTER 10: THE DESTINY OF AMERICA

1. Shoghi Effendi, *The Advent of Divine Justice*, ¶28.

2. Ibid., ¶29.

3. Ibid., ¶29.

4. Ibid., ¶30.

5. Ibid., ¶31.

6. Ibid., ¶31; Shoghi Effendi, *God Passes By*, p. 5; Shoghi Effendi, *The Advent of Divine Justice*, ¶32, 31.

7. Ibid., ¶32.

8. Ibid., ¶32.

9. Ibid., ¶32.

10. Ibid., ¶33.

11. Shoghi Effendi, extract from a letter dated 28 March 1941, *The Promised Day Is Come*, ¶291.

12. 'Abdu'l-Bahá, cited in a letter dated 28 November 1931 by Shoghi Effendi, *The World Order of Bahá'u'lláh*, p. 36; Shoghi Effendi, extract from a letter dated 28 March 1941, *The Promised Day Is Come*, ¶293, 294.

13. 'Abdu'l-Bahá, *Selections from the Writings of 'Abdu'l-Bahá*, no.15.6.

14. Shoghi Effendi, *The Advent of Divine Justice*, ¶85.

15. 'Abdu'l-Bahá, cited in a letter dated 28 November 1931 by Shoghi Effendi, *The World Order of Bahá'u'lláh*, p. 36.

16. Shoghi Effendi, extract from a letter dated 28 November 1931, *The World Order of Bahá'u'lláh*, pp. 42–43.

17. Shoghi Effendi, extract from a letter dated 11 March 1936, *The World Order of Bahá'u'lláh*, p. 163; Shoghi Effendi, extract from a letter dated 28 November 1931, *The World Order of Bahá'u'lláh*, p. 37.

18. Shoghi Effendi, extract from a letter dated 11 March 1936, *The World Order of Bahá'u'lláh*, p. 163.

19. Ibid., p. 164.

20. Shoghi Effendi, extract from a letter dated 28 March 1941, *The Promised Day Is Come*, ¶301–2.

21. Shoghi Effendi, extract from a letter dated 8 February 1934, *The World Order of Bahá'u'lláh*, p. 156.

22. Ibid., p. 144.

23. Ibid., p. 157.

24. Shoghi Effendi, extract from a letter dated 5 June 1947, *Citadel of Faith*, p. 32; Ibid., pp. 31–32.

25. Ibid., pp. 32–33.

26. Ibid., pp. 34–35.

27. Shoghi Effendi, *God Passes By*, p. 215; 'Abdu'l-Bahá, *The Promulgation of Universal Peace*, p. 103.

28. Shoghi Effendi, extract from a letter dated 5 June 1947, *Citadel of Faith*, p. 35.

29. Ibid., p. 35.

30. Ibid., p. 36.

31. 'Abdu'l-Bahá, *Selections from the Writings of 'Abdu'l-Bahá*, no. 71.2; Shoghi Effendi, extract from a letter dated 11 March 1936, *The World Order of Bahá'u'lláh*, pp. 191–92.

32. Shoghi Effendi, extract from a letter dated 5 June 1947, *Citadel of Faith*, p. 36.

33. Shoghi Effendi, extract from a letter dated 28 November 1931, *The World Order of Bahá'u'lláh*, pp. 36–37.

34. 'Abdu'l-Bahá, *The Promulgation of Universal Peace*, p. 167.

35. Shoghi Effendi, extract from a letter dated 11 March 1936, *The World Order of Bahá'u'lláh*, p. 165.

36. Shoghi Effendi, *The Advent of Divine Justice*, ¶122; Shoghi Effendi, extract from a letter dated 28 July 1954, *Citadel of Faith*, p. 126; Shoghi Effendi, *The Advent of Divine Justice*, ¶122.

37. Shoghi Effendi, *The Advent of Divine Justice*, ¶19.

38. Ibid., ¶15.

39. 'Abdu'l-Bahá, *The Promulgation of Universal Peace*, p. 122; Shoghi Effendi, *The Advent of Divine Justice*, ¶124.

40. Shoghi Effendi, *The Advent of Divine Justice*, ¶124.

A SELECTED BIBLIOGRAPHY

WORKS OF BAHÁ'U'LLÁH

Epistle to the Son of the Wolf. New ed. Translated by Shoghi Effendi. 1st ps ed. Wilmette, IL: Bahá'í Publishing Trust, 1988.

Gleanings from the Writings of Bahá'u'lláh. Translated by Shoghi Effendi. Wilmette, IL: Bahá'í Publishing, 2005.

The Kitáb-i-Aqdas: The Most Holy Book. 1st ps ed. Wilmette, IL: Bahá'í Publishing Trust, 1993.

The Kitáb-i-Íqán: The Book of Certitude. Translated by Shoghi Effendi. Wilmette, IL: Bahá'í Publishing, 2003.

The Summons of the Lord of Hosts: Tablets of Bahá'u'lláh. Wilmette, IL: Bahá'í Publishing, 2006.

WORKS OF THE BÁB

Selections from the Writings of the Báb. Compiled by the Research Department of the Universal House of Justice. Translated by Habib Taherzadeh et al. Wilmette, IL: Bahá'í Publishing Trust, 2006.

WORKS OF 'ABDU'L-BAHÁ

Memorials of the Faithful. New ed. Translated by Marzieh Gail. Wilmette, IL: Bahá'í Publishing Trust, 1996.

Promulgation of Universal Peace: Talks Delivered by 'Abdu'l-Bahá during His Visit to the United States and Canada in 1912.

Compiled by Howard MacNutt. 2d ed. Wilmette, IL: Bahá'í Publishing Trust, 1982.

Selections from the Writings of 'Abdu'l-Bahá. Compiled by the Research Department of the Universal House of Justice. Translated by a Committee at the Bahá'í World Center and Marzieh Gail. 1st pocket-size ed. Wilmette, IL: Bahá'í Publishing Trust, 1996.

Tablets of the Divine Plan. 1st pocket-sized ed. Wilmette, IL: Bahá'í Publishing Trust, 1993.

A Traveler's Narrative Written to Illustrate the Episode of the Báb. Translated by Edward G. Browne. New and corrected ed. Wilmette, IL: Bahá'í Publishing Trust, 1980.

WORKS OF SHOGHI EFFENDI

A World Survey, the Bahá'í Faith 1844–1944. Wilmette, IL: Bahá'í Publishing Committee, 1944.

Advent of Divine Justice. 1st pocket-size ed. Wilmette, IL: Bahá'í Publishing Trust, 1990.

Bahá'í Administration: Selected Messages 1922–1932. 7th ed. Wilmette, IL: Bahá'í Publishing Trust, 1974.

Citadel of Faith: Messages to America, 1947–1957. Wilmette, IL: Bahá'í Publishing Trust, 1965.

God Passes By. New ed. Wilmette, IL: Bahá'í Publishing Trust, 1974.

Messages to the Bahá'í World, 1950–1957. Wilmette, IL: Bahá'í Publishing Trust, 1971.

Messages to Canada. 2nd ed. Thornhill, Ont.: Bahá'í Canada Publications, 1999.

The Bahá'í Faith 1844–1952, Information Statistical and Comparative. Wilmette, IL: Bahá'í Publishing Committee, 1953.

"The Faith of Bahá'u'lláh, A World Religion," *World Order Magazine*, volume XIII, number 7, October 1947.

The Promised Day Is Come. 1st pocket-size ed. Wilmette, IL: Bahá'í Publishing Trust, 1996.

This Decisive Hour: Messages of Shoghi Effendi to the North American Bahá'ís, 1932–1946. Wilmette, IL: Bahá'í Publishing Trust, 2002.

The Unfolding Destiny of the British Bahá'í Community: The Messages from the Guardian of the Bahá'í Faith to the Bahá'ís of the British Isles. London: Bahá'í Publishing Trust, 1981.

The World Order of Bahá'u'lláh: Selected Letters. 1st pocket-size ed. Wilmette, IL: Bahá'í Publishing Trust, 1991.

WORKS OF THE UNIVERSAL HOUSE OF JUSTICE

Messages from the Universal House of Justice, 1963–1986: The Third Epoch of the Formative Age. Compiled by Geoffry Marks. Wilmette, IL: Bahá'í Publishing Trust, 1996.

COMPILATIONS OF BAHÁ'Í WRITINGS

Bahá'u'lláh, 'Abdu'l-Bahá, Shoghi Effendi and Universal House of Justice. *The Compilation of Compilations: Prepared by the Universal House of Justice, 1963–1990.* 2 vols. Australia: Bahá'í Publications Australia, 1991.

Hornby, Helen, comp. *Lights of Guidance: A Bahá'í Reference File.* New ed. New Dehli, India: Bahá'í Publishing Trust, 1994.

OTHER WORKS

Atkinson, Ann Gordon. *Green Acre on the Piscataqua, A Centennial Celebration.* Eliot, Maine: Green Acre Bahá'í School Council, 1991.

Bahá'í International Community. *Bahá'í Appeal for Religious Freedom in Iran.* Wilmette, IL: National Spiritual Assembly of the United States, 1956.

Balyuzi, H. M. *Eminent Bahá'ís in the Time of Bahá'u'lláh*. Oxford: George Ronald, 1985.

———. *Bahá'u'lláh, the King of Glory*. Oxford: George Ronald, 1991.

Bennis, Warren. "The Challenges of Leadership in the Modern World," *American Psychologist*, vol. 62, no. 1, (January 2007), pp. 2–5.

Etter-Lewis, Gwendolyn and Richard Thomas (eds). *Lights of the Spirit, Historical Portraits of Black Bahá'ís in North America 1898–2000*. Wilmette IL: Bahá'í Publishing, 2006.

Fields, Rona M. (ed). *Martyrdom, The Psychology, Theology, and Politics of Self-Sacrifice*. Westport, Ct.: Praeger, 2004.

Gail, Marzieh. *Other People, Other Places*. Oxford: George Ronald, 1982.

Garis, Mabel R. *Martha Root: Lioness at the Threshold*. Wilmette: Bahá'í Publishing Trust, 1983.

Ghadirian, Abdu'l-Missagh. "Intergenerational Responses to the Persecution of Bahá'ís of Iran," in Yael Danieli (ed.) *International Handbook of Multigenerational Legacies of Trauma*. New York: Plenum Press, 1998.

Hatcher, William S. & J. Douglas Martin. *The Bahá'í Faith, The Emerging Global Religion*. Wilmette IL: Bahá'í Publishing, 2002.

Hollinger, Richard (ed.) *'Abdu'l-Bahá in America: Agnes Parsons' Diary*. Los Angeles: Kalimát, 1996.

Jaeger, John. "Muslim Extremists and Violence, Bibliographic Essay", in *Choice*, December 2006, pp. 587–95.

Khan, Janet A. "Rank and Station: Reflections on the Life of Bahíyyih Khánum", *Journal of Bahá'í Studies*, volume 17, no. 1/4, March-December 2007, pp. 1–26.

Lewis, Bernard. *The Crisis of Islam, Holy War and Unholy Terror.* London: A Phoenix Paperback, 2003.

Maḥmúd, Mírzá. *Maḥmúd's Diary, The Diary of Mírzá Maḥmúd-i-Zarqání Chronicling ʿAbduʾl-Baháʾs Journey to America.* Oxford: George Ronald, 1998.

Martin, Douglas. "The Persecution of the Baháʾís in Iran 1844–1984," *Baháʾí Studies,* volume 12/13, 1984.

Momen, Moojan. *The Bábí and Baháʾí Religions 1844–1944, Some Contemporary Western Accounts.* Oxford: George Ronald, 1981.

Morrison, Gayle. *To Move the World.* Wilmette, IL: Baháʾí Publishing Trust, 1982.

Nábil-i-Aʿẓam [Muḥammad-i-Zarandí]. *The Dawn-Breakers: Nabíl's Narrative of the Early Days of the Baháʾí Revelation.* Translated and edited by Shoghi Effendi. Wilmette, IL: Baháʾí Publishing Trust, 1932.

Pedahzur, Ami. Cited in Christian Caryl, "Why They Do It," in *The New York Times Review of Books.* Volume 52, number 14, September 22, 2005.

Rabbani, Rúḥíyyih. *The Priceless Pearl.* London: Baháʾí Publishing Trust, 2000.

Reardon, Kathleen K. "Courage as a Skill," *Harvard Business Review,* January 2007, pp. 58–64.

Rutstein, Nathan. *Corinne True, Faithful Handmaiden of ʿAbduʾl-Bahá.* Oxford: George Ronald, 1987.

Stockman, Robert H. *The Baháʾí Faith in America, Origins 1892–1900,* vol. 1. Wilmette, IL: Baháʾí Publishing Trust, 1985.

———. *The Baháʾí Faith in America, Early Expansion 1900-1912,* vol. 2. Oxford: George Ronald, 1995.

The Baháʾí World volumes.

United States *Bahá'í News*. Various issues of this periodical.

Wegener, Daniel Nelson. *Divine Springtime, Louise Caswell Recalls the Early Years of the Bahá'í Faith in Central America and Panama*. Tegucigalpa, Honduras: Union Press, 1977.

Whitmore, Bruce W. *The Dawning place: the building of a temple, the forging of the North American Bahá'í community*. Wilmette, IL: Bahá'í Publishing Trust, 1984.

INDEX

Bahá'í
PUBLISHING

AND THE BAHÁ'Í FAITH

Bahá'í Publishing produces books based on the teachings of the Bahá'í Faith. Founded over 160 years ago, the Bahá'í Faith has spread to some 235 nations and territories and is now accepted by more than five million people. The word "Bahá'í" means "follower of Bahá'u'lláh." Bahá'u'lláh, the founder of the Bahá'í Faith, asserted that He is the Messenger of God for all of humanity in this day. The cornerstone of His teachings is the establishment of the spiritual unity of humankind, which will be achieved by personal transformation and the application of clearly identified spiritual principles. Bahá'ís also believe that there is but one religion and that all the Messengers of God—among them Abraham, Zoroaster, Moses, Krishna, Buddha, Jesus, and Muḥammad—have progressively revealed its nature. Together, the world's great religions are expressions of a single, unfolding divine plan. Human beings, not God's Messengers, are the source of religious divisions, prejudices, and hatreds.

The Bahá'í Faith is not a sect or denomination of another religion, nor is it a cult or a social movement. Rather, it is a globally recognized independent world religion founded on new books of scripture revealed by Bahá'u'lláh.

Bahá'í Publishing is an imprint of the National Spiritual Assembly of the Bahá'ís of the United States.

For more information about the Bahá'í Faith,
or to contact Bahá'ís near you,
visit http://www.bahai.us/
or call
1-800-22-UNITE

OTHER BOOKS AVAILABLE FROM
BAHÁ'Í PUBLISHING

ILLUMINE MY WORLD
Bahá'í Prayers and Meditations for Peace
Bahá'u'lláh, the Báb, and 'Abdu'l-Bahá
$14.00 US / $16.00 CAN
Trade Paper
ISBN 978-1-931847-65-0

A heartwarming collection of prayers designed for people of all faiths during times of anxiety and chaos in the world

Illumine My World is a collection of prayers and meditative passages from the writings of the Bahá'í Faith that will help bring comfort and assurance during a time of growing anxiety, chaos, and change in the world today. As financial and religious institutions crumble and fall, as the tide of refugees from countries torn by civil strife continues to grow, as the oppression of women and minorities are brought to light more and more in so many parts of the world, readers can take comfort from these soothing passages. The prayers included specifically ask, among other things, for protection, for unity, and for assistance from God. Individuals from all religions will find strength and assurance in this inspiring collection.

UNDERSTANDING DEATH
The Most Important Event of Your Life
John S. Hatcher
$18.00 US / $20.00 CAN
Trade Paper
ISBN 978-1-931847-72-8

A personal exploration of mortality and death, the inevitable journey of human life, and the acceptance of faith

Understanding Death: The Most Important Event of Your Life illustrates the need to prepare for this important moment, even though many ignore its inevitability. There is no escape from death and the grief that can consume one when faced by the loss of family and friends. The author's personal insight offers encouragement that death is not the end but the beginning of a new spiritual existence. Author John Hatcher surveys his own life, the decisions he has made over the years, and how those experiences have impacted him. He especially focuses on his discovery and exploration of the Bahá'í Faith and his eventual acceptance of Bahá'u'lláh's teachings. Accepting that death is not the end, that there is another journey, and that there is time to accept the inevitable and prepare for the life hereafter can bring peace and comfort to all.

MIND, HEART, & SPIRIT

Educators Speak

Heather Cardin

$18.00 US / $20.00 CAN

Trade Paper

ISBN 978-1-931847-66-7

Real-life stories from teachers who share their passion for shaping the lives of young people today

Mind, Heart, and Spirit: Educators Speak is a collection of real-life stories from a diverse group of educators on a wide range of issues such as how to deal with difficult students, the role of parents and religion in a child's education, and the similarities and differences in educating children in different cultures across the globe. Filled with interesting anecdotes and personal accounts, this is an intimate, sometimes frustrating, sometimes exhilarating insight into the experiences of all these educators as they have struggled to overcome various challenges in educating children. Their passion for teaching and their devotion to their students come shining through and offer a glimpse of the important role that Bahá'í education—with its emphasis on unity, tolerance, and diversity—can play in shaping the lives of young people today.

MARRIAGE
A FORTRESS FOR WELL-BEING
Bahá'í Publishing
$15.00 US / $17.00 CAN
Trade Paper
ISBN 978-1-931847-63-6

Valuable insight about applying spiritual principles to the practical realities of the marital relationship

Marriage: A Fortress for Well-Being offers valuable insight for every couple, whether married or in preparation for marriage, to apply spiritual principles to everyday needs. Redefining marriage as the basic building block for world peace and unity, the book explores issues such as dating, how to prepare for marriage, the purpose of marriage, conflict resolution, interracial marriage, raising children, divorce, and more. By taking an in-depth look at what the Bahá'í writings say about marriage, the book examines the institution in light of God's purpose for humanity and provides guidance for building spiritually founded marital unions. Coming at a time when modern social conditions are forcing a reexamination of the institution of marriage, the book offers sound advice, encouragement, and tremendous hope for the future. This new edition has a foreword by Elizabeth Marquardt, author of *Between Two Worlds: The Inner Lives of Children of Divorce,* and an affiliate scholar at the Institute for American Values.